IN THE MOOD FOR TEXTURE

IN THE MOOD FOR TEXTURE

The Revival of Bangkok as a Chinese City

DUKE UNIVERSITY PRESS
Durham and London 2026

Arnika Fuhrmann

Printed in the United States of America on acid-free paper ∞
Project Editor: Livia Tenzer
Designed by Matthew Tauch
Typeset in Garamond Premier Pro and General Sans
by Copperline Book Services

Library of Congress Cataloging-in-Publication Data
Names: Fuhrmann, Arnika author
Title: In the mood for texture : the revival of Bangkok as a Chinese city /
Arnika Fuhrmann.
Description: Durham : Duke University Press, 2026. | Includes
bibliographical references and index.
Identifiers: LCCN 2025027899 (print)
LCCN 2025027900 (ebook)
ISBN 9781478032991 paperback
ISBN 9781478029540 hardcover
ISBN 9781478061748 ebook
Subjects: LCSH: Arts, Thai—Foreign influences | Bangkok (Thailand)—
History | Thailand—Civilization—Chinese influences | Shanghai
(China)—History | Hong Kong (China)—History | Southeast Asia—
Colonial influence | East Asia—Colonial influence
Classification: LCC DS589.B2 F84 2026 (print) | LCC DS589.B2 (ebook) |
DDC 305.8009593/3—dc23/eng/20250903
LC record available at https://lccn.loc.gov/2025027899
LC ebook record available at https://lccn.loc.gov/2025027900

Cover art: Film still from Nawapol Thamrongrattanarit,
Happy Old Year, 2019.

DUKE UNIVERSITY PRESS GRATEFULLY ACKNOWLEDGES
THE SUPPORT OF THE GRAHAM FOUNDATION FOR ADVANCED
STUDIES IN THE FINE ARTS, WHICH PROVIDED FUNDS
TOWARD THE PUBLICATION OF THIS BOOK.

Graham Foundation

Contents

Acknowledgments

I had the great fortune to develop this book alongside numerous scholars, writers, filmmakers, and cultural activists engaged in reviving and telling Chinese Thai history from novel perspectives. I thank especially Veeraporn Nitiprapha for introducing me to her Bangkok as a Chinese city. Wasana Wongsurawat's insights on Chinese Thai history and its materialization proved invaluable. I am further grateful to all who explored Bangkok as a Chinese city with me. Over coffee, conversation, and meals, Anjana Suvarnananda, Ranwarat Kobsirithiwara, Phatthanaphol Engsusophon, Paphonphat Kobsirithiwara, Chairat Polmuk, Salee Art Every, and I attempted to decode the different textures of the revival. When I was not in Bangkok, friends, colleagues, and students continuously alerted me to new venues and writing about the reviving Chinese city.

When it was time to put the book together, Viranjini Munasinghe provided rigorous readings of all chapters. Only with her generous input was I able to turn my manuscript into a book. Tani Barlow's succinct critique proved invaluable, and her foundational work on Asia, history, and femininity continues to inspire. Lucinda Ramberg and Feng-Mei Heberer's sustaining and invigorating friendship and sharp feedback have been great gifts.

I had the great fortune to receive helpful critical feedback from audiences in Minneapolis–St. Paul, Minnesota; Lexington, Kentucky; Toronto; Berlin; Düsseldorf; Hamburg; Cambridge, Massachusetts; New York; Singapore; Bangkok; Bielefeld; Syracuse, New York; Hanoi; New Brunswick, New Jersey; Princeton, New Jersey; Claremont, California; Poughkeepsie, New York; Chicago; and Ithaca, New York. I thank a diverse contingent of interlocutors that include beloved friends and colleagues Jonathan M. Hall, Elizabeth Wijaya, Erin Huang, Bliss Cua Lim, Gina Marchetti, Justin McDaniel, Pheng Cheah, Nadja-Christina Schneider, Lawrence Chua, Sophia Siddique Harvey, Romita Ray, Sunait

Chutintaranond, Suradech Chotiudompant, Kong Rithdee, Cheng-Chiang Chai, Brett de Bary, Naoki Sakai, Nick Admussen, Joshua Young, Shaoling Ma, Tim Murray, Natalie Melas, Tamara Loos, Naminata Diabate, Lily Chi, Shiqi Lin, Wujun Ke, Shuang Shen, Xiao Liu, Suzy Kim, Chie Ikeya, Shui-yin Sharon Yam, Charlie Yi Zhang, Srimati Basu, Sirithorn Siriwan, Tinakrit Sireerat, Manasicha Akepiyapornchai, Kasidit "Gunn" Phikrohkit, Nida Sanglimsuwan, Anna Naiyapatana, Moodjalin Sudcharoen, Cathy Davidson, Don Robotham, Denise Tang, Ajjana Thairungroj, Palita Chunsaengchan, Travis Workman, Lucetta Kam, Hwa-Jen Tsai, Alex Zahlten, Tomiko Yoda, Jie Li, Jon Solomon, Peter Osborne, Soyi Kim, Jonathan Boyarin, Julia Cassaniti, Claudia Derichs, Jörg Engelbert, Itty Abraham, Joanna Pfaff-Czarnecka, and Eric Beverley.

I thank Marco Wilms for making his beautiful film about Bangkok, *Durch die Nacht mit Christopher Doyle und Nonzee Nimibutr*, available to me; and Salee Art Every (Waraluck Hiransrettawat) for providing me with a sample of her exciting film *Kith and Kin*.

At Cornell University I thank the entire traveling Mellon Collaborative Studies in Architecture, Urbanism and the Humanities seminar "Flux Navigations" (2014) and my co-instructor Jeremy Foster, who first taught me to perceive the city's material properties.

Several institutions supported the writing of this book. I gratefully acknowledge the support of a Distinguished Research Fellowship at the Advanced Research Collaborative of the City University of New York's Graduate Center in New York in spring 2020 and a "Global Dis:connect" Fellowship at the Käte Hamburger Research Centre at Ludwig-Maximilians-Universität München in 2024–2025. I am indebted to the Graham Foundation for Advanced Studies in the Fine Arts for generous support of this project through a publication grant (2023). Finally, a Cornell-Chulalongkorn Strategic Collaboration Grant (2024) is allowing Napong Tao Rugkhapan (Chulalongkorn University) and me to continue research on Bangkok's Chinese revival.

Both of Duke University Press's initially anonymous readers have allowed me to thank them by name. For more than two decades, I have been fortunate to be able to witness Jean Ma's generous critical intellectual energy. I am extremely grateful for her in-depth engagement with my manuscript. Since I first met Nguyen Tan Hoang almost twenty years ago, he has been an incredibly supportive and insightful interlocutor. I have immense gratitude for the intellectual energy that he invested in the critique of my manuscript. Both readers challenged me to make the book better than it could otherwise have been.

I was extremely fortunate to be able to develop this project with my editor Ken Wissoker's enthusiastic support and sharp insight. Through the long process of shaping the book, Ken was there through thick and thin. I thank also Duke University Press's Ryan Kendall and Livia Tenzer, who shepherded this project with great expertise. I am grateful to Daniel McNaughton for lending his sharp eye to the indexing and proofing process.

Finally, this book is dedicated to the city of Bangkok, its stellar inhabitants, and those who first took me there many decades ago.

The Revival of Bangkok as a Chinese City

The larger-than-life portrait of a woman in a long red gown, circa the nineteenth century, greets visitors to the Shanghai Mansion Bangkok. Brightly lit, the floor-to-ceiling painting at the far end of the hotel's entrance occupies all visual attention. Whether the painting is antique or merely distressed, the femininity featured in it evokes the Shanghai of a bygone era. A more proximate eye-catcher is the red floor shrine that bears the Chinese characters for "landlord" and is adorned with offerings, the pineapple placed before it the most striking (fig. I.1).

This Bangkok venue is suffused with the aesthetics of Shanghai, but the pineapple offering at the shrine draws visitors back to Southeast Asia.[1] As visitors walk into the hotel's Red Rose bar and restaurant, a 1960s Hong Kong aesthetic is moreover superimposed on this mix of styles. What does it mean when a Bangkok hotel combines referents of Shanghai, Hong Kong, and Straits Chinese modernities while also highlighting the Chinese histories of Bangkok? More intriguingly yet, how might one understand Shanghai Mansion Bangkok's simultaneous foregrounding of the aesthetics of colonial modernity? What insights into new understandings of Asia emerge from this contemporary Bangkok with its citations of transregional Chineseness? Taking Asia as a question rather than a certainty, this book examines current reimaginations of region and identity in Bangkok.[2]

Thinking Region from Urban Southeast Asia

This book inquires into two concomitant occurrences: The first is the superimposition of three cities in East Asia and Southeast Asia onto one another in contemporary Thai cultural production and hospitality venues; the second consists of the simultaneous revival of Chinese pasts and the

I.1 Entrance of the Shanghai Mansion Bangkok hotel.
Photograph by the author, 2018.

aesthetics of colonial modernity. Examining the doubling of Hong Kong, Bangkok, and Shanghai across literature, cinema, digital media, and the hospitality industry of Bangkok, I gauge the valences of a transregional Chineseness that is both virtual and anchored in material structures. I analyze these contemporary texts and sites to learn how they mobilize a colonial modernity inhabited by Chinese persons and signal alternative desires for region, identity, and collectivity.

The colonial aesthetics and transregional span of Hong Kong director Wong Kar-wai's iconic film *In the Mood for Love* (2000; rerelease, 2020) centrally instantiate these conditions. The film's 1960s settings extend from the colonized locations of Hong Kong, Singapore, and Phnom Penh to the not formally colonized location of Bangkok, as the film's production site, and an implied semicolonial Shanghai. Wong's film features a colonial modernity that includes only Chinese persons, yet it turns precisely on the ways that these characters consume, produce, and trade goods circulated through colonial networks across Asia. At times in this book the term "Chinese colonial modernity" is used to denote the concomitant revival of Chinese pasts and the aesthetics of colonial modernity. Nowhere does the term refer to a Chinese colonialism; rather, it connotes the features of a nineteenth- and twentieth-century treaty port culture and transregional modernity that vitally drew on colonial networks and products yet always exceeded conditions of imperial and national governance.[3] Cultural producers and designers call into play this colonial modernity to proffer critiques of national and regional formations in Asia today.

Across Southeast and East Asia real estate and hospitality ventures, cinema and new media, lifestyle brands, and wellness businesses draw on the colonial as the privileged aesthetics of the good life.[4] In urban locations practices of consumption, art, and the logics of real estate markets blend in unpredictable ways with the more ephemeral networks of taste cultures, nostalgia, and texture to produce new, transregionally informed cosmopolitanisms.

As film directors, hotels, bars, and clubs revive 1930s Shanghai and 1960s Hong Kong modernities—and exploit the Chinese past of Bangkok's old European trading quarters—these (semi)colonial urban histories are emerging as primary signifiers of a desirable Asian cosmopolitanism. Rather than invoke only the local histories of Bangkok's Chinese neighborhoods, contemporary cultural production and leisure venues blend these with Shanghai's and Hong Kong's aesthetics of colonial modernity.

I track the revivification of Chinese pasts and colonial modernity across locations and cultural domains. Why does a Shanghai-themed club in Bangkok or Hong Kong cinema's use of Bangkok as a filming location rely on referencing a transregional Chinese production and occupation of colonial modernity? My analysis seeks to understand the confluence of the spatial and temporal properties produced by this superimposition of the colonial modernities of the three Chinese cities onto one another. My initial primary interest lay in the intricate relationship between Bangkok and Hong Kong, but this relationship proves to be haunted also by the imaginary of semicolonial Shanghai. Bangkok as a Chinese city stands at the center of these inquiries. Both nationally and internationally the city represents a paradigmatic site of fantasy that provides for a particular elasticity of place and time and, by extension, personhood and belonging.

One would be able to relegate the temporal and spatial relays between the three cities to taste cultures, the exigencies of real estate arbitrage, or the continued tendency in the Hong Kong cultural imaginary to view Thailand as a terrain of ghostly alterity, sexual license, and financial corruption.[5] These would all be good interpretations, yet I aim to glean knowledge about a different kind of intraregional desire from this confluence of time and space.

My investigation tracks the vestiges of urban imaginaries that are counterposed to a present in which city space is overwhelmingly corporately owned and regional imaginaries overdetermined by the aftermath of the Cold War (in formations such as the Association of Southeast Asian Nations) and affected by the economic and political ascension of the People's Republic of China (PRC) as well as the resurgence of the Thai military since 2006. I ask how invocations of twentieth-century translocal Chinese modernity point to enduring regional imaginaries that diverge from global notions of "China Rising," the goals of the PRC's Belt and Road Initiative (BRI), Western Orientalisms, and the policies of national governments. At the moment of the disappearance of the material remnants of Chinese pasts—as Bangkok undergoes massive transformation—ephemeral infrastructures take up the work of historical memory. In a period of impoverished geopolitical imaginaries, one can track the submerged persistence of other regional formations in contemporary design, writing, and media. In the global Asian city, lifestyle venues and cultural production represent key sites that store, visualize, and transform such prior cultural and social models.

To unearth the material, affective, and historical doublings that occur between Bangkok, Hong Kong, and Shanghai, I examine a transmedia archive that centers on Wong's *In the Mood for Love* (*Fa yeuhng nihn wah* [Age of blossoms] in Cantonese). This archive also includes Marco Wilms's *Durch die Nacht mit Christopher Doyle und Nonzee Nimibutr* (Into the night with Christopher Doyle and Nonzee Nimibutr, 2010), other transnational Chinese and Thai cinematic materials (*Chalad kem kong* [Bad Genius, 2017]; *How to Ting . . .* [Happy Old Year, 2019]; *Rouge* [1987]; *Baober in Love* [2004]), selected social media pages ("Kratham khwam Wong" [Doing Wong-ness]), literature (*Phutthasakarat atsadong kab song jam khong song jam khong maeo kulab dum* [Dusk of the Buddhist era and the memories of the memories of the black rose cat, 2016], published in an English translation as *Memories of the Memories of the Black Rose Cat* [2022]), other print media, and new ventures in Bangkok's hospitality industry. The latter include the nightclub Maggie Choo's, the Shanghai Mansion Bangkok, multiple bars and cafés in Bangkok's Chinatown, and the Lhong 1919 commercial complex. My rationale for choosing these materials is their proliferation, mobility, and appeal across locations; role in the resignification of Chineseness in Thailand; and renegotiation of a regional imaginary.

My analysis concentrates especially on texture, or the features of the built environment and the feminine sartorial styles highlighted in the cinematic materials and exploited in Bangkok's hospitality industry. Thus in Wong's *In the Mood for Love* the revivification of cosmopolitan Chinese modernity is anchored and actualized in the materiality of the urban environment that the film obsessively details, especially in the colonial ruin. At the heart of Wong's films lies also the nostalgic-futuristic distressing of a particular kind of Chinese femininity. His films undertake this distressing in conjunction with referencing the modernities of 1930s Shanghai and 1960s Hong Kong. These are likewise the aesthetics exploited in Bangkok's hospitality industry, where historical surfaces and representations of femininity furnish frontiers for the expansion of capital in the transforming city.

I use the notion of distressing in Susan Stewart's sense of "to make old, to antique." Stewart notes that "if distressed forms involve a negation of the contingencies of their immediate history, they also involve an invention of the past that could only arise from such contingencies. We see this structure of desire as the structure of nostalgia."[6] Distressed genres rely on operations of fantasy and improvise on time and history. These dynamics are at play in Wong's films and sections of the Bangkok revival that "[negate] the contingencies of their immediate history": the current structures of governance, the colonial heritage of the Thai polity, nonredemptive aspects of Chinese Thai history, neoliberal urban transformation, and the role that femininity plays in this context.[7] Others represent imaginative contentions with precisely these conditions.

The array of textures materializing in architecture, design, and the sartorial links 1920s and 1930s Shanghai and 1950s and 1960s Hong Kong with Bangkok past and present. The current reoccupation of physical sites relies on actual histories of transregional exchange linking the trade port cities of East and Southeast Asia. At the same time, it responds to contemporary desires for the imagined affective plenitude, atmospheres, and political affordances of these cultural histories. The actuality of their material remnants and the affects and practices surrounding them come together to form one textured field.

The focus on the texture of the ruin and of feminine style allows us to understand the doubling between Bangkok, Shanghai, and Hong Kong as something other than merely metaphor. Texture and surface constitute conduits between urban pasts and presents and between the "looks" of the city and the material grounds of its transformation. If it is to be criti-

cal, a history of the recoveries of Bangkok's Chinese pasts must be a material and materialist one. An investigation of contemporary design's focus
on urban materiality is thus not merely frivolous. The analysis of texture
reveals the city as composed of an infrastructure that exists at the seam-
lines of the virtual and the material. With Eve Sedgwick, Tom McEnaney,
and Michael Lucey, I understand texture as indexical of the contexts of its
emergence, allowing us to connect the present with often-obscured historical occurrences.[8]

I classify the Chinese pasts and colonial modernities invoked as *cosmopolitan* on the grounds of their hybrid and translocal character. The concept of cosmopolitanism denotes the plural composition of culture as well
as a particular mode of cultural circulation.[9] "Cosmopolitan" describes
cultural formations that envision themselves as transcending immediate
locale and laying claim to at least regional universal validity. With regard
to figurations of femininity, Su Lin Lewis's delineation of the global appearance of the Modern Girl is a persuasive example of the cultural work
of a cosmopolitan trope in the colonial context: "She did not come from
any one center, but emerged in cities everywhere, as a worldwide phenomenon consolidated through the newly international media of newspapers
and cinema. Viewed within the context of colonial and world history, the
Modern Girl completely collapses traditional dichotomies between the
modern imperial métropole and a 'backward,' colonial periphery."[10]

Bangkok's Chinese revival recuperates ideals that lay claim to transregional cultural universality, are multiply constituted, and reference
distinct figures such as the Modern Girl from an early and mid-twentieth-
century trans-Asia colonial modernity. The ways that participants access
this culture is predominantly through the textured, material remnants of
Chinese and colonial histories extant in Bangkok as well as through contemporary design and cultural production.

Rather than dismiss it as merely bad taste or questionable politics, I
understand the revival of colonial modern feminine styles as a fetish in
the Marxian and psychoanalytic senses. What can the prevalence of distressed, translocal Chinese femininities tell us about alternative regional
imaginaries in the present? The textures of femininity and of the ruin
emerge as elements of film syntax as well as of club and hotel décor but
also furnish a material substrate that breathes life into regional imaginaries
that exceed those of the post–Cold War and of an Asia "rising" under the
dominance of the PRC. Thailand's semicolonial temporality, the anomalous colonial temporalities of Shanghai and Hong Kong, and the func-

tions that their aesthetics, regional networks, and notions of sovereignty take on in the present stand at the heart of this inquiry.

In the context of my analysis, identity and region—notions of Chinese Thai personhood and Asian interconnection—inflect each other. Area and identity formation are intricately bound with each other and premised on violent processes. Naoki Sakai and Gavin Walker investigate "area as an epistemological-political technique."[11] As they explain, "Area is a technology according to which elements—which may or may not have been thoroughly heterogeneous to each other—are gathered and redeployed as a point of reference for a variety of social—racial, class, religious, gender, and so forth—distinctions."[12]

Walker argues that the notion of area is premised on capture and enclosure, and as such is closely tied to the clearing of new terrain for capital, or primitive accumulation. Most pernicious, however, is area's definitional power—the ways in which area determines the parameters of belonging.[13] In the materials analyzed here it is predominantly from the area of the city that region is reenvisioned. The city and its surfaces, its digital spaces, and the gendered, racialized, and ethnicized bodies inhabiting it represent prime "areas" for the expansion of capital and the realization of divergent political projects.

Against this background, my inquiry into urban trans-Asia revivals of Chinese colonial modernities does not merely substitute one notion of region for another. Rather, it aims to uncover the ways that contemporary cultural production, hospitality venues, and leisure practices either conjure or aim to undo the violence at the heart of belonging itself. My project draws on ethnographic and archival research undertaken in Bangkok and Hong Kong from 2014 to 2020 and from 2022 to 2023. Engaging scholarship in urban studies, Chinese history, media studies, semicoloniality, critical regional and area studies, gender studies, and theories of surface and image, this book sheds light on the current conjuncture of historical imagination, reregionalization, and the transformation of cities in Asia.

Bangkok as a Chinese City

Physically, materially, and affectively, the location of (post)colonial Bangkok and the styles of femininity referenced here furnish the raw material for the layering of cosmopolitan moods, textures, and histories. Since 2000 all of Wong Kar-wai's films about colonial Hong Kong have in fact been shot in Bangkok. I argue that it is especially the chronotope of Bangkok's disavowed coloniality that allows for the mobility in time necessary for the visceral reliving of a colonial ideal. I thus focus on uncovering the (post)colonial temporalities of the Chinese modernity of Bangkok—a city that remains under-studied and that may not primarily be understood as Chinese.[14]

But Bangkok as a Chinese city stands at the center of prominent reconceptualizations of region; its study may hold out more fine-tuned, egalitarian perspectives on region than the East Asia–based inquiries to date. In Bangkok, abiding, alternative notions of culture, ethnicity, and regional connectivity persist—shadow memories of *other* regional networks that manifest in ruins, bodies, and affect. What does it mean to understand Chineseness from this location? Why does Bangkok currently figure as one of the most "originary" Chinese cities? What happens when Bangkok urbanites and visitors imagine Asia beyond reductive, hegemonic visions?

While much Chinese history in Bangkok has been lost or is on the brink of disappearance, several material histories persist. Opened in 1997, About Studio About Café anticipated the occupation of material Chinese Bangkok for artistic and lifestyle purposes in later decades. The venue inhabited a historical corner shophouse on Maitrichit Road near the Roundabout of 22 July, in the vicinity of auto shops, the Khristhajak Maitrichit Chinese church, massage parlors, and other small businesses in the Pom Prap Satru Phai district of Bangkok's Chinatown. In a multifloor café and pub space, the avant-garde About Studio About Café featured performances and exhibitions.[15] Only in the 2000s and 2010s did other individual bars, clubs, and hotels draw on the city's Chinese pasts, when FooJohn Building, Maggie Choo's, Shanghai Mansion Bangkok, and Lhong Tou Café began to open. By the early 2020s revival venues were burgeoning all over the city, too numerous to track. Thus the 2023 bilingual *Song Wat Guidebook* lists dozens of leisure venues clustered around Song Wat Road alone in the historically Chinese and Indian neighborhood of Song Wat in the Samphanthawong district.[16]

At present Chinese revival venues augment—rather than replace—established community venues. The revival thereby brings into being a contemporaneity of cultural practices across generations. It valorizes that which is about to disappear, while also recurring to that which cannot be recovered in originary form—a counterfactual relation to the present and skeptical-hopeful anticipation of futurity. Two different modes of "assay-

I.2 The historical coffee shop Eia Sae, one of Bangkok's "six most classical Chinese-style cafés." Photographs: *BKK Menu*, February 20, 2018.

ing" history manifest concurrently in two venues in Bangkok's Chinese neighborhood of Yaowarat.[17]

The nearly century-old coffee shop Eia Sae historically functioned as a venue frequented by Chinese migrants of different vocations, serving as a place to find work and orientation for those newly arrived from China.[18] Today the café continues to be popular with the older denizens of the neighborhood. At the same time, Eia Sae has become a lifestyle destination: The website *BKK Menu* features it as one of the "six most classical Chinese-style cafés" (fig. I.2).[19]

Almost concurrently BKK *Menu* introduces the newly designed Lhong Tou Café, located just one minute away from Eia Sae.[20] Approximating the style of historical coffeehouses, Lhong Tou opened in 2018, roughly ninety years after Eia Sae. BKK *Menu* nevertheless classifies the venue as "Vintage / Chinese," reviewing favorably its design and a menu curated to offer stylized versions of "Chinatown" favorites.

In contemporary Bangkok both Eia Sae and Lhong Tou represent Instagrammable locations. While the older Chinese residents of Yaowarat do not frequent the stylish Lhong Tou, younger Bangkokians haunt both the new and old cafés. Both modes of engaging the city's Chinese history will eventually be superseded by more lucrative real estate developments but, for the moment, the historical and a curated patina coexist in Bangkok.[21] As revival destinations like Lhong Tou join established venues like Eia Sae, the city's Chinese culture enters a new temporality, in which quotidian cultural rituals coexist with new prosthetic lifestyle practices. As embodied and material histories disappear, the task of memory devolves onto cinema, digital media, print media, and new embodied publics. Alison Landsberg has described contemporary medial and embodied transgenerational and transethnic witnessing as "prosthetic memory."[22] In Bangkok's Chinese revival, texture plays an important role in prosthetic remembering.

Texture

The lens of texture facilitates an understanding of the ways in which urban venues and media store and invoke local pasts and regional imaginaries. Texture points beyond immediate historical context and can move analysis beyond "genre," so that film does not stand in opposition to urban design, nor the virtual to the material. When Bangkok urbanites frequent the cafés, hotels, and bars that are textured by the city's enduring pasts or consume revival media, what might they be looking for?

Sedgwick's delineation of texture's intersubjective logic and its link to affect helps to elucidate the participatory, sensory elements of Bangkok's Chinese revival. For Sedgwick "affect and texture . . . seem to belong together" and "both are irreducibly phenomenological."[23] Texture is moreover closely connected to touch as well as to (historical) intersubjectivity: "To touch is . . . always also to understand other people or natural forces as having effectually done so before oneself, if only in the making of the textured object."[24] As Sedgwick further explains, "Perceiving texture is never only to ask or know What is it like? nor even just How does *it* impinge on *me*? Textural perception always explores two other questions as well: How did it get that way? and What could I do with it?"[25]

In Sedgwick's conceptualization, texture always allows for an etiology of the object or context as well as bearing a conjectural dimension. This notion facilitates insight into how Bangkokians are touching (Chinese) history and interpreting it for the future-present. As an online review of the then newly opened Lhong Tou in Yaowarat notes, the café "presents the particular charm of traditional Chineseness but reinterprets it through the fun and fresh tactics of the new generation; it is able to communicate these concepts through the design of the space, the decoration of the venue, and of course through the food and drinks menu, with an identity unlike any other."[26] When patrons experience Lhong Tou and taste the café's *kiao* (wontons), *bao* (buns), *khao tom* (congee), desserts, and flower teas, flavors are carefully evaluated, but the venue's menu and atmospherics also index the pasts of Bangkok's Chinese neighborhoods, of Hong Kong and Shanghai, as well as of the patrons' (or others') immigrant grandparents and great-grandparents.

In appraising the textures of Chinese Bangkok, this book thus explores what C. Nadia Seremetakis would call a commensal event: I understand the Bangkok revival as propelled equally by objects and by consciousness, the material and the phenomenological. In Seremetakis's theory, memory bears a material dimension, and its storage is equally distributed across bodies and artifacts.[27] When bodies and artifacts come together in a commensal encounter, lost histories can be reanimated and remembered. In Bangkok the past is simultaneously enlivened by the material remnants of Chinese and colonial textures and texts and by the sensory perceptions, experiences, and memories that patrons or consumers of culture produce in relation.

In the Mood for Love provides a kind of supertexture for the media, design, and consumptive experiences of the Bangkok revival. *In the Mood for Love*'s multiple media lives unfold as a citational creative-consumptive loop that extends across the filmic and built environment in East and Southeast Asia. Shot in Bangkok, Wong's film exploits the city as a "raw material" that lends texture to a Chinese-inhabited colonial modernity.[28]

Wong's celebrated work tells the story of the epochal love between So Lai-Chen (in Cantonese; Su Li-Zhen in Mandarin) and Chow Mo-Wan: "Wong's *In the Mood for Love* is a romance melodrama, which tells the story of a married man (played by Tony Leung) and a married woman (played by Maggie Cheung), living in rented rooms of neighbouring apartments, who fall in love with each other while grappling with the infidelities of their respective spouses whom they discover are involved with each other."[29] Set in a Shanghai émigré community in 1960s colonial Hong Kong, with scenes also in Cambodia and Singapore, Wong's atmospheric love story is closely connected to social and political transformations underway in Asia in the second half of the twentieth century.

In the Mood for Love's outdoor scenes of 1960s Hong Kong were shot at Bangkok's 1880s Customs House, its worn-out shutters and textured walls suturing affect and history. In this location the lovers play out scenes of attachment and weigh the "what could have been" and the "what could still be" of their affair.[30] By extension the Customs House anchors the collective vision of region, style, and community that the love relationship personalizes. As the nostalgic conditional of the affair comes together with a regional vision, Bangkok emerges as the iconic site of (post)colonial fantasies of the good life in Asia.

With Giuliana Bruno I also understand texture as a bridge between the material and virtual. Her analysis of *In the Mood for Love* further provides insight into how texture is connected to a particular fashioning of time: "In this film attire is carefully constructed, as if it were a tangible form of architecture, while the city's fabric, in turn, is fashioned as if it were an enveloping dress, a second skin. In fact, tailored in the guise of one of Maggie Cheung's cheongsams, the city of Hong Kong appears itself encased, tightly wrapped in time and sheathed in space, somewhere in the 1960s."[31]

While the city in question is Hong Kong, the fabric of its 1960s ambiance materializes in Bangkok, the quintessential Chinese and colonial city. At present Bangkok's revival bars, clubs, cafés, and restaurants host patrons craving new consumptive experiences. But they also attract second- and third-generation Chinese Thai writers, intellectuals, and filmmakers engaged in a new wave of cultural production that revives Thailand's Chinese pasts with a difference. What "second skin" can a filmmaker like Salee Every (Waraluck Hiransrettawat), who makes films about her Chinese Thai family, or the novelist Veeraporn Nitiprapha, who chronicles Chinese migration to Thailand, take on in these locales? In their leisure practices the patrons of Chinatown hospitality venues are "sheathing" themselves in the fabric of an imaginary that ties in to pasts that are about to be erased—as well as into an indeterminate future.

Across textured exteriors and interiors, *In the Mood for Love*'s melancholy love story unfolds the temporalities of the "what could have been" and the "what could still be." In Bangkok these temporalities meet the "never" and "yet still" of Siam/Thailand's semicoloniality. Both temporalities provide ample room for fantasy. In Bangkok hospitality venues, *In the Mood for Love*'s regional cultural imaginary collides with the material actuality of the Chinese modernity that the film foregrounds. Wong's film in turn furnishes a blueprint for the design of clubs, restaurants, and hotels. Together the venues and the film provide the virtual and material basis for the ways in which Bangkok urbanites can reimagine their lives as cosmopolitan and transnational. In locations such as the Shanghai Mansion Bangkok the citation of Wong's film becomes explicit; several additional Bangkok venues will reveal themselves as cognate with Wong's 1960s Hong Kong.

Temporality in Hong Kong Cinema

That a film by a Hong Kong director would come to stand at the center of the Bangkok revival is apt. Around the turn of the twenty-first century Hong Kong cinema probed novel temporalities and recalibrated the past. The scholarly literature variously classifies the productions around the time of the city-state's 1997 handover from Britain to China as nostalgic, future-oriented, evincing a heightened concern with temporality, or postnostalgic.[32] Stanley Kwan's film *Rouge* (1987) is exemplary for the consideration of urban historical revival because it excavates the city as multiply constituted in place and time. Part of the nostalgic contingent of the Hong Kong New Wave, it tracks the ghostly reappearance in 1980s Hong Kong of the 1930s courtesan Fleur.[33] In an iconic scene Fleur stands in front of a modern-day department store. Its mirrored façade gives way to the view of a Cantonese opera performance in the 1930s teahouse that Fleur remembers in its stead. Bliss Lim writes that "this film sequence depicts one space as splintered yet whole." She notes that instances such as these constitute "'spatial palimpsests' traversed by divergent temporalities."[34] Kwan's use of this palimpsestic device is pertinent for my analysis as it breaks open the supposed unity of space and time and shows the city as possessed of sedimented temporalities and spaces instead.

Vivian P. Y. Lee underlines the significance of the new Hong Kong cinema for historical revision: "Within the fissures of colonial and national histories, and the temporal-spatial displacements that result, the local cinema has reinvented itself as a form of visual history.... This visual history is a dynamic register of codes, styles, and images that help to recall and critically reposition the historical in a popular and highly idiomatic visual medium."[35]

In the Mood for Love premiered in 2000, shortly *after* Hong Kong's 1997 transition from British colony to Special Administrative Region of China. Wong's work is frequently situated in a "'second wave' of the Hong Kong New Wave," immediately after that of Stanley Kwan, Ann Hui, Tsui Hark, and Yim Ho.[36] Lee classifies Wong's *In the Mood for Love* as postnostalgic, noting that the film deploys nostalgia but reflects on it critically.[37] With its facility for critical historical inquiry, atmospheric design, and affective density, Wong's film thus provides a generative paradigm for the temporal experiments of the Bangkok revival.

Chinese Thai Histories

To unpack the complex temporality that the Chinese revival summons, we have to consider the fact that Siam/Thailand's coloniality remains largely unacknowledged. On the one hand, the country's semicolonial status meant that its sovereignty was compromised by laws of extraterritoriality. On the other hand, Siam/Thailand itself acted as a colonizing power.[38] Lysa Hong argues that Siam declared itself postcolonial already in the nineteenth century while remaining colonized by its elites until today.[39] While the dominant nationalist discourse foregrounds the fact of Thailand's not having been formally colonized, critical historiographies uncover the disavowal of enduring authoritarian power structures that bear colonial elements. I take up Hong's argument to posit that Thailand's semicolonial history engenders a temporality of the "never/yet still." This temporality provides the grounds for the elasticity of the colonial imaginary that makes Thailand and its capital city a local and global subject of fantasy. It moreover allows for the imaginative importing of the colonial temporalities of Hong Kong and Shanghai. The time of contemporary Bangkok is determined by the "never" and "yet still" but also augmented by "that which will not have been."

Wasana Wongsurawat's *The Crown and the Capitalists: The Ethnic Chinese and the Founding of the Thai Nation* positions Siam/Thailand's ethnic Chinese populations as pivotal in the country's nineteenth- and twentieth-century history. Especially the merchant, middle-class, and upper-middle-class Chinese populations represented linchpins for the country's political development and relations to larger powers. From the Qing era (that ended in 1911/1912), to the rise of imperial Britain in nineteenth-century Southeast Asia (culminating in the 1855 Bowring Treaty), Thailand's alliance with Japan (1930s–1940s), and US Cold War dominance, Thailand's Chinese populations mattered for the country's educational, medial, economic, political, and social formation.[40] What happened in China's history remained foundational for Siam/Thailand's history throughout this time. Monarchical rule, republicanism, and communism; language, identity, and education; as well as China's relation to the (other) superpowers were watched closely and had an impact on Siam/Thailand's political systems.

Wongsurawat studies Chinese Thai history in proximity with colonial history and argues that the first event that vitally reconfigures Siam's position in the region is the nineteenth-century shift from "the economic context of the Chinese tribute system" to a world in which "the center of the universe regarding trade and political power had been relocated from the Great Qing Empire to the British Empire."[41] Siam's extraterritorial conditions from 1855 to 1938 allowed Chinese entrepreneurship to flourish and accorded Chinese traders, who were often subjects of a colonial nation (e.g., Britain or the Dutch Empire), a particular place within the polity.[42]

The largest waves of Chinese migration arrived from the second half of the nineteenth century until the 1920s.[43] These migrations occurred in part to satisfy Siam's need for large, new labor contingents to replace slave and corvée labor.[44] Jeffery Sng and Pimpraphai Bisalputra designate the years 1855 to 1900 the "Age of Emigrants": "The second half of the 19th century saw a flood of Chinese emigrate to Siam . . . form[ing] an enormous non-native population in Siam."[45] The years from 1855 to 1925 also saw the emergence of new infrastructures, markets, and ideas that were significantly propelled by these migrations.[46]

Total population numbers remain unclear, but some figures regarding migration are extant. Brian Bernards writes: "From 1876–98, nearly 185,000 Chinese passengers came from Swatow directly to Siam, with only about 27,000 returning. Between 1906 and 1918, the number of total Chinese arrivals increased substantially to more than 630,000, while the number of returnees also increased to nearly 250,000, showing the growth of circular migration after earlier pioneer settlement drew Siam into the South Seas network. In total, nearly 3.7 million Chinese settled in Siam throughout a century of emigration following the Opium Wars."[47] Lawrence Chua presents similar figures for the late nineteenth and early twentieth centuries.[48] By the 1930s, Wongsurawat reports, Kuomintang sources estimated the Chinese population as making up approximately one-third of the total population.[49]

Key events in twentieth-century Chinese Thai history include the 1910 Chinese general strike, "which brought the kingdom to a virtual standstill for nearly three days," and indicated the growing economic significance of Chinese entrepreneurs and laborers.[50] In the early 1910s Rama VI Vajiravudh designated the Chinese the "Jews of the Orient"; this constituted a first wave of anti-Chinese sentiment during which "substantive anti-Chinese policies were [however] relatively few. Vajiravudh's anti-Chineseness was only ideological; it was never operationalized into immigration, economic or social measures."[51] A second wave of anti-Chinese sentiment occurred under Phibun Songkhram (1938–1944), whose policies included arrests, deportations, the nationalization of Chinese businesses, the closing of two hundred Chinese schools and all newspapers except one, and the reservation of positions for ethnic Thais only.[52]

In the postwar period Wongsurawat draws particular attention to two nearly forgotten race riots, the 1945 Yaowarat and 1974 Phlapphla Chai incidents. In late September 1945 police forbade the display of Republic of China flags for National Day celebrations without the concurrent hoisting of Thai flags. The military was called in to subdue ensuing protests. In the immediate aftermath residents of the area experienced "violent repercussions not only from military forces but also from the non-Chinese general public."[53]

In early July 1974 a Chinese taxi driver's resistance to police extortion sparked multiday clashes with police and military that spread from Chinatown's Phlapphla Chai police station. A national state of emergency was declared.[54] Wongsurawat underlines the anti-Chinese tenor of both state documentation and Thai-language news reporting of the Phlapphla Chai incident.[55] Both incidents have nearly been expunged from historical memory.[56]

Multiplicities of Migration

I review the present-day shifts in understandings of region and identity against the background of narratives regarding Chinese migration to Thailand that are marked by contradictory elements and significant elision.

The specific question that this analysis asks about Chinese Thai history is the following: What happens when a history of oppression and disavowal meets a present of cultural revival? The historiography of Chinese migration and integration is overdetermined by discourses of the radically unassimilable difference of the Chinese, on the one hand (the "Jews of the Orient"), and their complete assimilation into Thai society, on the other (the disavowal of histories of adversity and dissent).[57] Historically minoritized persons are thereby conceptually situated between notions of radical difference and complete disappearance. As in other Southeast Asian contexts, Chinese migrants to Thailand are credited with bringing about Thai modernity. At the same time, they were charged with extraterritorial loyalties and with depleting the resources of the country. What does it mean to live in a context in which the current taken-for-granted ubiquity of Chinese persons and culture coexists with the consistent disavowal of details of their history?

In *Ghostly Desires: Queer Sexuality and Vernacular Buddhism in Contemporary Thai Cinema* I analyzed the dynamics of a revival that since the 2000s valorized the very features of Chinese femininity that were once disparaged in Thailand.[58] In order to situate these dynamics historically, I reviewed the narratives of difference and assimilation that constituted the majority of dominant and vernacular accounts of Chinese Thai history. I examined both the logics of assimilation derived from self-positioning and those that are externally imposed:[59]

> The vast majority of overseas Chinese reside in Southeast Asia; in the scholarly literature about this geographic context, Thailand has represented the paradigmatic example for the notion of Chinese assimilation since the 1950s. Yet it is currently this site from which notions of Chineseness are being reconfigured.
>
> Not only academic perspectives on Chinese Thai history have espoused the idea of assimilation. In popular discourse denials of Chineseness stem from negations by the Thai ethnic majority of a history of denigration or can come from a refusal of essentialist notions of Chineseness on the part of Thais of Chinese descent. As Ien Ang writes with regard to Chineseness in Southeast Asia, "In these narratives, the very validity of the category of Chineseness is in question, its status as a signifier of identity thrown into radical doubt."[60]

Conversely, "Discourses of assimilation become particularly problematic when they deny a notion of agency to the ethnic subject yet fail to protect from violence whenever notions of ethnic difference are reanimated. Significantly the notion of assimilation obscures past suffering and trivializes ongoing discriminations."[61]

Older scholarly analyses tend either to espouse notions of the harmonious assimilation or of the discrimination of the Chinese in Thailand. This scholarship also frequently invokes the idea of Chinese economic centrality and political and social marginality.[62] By contrast, recent scholarship concentrates increasingly on the simultaneous operations of centrality and marginality, of Thainess and Chineseness, and of allegiance to the Thai nation and transnational political projects. Thus Sittithep Eaksittipong and Saichol Sattayanurak assert in their history of Chinese emotion in 1950s–1970s Thailand that migrants always maintained complex links to their Chinese heritage as well as to their positioning in Thai society.[63] At present Chineseness as social positionality exceeds the formula of a "historical status of economic centrality and social and political marginality."[64] Present-day shifts have transformed Chinese heritage from "a racialized minority position to one of increasingly desirable ethnic membership."[65]

But why is it a *Chinese* historical modernity that informs the desire for new transregional collectivity in the first place? For one, the Chinese represent the paradigmatic transnational figure in the modern history of Southeast Asia. To an extent historical Chinese migration to Thailand has come to figure as a blueprint for the notion of the diasporic: The term *phon thale*, "overseas," is synonymous with Chinese migrants. The ways in which historical Chinese migration today stands in for the diasporic as such is indexed in the title of Anocha Suwichakornpong's short film *Phon Thale (Overseas*, 2012), which alludes to the notion of historical Chinese migration in order to address the plight of contemporary *Burmese* labor migrants in Thailand.

China's current increased agentive power in regional economies and politics also inflects narratives regarding Chinese migration to Southeast Asia in complicated new ways. The facile assumption that a resurgent converging of center and diaspora is responsible for the revivals of Chinese identity in Southeast Asia is erroneous. While the Chinese revival in Thailand is in many ways connected to the PRC's ascendancy, a unity between a hitherto-disparaged minority and a new regional hegemon cannot be assumed. Such conflation disregards the many disjunctures between Chinese Thai and mainland Chinese histories, interests, and practices.

China's BRI is frequently taken to overdetermine all current PRC–Southeast Asia relations. As David Lampton, Selina Ho, and Cheng-Chwee Kuik write, "The strategic intent of Beijing's policy is to make China an economic hub for its vast periphery, provide connectivity nodes for military power projection, drive China's move up the value-added ladder, and increase its neighbors' dependence on the PRC. The... BRI... is the broad signboard under which these objectives are articulated and advanced." The authors are quick to qualify, however, that the BRI designates a conglomerate of dispersed projects, rather than emanating from an all-powerful center.[66] State and commercial initiatives have powerful impacts yet do not exhaust the multiple factors that determine regional relations.

China's involvement in Thailand includes infrastructural, military, and cultural projects. Infrastructural projects include a high-speed rail network, an economic corridor, a potential canal across the Isthmus of Kra, and digital infrastructures as well as projects on the Mekong River. "Soft-power" projects extend to tourism, language teaching (Confucius Institutes), media, and cultural and religious initiatives. While Benjamin Zawacki notes Thai civil society's highly divergent responses to China's activities in the country, Kornphanat Tungkeunkunt claims that most cultural initiatives are welcomed.[67] Sittithep argues that the PRC does not provide inspiration for Thais of Chinese descent on account of its handling of COVID-19 as well as its involvement in Hong Kong, Tibet, and Xinjiang.[68]

In the current conjuncture, neoliberalism constitutes the dominant idiom of economy, politics, and subjectivity. The nostalgic longings for past regional coherences evident in revival cultural production and Bangkok hospitality venues are closely, though not symmetrically, connected to neoliberal paradigms. Wendy Brown stresses that neoliberalism has to be understood as "more than a set of free market economic policies that dismantle welfare states and privatize public services," but rather as the "explicit imposition of a particular form of market rationality" on "the social, the subject, and the state."[69] A neoliberal order thus manifests also in technologies of the self that include the professional sphere, affective dispositions, and the domains of belief and aspiration.

The ways that neoliberalism comes into play in the visual materials and writing of the Chinese revival are manifold. It centrally informs not only the mode in which relations of center and diaspora are imagined but also the negotiations of personhood in the contemporary city. Chinese femininity in particular is invested with the capacity to figure optimal productivity in changing economic systems. The flexibility demanded of markets is demanded also of persons, and the female protagonists of the films and stories under consideration are tasked with accelerating and stretching to actualize it.[70]

Why is colonial modernity associated with the aesthetics of the good life? The splendors associated with coloniality in Asia were possible only through the "superfluity" of immense labor forces.[71] Conditions such as these lie at the heart of, and are obscured by, the fetish of a revived colonial modernity. This fetishization also draws attention to the relative absence of a temporality of the present in the sites and materials under consideration. At the same time, the draw of transregional Chinese cosmopolitanisms is hardly exhausted by desires for the colonial. Instead multiple causalities determine the desirous gaze on a Chinese-inhabited colonial modernity. In a dispiriting present, in which authoritarian national politics generate oppressive structures, people are turning to spatialities, eras, and collectivities that extend beyond their immediate purview. In Bangkok, Hong Kong, and other parts of Asia this includes what Koichi Iwabuchi terms the "nostalgia for a different Asian modernity."[72] These feelings are prompting imaginary and imaginative migrations into the past and across the region.

The City and the Modern Girl

In the pages that follow, a woman will make a prominent appearance, or rather a reappearance, in Bangkok, Hong Kong, Shanghai, Singapore, and Phnom Penh, as well as ultimately in New York.[73] She is the Modern Girl of 1930s Shanghai or 1960s Hong Kong—but her look is cognate with that of her peers across the globe in the twentieth century.[74] She stands at the center of the contemporary revival in media and urban design that brings to life Chinese pasts and the aesthetics of colonial modernity. Thus upon entry to the Shanghai Mansion Bangkok's Red Rose bar, one will find the walls adorned with photos of this Modern Girl embarking on a transnational nightlife.

The Chinese and colonial modern femininity that she embodies is generic in the sense in which Lauren Berlant defines the relation between gender and genre: "To call an identity like a sexual identity a genre is to think about it as something repeated, detailed, and stretched while retaining its intelligibility, its capacity to remain readable or audible across the field of all its variations. For femininity to be a genre *like* an aesthetic one means that it is a structure of conventional expectation that people rely on to provide certain kinds of affective intensities and assurances."[75] To think of the contemporary Modern Girl as a genre allows us to recognize her appearance across fields and to claim her significance for the present. At the same time, understanding the Modern Girl as a genre still accounts for the varied, at times contradictory, kinds of work that she performs in the present. A genre, according to Berlant, is a form of aesthetic expectation "with porous boundaries allowing complex audience identifications."[76] In her analysis many of the identifications and expectations attached to femininity have to do with hopes for the "good life." In the context studied by Berlant this desired good life consists of an emotional richness and reciprocity that is both generated and experienced by women. In the case of the revived Modern Girl in Bangkok, the focus of the analysis lies on expectations especially for the collective good life. Her location in Thailand and in Asia endows this figure with a particular recent history.

The figure of "woman" in Asia has in the past decades above all encoded new forms of efficacious labor. "Woman" was the agentive figure of a continent that manufactures nearly the majority of the world's products, as "Asian nation-states have become the world's manufacturing center of gravity."[77] The female figure haunting contemporary cultural production and leisure venues in Bangkok can also be linked with wage labor, yet she becomes most efficacious through other kinds of work. She is instrumental in three processes: the leap from the historical denigration of Chineseness into present-day desirability in Thailand (a local phenomenon); the denotation of a particular continental past and the key to a transregional future (a regional phenomenon); and, finally, the encoding of the changing forms of value in the city under finance capitalism (a global phenomenon).

To undertake a transcultural inquiry such as the present one, we have to pay attention to both "history" and "style." My inquiry into style includes an investigation of cinematic, digital, and literary forms. By history I mean the past, but also the current social, political, and economic contexts in which the recuperated Modern Girl lives. Within such a history Asian femininity currently exemplifies the collapsing of pasts, presents, and futures into a single temporality. According to Harry Harootunian such temporal collapse is a hallmark of the global present.[78] His paradigm of an undifferentiated historical present attains great salience in Asia, where both cities and bodies are transforming quickly.

Femininity is not a transhistorical concept and still in nineteenth-century China was not a quality attributed solely to female bodies.[79] But when the Chinese femininity of a colonial modern era appears en masse across social fields, the proliferation of this trope points to "highly charged areas in the social fantasy that produced it."[80] What kinds of questions should we ask about the ubiquity of this distressed Chinese femininity across national locations and fields of inquiry? How might this figure aid in the critique of Asia as a spatial and temporal construct—but also of what is conventionally assumed to be China or a Chinese city? What account of this figure's aesthetic form can we provide and what information does it transmit? What animates her? What kind of "social theory" does she enable that another figure cannot?[81]

A distressed Chinese femininity drives *In the Mood for Love* and also appears prominently in Bangkok's leisure venues, where the textures of her sartorial style are set in scene before those of crumbling colonial ruins. In Bangkok she is a particular kind of avatar. As such she allows for the suturing of historical temporalities; she salvages a past whose material disappearance is imminent; she provides for a bridge between the material and the virtual; and she facilitates new ways of encoding history.

In the contemporary city the distressed Modern Girl often recuperates a market-friendly, easily consumable multiculturalism. Most recently the notion of "women" in Asia has moreover shifted from encoding labor to encoding surplus value, to standing in for compounding forms of value under finance capitalism in the present.[82]

At the heart of the work that femininity performs across contemporary Asia stand particular histories of associating women with a "more"—the more of excess and surplus as well as of consumption and production. In early twentieth-century Chinese history, Tani Barlow has shown femininity to be located at the heart of notions of the productive, specifically of logics of eugenics and capitalist social progress.[83] In the past few decades Asia has stood at the center of a recoding of femininity as surplus value.[84] This propensity of the feminine not merely to embody but rather to produce the "more" is currently heightened, making femininity the quintessential figure of a finance capitalism that needs to create pricelessness in commodities in order to produce enhanced forms of value.[85] In this incarnation the figure of woman lends style and history to mundane urban surfaces. She thus underwrites the neoliberal phenomenon in which urban locales are given patina and invested with historical cachet in order to both absorb and increase spiraling real estate values.[86]

At the same time, as Jean Ma teaches us, the task of telling history—especially that which centers on traumatic events—has in many locations in Asia devolved onto women.[87] In Thailand the revived Modern Girl allows us to track the minoritized histories of Chinese femininity and this femininity's rise into mainstream desirability. This figure both recalls a denigrated form of personhood *and* reasserts it precisely in a location in which it was previously disparaged. In the elastic fantasy space of Bangkok a repositioning of minoritized identities thus also finds great traction.

Locally and regionally this incarnation performs the work of a lived deconstruction of area—of Asia and its dominant geopolitics—and makes different forms of personhood and belonging available to anyone in Bangkok, or indeed to visitors from Hong Kong, Shanghai, and elsewhere. In Bangkok almost everyone can inhabit a "better" Chinese cosmopolitanism than that of present-day trans-Asia geopolitical alliances. Here a distressed Chinese femininity represents a compact figure of thought that allows insight into processes and desires that define the global present. The revival makes this figure available to the present as "intellection"—that cognitive effort that appraises the present and anticipates the future in transformative ways.[88]

The Bangkok revival draws on templates of female consumptive and productive power from semicolonial Shanghai and from a burgeoning 1960s industrial Hong Kong. This figure of trans-Asia Chinese femininity is both elastic and bears great synthesizing capacities. As such she represents a "dense transfer point" for desires that both exemplify and stand in strong contrast to impoverished geopolitical imaginaries.[89] Stretching across eras and modes of production, the figure of Chinese femininity encodes all-encompassing neoliberal demands for ever-greater malleability and flexibility and at the same time reveals loopholes in these frameworks.

A few key figures, texts, and sites recur throughout this book. The spotlight on femininity guides the reader through different registers of the revival: the opulent, fantastic registers of the heritage revival; the material registers of hegemonic, statist revivals; and the understated, citational registers that revive forgotten histories of labor and dissent. *In the Mood for Love* weaves through the book as a supertexture. Bangkok's 1880s Customs House instantiates Thailand's semicolonial conditions in chapters 1 and 2, and the analysis circles back repeatedly to the Shanghai Mansion Bangkok with which I opened this chapter. The hotel is pivotal because of its heightened attention to Chinese history on the levels of architectural materiality, design, and publicity. The digital Shanghai Mansion Woman also appears twice; she illustrates the role of femininity in contemporary urban transformation (chapter 2) but also rewrites the possibilities of the minoritized actor in the present (chapter 3).

Structure

The book proceeds by immersing the reader in the affective experience and textures of the revival and its foundational filmic inspiration in part I. After introducing intercity referencing between Bangkok, Shanghai, and Hong Kong, it analyzes *In the Mood for Love*. Part II examines the revival's concrete instantiations in Bangkok in more depth: After exploring the materiality of Chinese Bangkok, it investigates a progressive style of revival in conjunction with a film analysis. Part III reflects on the potential of this Southeast Asian location for new understandings of identity, belonging, and region. It examines a literary account of Chinese migration, homes in on the function of femininity in the city, and returns to the question of Southeast Asia's role in the reimagination of region and identity. The book thereby theorizes "up" from the individual contexts in Bangkok to speculate on the significance of Southeast Asia as an intellectual site. Individual chapters are weighted toward medial or material questions, yet most combine the investigation of the city's materiality with media analysis.

Part I: In the Mood for Texture

This section investigates the theoretical implications and aesthetic features of the Chinese revival in media and sites that immerse viewers and visitors in the aesthetics of colonial modernity. It introduces the superimposition of Bangkok, Shanghai, and Hong Kong onto one another and the revival of colonial modern style. Its primary cinematic text is *In the Mood for Love*, set in 1960s colonial modern Hong Kong but shot entirely in Bangkok. For present-day Bangkok hospitality venues, *In the Mood for Love* functions as a framework for design.

My investigation centers on the texture of the built environment (the colonial ruin) and the feminine sartorial styles (the high-modern *cheung sam*) highlighted in the cinematic materials and exploited in Bangkok's hospitality industry. The ruin and the cheung sam, or *qipao* (Mandarin), emerge as switch points that allow for the bridging of historical and present-day plurality, affective and historical contexts, and national and regional divides. They instantiate the ways that neoliberal urban governance markets city and femininity as surface and image in order to maximize not only surplus value but also compound value.

Chapter 1, "City Connectivities," presents a first foray into Bangkok's historical and imaginary, material and medial constitution, and its connection with Hong Kong and Shanghai. It weighs the significance of the semicolonial and shows how it materializes in Bangkok. The discussion lays out the elements of the contemporary urban condition and introduces the medial and material recuperations of Bangkok's Chinese pasts and colonial modern elements. Chapter 2, "In the Mood for Texture: Transmedia Revivals of Hong Kong's, Bangkok's, and Shanghai's Chinese Pasts and Colonial Modernities," analyzes *In the Mood for Love* but underlines the film's imbrication with the material city.

Part II: Bangkok: Originary Chinese City

To think about Bangkok as a Chinese city allows for the reconfiguration of notions of minoritarian and majoritarian citizenship in the context of shifting transregional desires. At present Bangkok figures as the most "authentic" Chinese city among the three under consideration: It consistently provides the raw material for the recovery of Chinese pasts in cinema, tourism, transregional spiritual activities, and the hospitality industry. I draw on ethnographic data acquired in my study of urban transformation and design in Bangkok's "Chinatown," the Samphanthawong, Bang Rak, and Pom Prap districts of the city south of the historical palace. This area is undergoing some of the most severe transformations in the history of Thai urban renewal.

What are the implications of thinking about Chineseness in a present in which it, while constantly referenced, cannot be recovered in genuine historical form? While Chinese Thais historically faced decades of discrimination, Chineseness became a valorized feature of personhood since the 1990s. What happens when a denigrated minority identity ascends into cultural desirability at the very time of its purported disappearance? To think about Chineseness from a site of heterogeneity—Bangkok, rather than cities assumed to be self-evidently Chinese—allows for the revision of the fixity of identities. The notions of ethnic personhood that emerge from this location do not merely stand in for the notion of difference in a national context (Chineseness as the other of Thai nationalism) or for regional difference (Chineseness in Southeast Asia) but present a general platform for future pluralities while retaining links to a particular history of migration.

Two different registers of revival are counterposed in this section: Chapter 3 focuses on dominant invocations of Bangkok's Chinese history, while chapter 4 shows the progressive referencing of Bangkok as a 1960s Chinese city in film and café culture. Thus chapter 3, "Bangkok: Chinese City of Colonial Modernity," primarily investigates dominant occupations of Chinese Bangkok as a material site and highlights temporalities of governance and updated narratives of development in the neoliberal era. By contrast, chapter 4, "*How to Dump*: Radical Revitalization in Thai Cinema and Hospitality Venues," draws out the concretely material and quotidian modes of revival projects that foreground submerged histories of labor migration and dissent. Investigating the vicissitudes of contemporary Chinese Thai identity, it works toward a notion of a prosthetic, post-migrant historical memory.

Part III: Thinking Region from Southeast Asia

This section deliberates on an understanding of region that emerges from Southeast Asia. Other current efforts to reconceptualize Asia originate in the field of East Asian studies. Here Southeast Asia at times appears as a "new" generic stepping-stone for interventions into notions of power, governance, and historical trajectory. By contrast, chapters 5 ("*Memories of the Memories of the Black Rose Cat*: Thai Literature as Contemporary Chinese Literature) and 6 ("Southeast Asia as Question: Thinking Region from Bangkok") argue that a method that privileges Southeast Asian texts, sites, and languages promises to produce a less monumental perspective than other reconceptualizations of Asia to date. It yields frames of reference that are less burdened than East Asia–based efforts that recur to problematic prior regional formations, such as that of Japan's Greater East Asian Co-Prosperity Sphere in the 1940s, or liken today's PRC expansion to a historical tributary system.

My claim is that the heterogeneity attributed to Southeast Asia as well as precolonial, colonial, and postcolonial conceptualizations of the region are all being reanimated productively in the Bangkok revival. Southeast Asia represents a site in which Chineseness becomes salient both in its historical trajectory of becoming-race and in its subsequent becoming-ethnicity. In the largest Chinese diaspora in the world, Chineseness bears historical traces; is an indelible element of national modernities; and furnishes an intricate part of reregionalization processes that involve Southeast Asian nations' fraught relations with the PRC. While Southeast Asia does not possess any "natural" unity but was created through political events such as World War II and the Cold War, it represents a site in which majority-minority relations take on instructive formats. Chapters 5 and 6 examine how two contemporary films and a novel reenvision region through their formulations of Chinese femininity. The coda, "Women in Asia and the World," closes the analysis with a glimpse of how such a formulation might play out in New York and speculates on the significance of a Chinese colonial modern revival beyond Asia.

I

IN THE MOOD FOR MOOD FOR TEXTURE

ONE

City Connectivities

In the contemporary city of Bangkok, traces of Shanghai, Hong Kong, and local urban history intersect in both material and virtual forms. A Facebook page, the city's 1880s Customs House, the club Maggie Choo's, and the Shanghai Mansion Bangkok hotel all animate multiple temporalities, locations, and histories. These sites elucidate the makeup of the historical and the contemporary city. The invocation of the semicolonial condition of Thailand, when it was Siam—and its treaty port culture—furnishes a vital link between the city's past and present.

The Facebook Community page for "Kratham khwam Wong" exemplifies the translocal and transmedia character of the Bangkok revival (fig. 1.1). Dedicated to re-creating the atmospheric settings of Hong Kong–Shanghainese director Wong Kar-wai's films, the page cites Hong Kong's and Shanghai's colonial modernities and brings the materiality of Bangkok into relief.[1]

"Kratham khwam Wong" means "doing, practicing—or even committing 'Wong-ness'"; the adjective "wong," derived from the director's name, has become a Thai neologism that is fairly broadly understood.[2] The Facebook page is at times merely citational of this coveted Wongness, featuring stills from Wong's films. But the page also stages scenes in Thailand that approximate the colonial modern ambiance of the director's work. "Doing Wong" means that the page produces wistful, artistic images that evoke the atmospheres and color schemes that define Wong's 1960s Hong Kong but are in fact composed in Bangkok—frequently of nighttime drinking in derelict locations across the city. Centrally connecting the Hong Kong director's films with the materiality of Bangkok, the Facebook page not only performs a cultlike reverence for Wong's oeuvre but also produces scenes of desire for a transregional colonial modernity extending across East and Southeast Asia. The page moreover invests citations of this history with progressive implications for the present, as it

กระทำความหว่อง
@whysowong · Community

Send Message

1.1 "Kratham khwam Wong" Facebook page, January 25, 2023.

links its colonial modern aesthetic with anti-establishment political critique.

City, Media, Migrations

The "Kratham khwam Wong" page exemplifies the regional vision, urban materiality, and migration of ideology that determine the shape of the city in present-day Southeast and East Asia. Material, sensory, and imagined remnants of past urban connections define the city as much as present-day relations wrought by media and capital. The historical linkages between Bangkok, Hong Kong, and Shanghai figure as precursors of today's interconnectivities. It is not that migrants to Thailand hailed primarily from these cities but rather that Hong Kong and Shanghai represent iconic locations and cultural intertexts with which Bangkok was always in conversation.[3] To do justice to this complex constitution of the urban, my analysis of media and features of the built environment that reference Hong Kong, Shanghai, and Bangkok relies on materialist critiques of contemporary urban development, the media archaeological notion of the city as a set of sedimented networks, and scholarship on colonial modernity and semicoloniality in East and Southeast Asia.

The contemporary city is already "wired" by communications networks and through its overdetermination by finance capital. Shannon Mattern argues that the city's history as a mediatized locale is not a recent phenomenon, however, but reaches back centuries and even millennia.[4] She shows how the city can be understood as mediatized not just on the basis of its close connection to the development of the cinema, or in the sense that our understanding of cities is (over)determined by visual media. Rather, Mattern understands the city as itself composed of media that include but also exceed visual media, such as sound, print culture, infrastructures, and material objects.

Determined by both virtual and material dimensions, the Facebook page "Kratham khwam Wong" represents an example of the continual transformation of the mediatized city. As a consistently updated social media page, it inhabits a medium of the present and shapes current imaginations of Bangkok's Chinese revival. At the same time, it draws on history in discerning ways, deploying both Bangkok's material encoding of colonial modernity and the cinematic history of Wong's work. As such, the page agglomerates the different historical layers and ontological dimensions of the city.

The route between Hong Kong and Thailand is marked by a long history in the traffic of ideas, persons, and (moving) images. When social media pages such as "Kratham khwam Wong," art-house films such as *In the Mood for Love*, documentary films, and hospitality venues resuscitate Chinese colonial modernities, they thus replicate actual histories of circulation and migration, playing off transnational business histories, trajectories of cultural production, and taste cultures.[5] These histories include the circulation of Chinese films in Southeast Asia (e.g., the Shaw Brothers' productions) as well as histories of transnational migration prompted by political circumstances, such as that of Chinese Thai dissidents to Hong Kong.[6] Bangkok remains enduringly connected to (other) Chinese cities through the material and affective traces of migration and through embodied memory, though the latter is precisely precarious. This moment at which embodied memory is endangered has also prompted the migration of memory to new prosthetic forms, however.[7]

While the transregional phenomena cited above are not always referenced explicitly in the films, novels, and venues under consideration, they furnish subtextual histories that nevertheless underwrite these materials' and sites' visions. As evident in the Facebook page and Wong's films, such transregional histories inform the desire to calibrate the possibilities of a different Chinese or Asian cosmopolitanism—at a time when the possibilities of most such formations have been foreclosed. Examining media, urban leisure practices, and material remnants in Bangkok, I use the notion of transmedia to describe an archive that allows us to track qualities of the urban across new media, the moving image, bodies, physical locations, objects, and fantasy.

The Urban Condition

I noted above that the "Kratham" Facebook page indicated the desire for a more habitable region and a different national politics. At the same time, the page can also be aligned with trends that exploit the Southeast and East Asian city as a commodity. In this, it partakes in trajectories that make the city a site for lifestyle rather than a place for living, substituting atmospherics for housing and backdrop for shelter. In the course of such developments the city becomes a place that selectively foregrounds the sheen of history but does not genuinely acknowledge the past. This has to do with the ways that the city is tasked with hosting and materializing new economic forms.

What marks the urban condition under "electronic capitalism" are the increased concentration of capital investment and infrastructures in the city and transnational and interurban rather than national connectivities; unprecedented corporate ownership of real estate; the stylization of urban living; and the generation of two divergent kinds of "superfluity"—of unprecedented capital accumulation and of increased labor precarity.[8] In materialist critiques of contemporary urban conditions, the city appears as hyperbolic, a site no longer merely of capital concentration but of capital *compounding*.[9] In close connection the urban appears as surface. As economic profit and notions of value spiral toward the immeasurable and "priceless," the aesthetic properties of the city compound into designed surfaces, rather than sites for public life, work, and everyday activity.[10]

Achille Mbembe develops the concept of superfluity to characterize the present of the city of Johannesburg, South Africa. Superfluity is particularly useful for drawing into relation the economic logic, historical background, psychic dynamics, and aesthetic properties of contemporary cities: "*Superfluity* does not refer only to the aesthetics of surfaces and quantities, and to how such an aesthetics is premised on the capacity of things to hypnotize, overexcite, or paralyze the senses. To my mind, superfluity refers also to the dialectics of indispensability and expendability of both labor and life, people and things."[11] The transformation of lives and livelihoods into "lifestyle" is a prominent component of urban development. Thus Mbembe relates the aestheticization of the urban sphere to contemporary economic forms: "Johannesburg's city space is a *product* that is marked, measured, marketed, and transacted. It is a commodity. And as such, its representational form has become ever more stylized."[12] Describing city space and design as "new public theaters of late capitalism," he further explains: "These developments are concomitant with the emergence of media and high-technology centers and new theaters of consumption in which space and images are both *figural forms* and *aestheticized commodities*."[13]

The ways in which both digital media and the Bangkok hospitality industry reference and "double" city space partake in the logic of superfluity, in which sites and surfaces are aestheticized precisely to obscure their historical singularity and economic function. Neither the Bangkok commercial ventures nor a transnationally circulating art-house cinema can be viewed as exempt from the constraints of contemporary urban capitalism. The distressing of the city spaces of Bangkok, Hong Kong, and Shanghai partakes in a nostalgia without history and the dynamic of lifestyle-instead-of-living that are prominent in today's urban contexts. Texture becomes a part of these logics when it provides an authentic lifestyle veneer to the becoming-product of the city.[14] In this context history, too, becomes merely another commodity in global real estate, as its textures add a desired patina to urban environments.[15]

Of the three cities referenced, Hong Kong has seen the fastest urban development and shift from industrial to financial capitalism as well as the highest real estate prices (exceeding those of Bangkok by up to 800 percent). Esther Cheung's interpretation of a Hong Kong cinema of haunting as providing a "metahistory of space" and critique of the overdetermination of urban life by real estate arbitrage is instructive: "It [the spectral city] corresponds to a dislocated affect produced by the transforming perception of the mutating urban environment, which has an intimate relationship with its own material, economic dimension."[16]

Notwithstanding these global, dominant patterns of city development, I take the analysis of the transregional filmic materials, literary texts, and leisure venues as an opportunity to explore fissures in the veneer of contemporary urban hegemonies. To be sure, these materials and sites are part of new monetized public spheres of literary and visual production and leisure practices. Yet entirely different connections between urban aesthetics, personhood, and belonging come into being on the basis of the same media, economic mechanisms, and aesthetics that overdetermine the city as a space of corporate venture. As Mbembe also stresses, contemporary electronic capitalism's urban projects can never be entirely totalizing ones.[17]

Colonial Modern Texture

My analysis of the revivals of the Chinese pasts of Bangkok vitally relies on the scholarship on colonial modernity in Southeast and East Asia. This body of work extends the notion of the colonial to include territories that remained formally noncolonized, such as Siam and China.[18] As work that focuses on the treaty port city—as the predecessor of the global city—this scholarship is of prime historical importance to this project. But the scholarship on colonial modernity also revises received notions of origin and derivation in colonial relations, highlighting primary and prescient forms of thought about gender, the social, and relations between capital, image, and personhood.[19]

Tani Barlow defines colonial modernity as follows: It "can be grasped as a speculative frame for investigating the infinitely pervasive discursive powers that increasingly connect at key points to the globalizing impulses of capitalism."[20] Using the notion of the semicolonial to describe such conditions, Barlow asks, "How could a lexicon forged in conditions of binary opposition of colonizer/colonized work in the manically proliferating conditions of difference that operated under the conditions of semicolonialism?"[21]

Bangkok's old Customs House (in Thai, Sulakasathan; colloquially, Rong Phasi) vitally embodies features of Siam's colonial modernity and semicolonial condition. Located in Bangkok's old European trading quarters in the Bang Rak district, the Customs House's colonial architecture is replicated by the area's other edifices, such as shophouses and *kodang* (warehouses), as well as the famous Oriental Hotel's Authors' Wing (1879) and the Danish East Asiatic Company's waterfront compound (1884). The Customs House, which long provided "public housing for families of the officers of the Bangrak Fire Brigade and the Marine Police," is marked by severe decay.[22] It is currently being developed into an upscale hotel.

The grand 1880s building signals both the Siamese royals' emulation of British colonial governance as well as the fact that a nominally independent Siam had to operate under conditions imposed by France and Britain. Rather than representatives of a foreign colonial power, it was once

Siamese officials of the Crown who worked in the Customs House, albeit constrained by the conditions of extraterritoriality in effect from 1855 to 1938. After the passing of the Bowring Treaty in 1855, this extraterritoriality limited Siam's tariff autonomy. Rather than possessing dominion over land concessions, Western countries controlled 75 percent of external trade. This is how Bangkok's extraterritoriality distinguishes itself from the better-known extraterritorial conditions operative in Shanghai.[23]

Wasana Wongsurawat argues that Siamese rulers benefited from extraterritoriality rather than being disadvantaged by it. They did so with the aid of a transnational Chinese merchant class who were colonial subjects and whose mobility and extraterritorial exemption from Siamese jurisdiction proved efficacious in producing wealth for Siam's royal elites.[24] What is more, Siam itself acted as a colonizing power, and its elites modeled the country's administrative structures on those of British India.[25]

The scholarship on colonial modernity in Asia argues for the contemporaneity of the modernities of metropole and colony—it is not that colonialism comes first and brings modernity; rather, colonization and modernity occur simultaneously. I adopt the idea that the modernities of cities like semicolonial Shanghai and Bangkok are primary and prescient, rather than derivative, from Barlow's work, which warns that "once modernity *is* construed to be prior to colonialism, it becomes all too easy to assume, wrongly, the existence of an originary and insurmountable temporal lag separating colonialism from modernity." Barlow asserts that, on the contrary, "the modernity of non-European colonies is as indisputable as the colonial core of European modernity."[26] I further rely on Ann Laura Stoler's formulations of a modernity that was coproduced in the colonies, rather than merely imported from the metropoles.[27] With regard to the Southeast Asian city, Robbie Goh and Brenda Yeoh stress "the co-causal relationship between Western colonial influence and the cultural particularities of the colonized peoples, in the creation of colonial urbanisms which leave their mark on the newly-independent nations."[28]

Bangkok's majestic Customs House embodies Siam/Thailand's specific colonial modernity in both historical function and architectural style. Even the very form of the 1880s building—its neo-Palladian architecture, designed by the Italian architect Joachim Grassi—can be aligned with a style prominent in the Anglophone world and emblematic of the British empire that Siamese royal elites emulated.

At present the Customs House is one of the city and region's most storied and imaged colonial-style edifices. Its atmospheric crumbling façades made it into a sought-after film location, photography site, and art exhibition venue. Mounted in the Customs House, the 2020 exhibition *Hundred Years Between* recaptured the edifice's royal, semicolonial, and cosmopolitan modern significations.[29] Royal family member Sirikitiya Jensen's curation exploited the building's derelict state to invoke the era of its contemporary, her great-great-grandfather, King Chulalongkorn, Rama V (1853–1910). Sirikitiya's exhibition improvised on Chulalongkorn's letters and photography and consisted of photographs that she herself produced on the trail of the king's 1907 expedition to Norway.

Hundred Years Between brought into view a Siamese project of modernity that was from its beginning always already liberal (transnationally modern) and always already Buddhist rationalist (locally modern). The medium of photography itself indexes a time in which Siamese elites used some of the first globally deployed photographic and filmic technology to construct a modernity that aligned local with transnational, colonial elements.[30] In the atmospheric fifth reign building of the Customs House, *Hundred Years Between* made a royal past uncannily present, while lending a royalist future-present authenticity and inevitability.

Occurring under conditions of capitalist expansion as it does, colonial modernity extends beyond national borders and the boundaries of empire. Such a perspective considers the movement of commodities and the activities of business empires as constitutive of transregional historical formations that exceed the nation.[31] These elements of colonial modernity are vital to my analysis, because the Bangkok revival recovers the aesthetics of particular transnational, colonial modern formations that arose in the region.

Bangkok's Customs House was used by Wong Kar-wai to embody 1960s Hong Kong, and the next chapter will investigate the significance of the ways that this Hong Kong colonial modernity is actualized in Bangkok. The remainder of this chapter, by contrast, focuses on the referencing of Shanghai's colonial modern past in Bangkok.

Throughout its commercial invocations across Bangkok hospitality venues, Shanghai frequently represents a Chinese cosmopolitanism that remains safely relegated to the past. According to Harry Harootunian, the collapse of the past, present, and future into an undifferentiated "historical present" is a pervasive characteristic of contemporary political temporalities. Yet there remain differences in how divergent temporalities comingle and compete in this "historical present."[32] The attempt to calibrate whether the invocations in Bangkok studied here neutralize the unruly and multivalent characteristics of historical Shanghai—or whether they reanimate these—therefore remains a worthy undertaking. In what follows I contrast two contemporary modes of referencing Shanghai in Bangkok.

Bangkok's Textures of Femininity

The revivification of Chinese pasts in film and hospitality venues relies on referencing a colonial modern femininity from 1930s Shanghai and 1960s Hong Kong. While the sartorial style of the iconic female protagonist of *In the Mood for Love* becomes part and parcel of this film's 1960s ambiance, and the plot of its quasi sequel, *2046*, engages the "pleasures of commodified flesh" as a theme, several business ventures in Bangkok also invoke colonial modernity and capitalize on the commodification of Chinese femininity.[33] Thus the upscale Oriental Hotel's China House restaurant relies on femininity as a central feature of its décor, as does the speakeasy-style bar Honest Mistake, which approximates the atmosphere of a historical pawnshop.

Less than a kilometer away from the Customs House, one finds the most striking Shanghai-informed business venture in the city: Maggie Choo's, a nightclub that opened in 2013 in Bang Rak, close to the heart of Bangkok's financial district. The so-called high-concept venue relies on a hyperbolic occupation of Shanghai femininity and urbanity.[34] Maggie Choo's draws centrally on the aesthetics of Chinese cosmopolitan modernity and incorporates the Shanghai of the 1930s into the scheme of its design theme and business plan. The club relies on what it presents as an authentic history of migration from Shanghai to Bangkok. Its Facebook page outlines what is intended to function as the tantalizing backstory of the venue:

> Maggie Choo's was named after [*sic*] Shanghai cabaret owner who fled her hometown in 1931 following the Japanese invasion that tore the city [*sic*]. Shortly after arriving in Bangkok, she found a 19th century Thai Chinese shoe box restaurant crammed into a basement 10 meters below Silom road serving authentic Thai chinese shophouse food. When one day, she discovered behind the walls in the corner of the restaurant an entrance that lead [*sic*] to a derelict 19th century East India company bank built in 1847 used for storing porcelain and spices that the British used to carry back

1.2 A hostess sits on a swing at the Bangkok club Maggie Choo's. Maggie Choo's Facebook page, May 23, 2017.

to England for Queen Victoria, her past caught up with her and she converted the old bank into a cabaret, just like when she used to [*sic*] back in Shanghai. Today the cabaret is yet to be revived again.[35]

In the club, women have to perform, embody, and offer up for consumption a Chinese modernity of the early twentieth century (fig. 1.2). Women literally constitute the décor of the venue, as they are positioned on swings, on the piano, and above the bar, in largely motionless roles (fig. 1.3). The attire of the club's hostesses takes the cheung sam, or qipao, the iconic garment of Chinese cosmopolitan modernity, to an extreme. With its high side slits and spare top design, the Maggie Choo version of the cheung sam hyperbolizes the high modern style of bourgeois femininity of *In the Mood for Love* as well as suggesting the availability for money of the women who wear them.

Maggie Choo's branding capitalizes on the sexual titillation associated with a 1930s Shanghai cosmopolitanism. The sex trade of the time, rooted in poverty and displacement, functioned as an organizing trope for influential discourses on social issues.[36] Transposed into the club's description and visual presentation in contemporary Bangkok, by contrast, it acquires solely debonair significance and connotes consumability. This occurs in the manner of the linkage between femininity and city that Shuh-mei Shih has identified in the "prototype of the modern Shanghai femme fatale.... Lodged in her are the characteristics of the urban culture of the

1.3 Women are positioned above the bar at the club Maggie Choo's. "Bangkok" Facebook page, September 12, 2014.

semicolonial city and its seductions of speed, commodity culture, exoticism, and eroticism."[37]

The high-concept venue further occupies the vault of a colonial bank, and the words "British East India Company" are emblazoned in neon on the walls. As in Sirikitiya Jensen's exhibition in the Customs House—or in Wong's *In the Mood for Love*—a colonial-style building, with an explicitly colonial history, provides the material edifice for the invocation of a geographically disparate colonial modernity that extends far beyond Bangkok.

Ackbar Abbas describes the city of Shanghai's historical cosmopolitanism as constituted by a multivalence of law, style, population, and attitude. Abbas stresses the city's "capacity to be all at once a space of negotiation, domination, and appropriation."[38] This cosmopolitanism, according to Abbas, was brash, always in a mode of contestation and, above all, ruthlessly indifferent. In these characteristics, he locates the emancipatory potential of Shanghai's cosmopolitanism.

With regard to the material remnants of this past in the current city of Shanghai, by contrast, Abbas describes the seamless incorporation of the old into present-day exigencies of real estate arbitrage. Here the remnants of the city's cosmopolitan heritage blend into the demands of late capitalist development. Abbas writes that in Shanghai "preservation produces not a sense of history but the virtuality of a present that has erased the distinction between old and new—or where local history is another gambit in the game of global capital."[39]

As material edifice, Maggie Choo's occupies the flattened temporality that Abbas outlines for contemporary Shanghai. Constrained by its high-concept framing, the colonial ruin does not appear as agentive in Bradley Garrett's sense of vernacular history telling, and its conventional historical signification remains unacknowledged.[40] Instead the ruin works merely to provide an ambiance of authenticity. Maggie Choo's deployment of the ruin thus approximates a "heritage" type of revival. Much like what May Adadol Ingawanij describes for the "heritage film," whose "distinguishing features include an emphasis on marketing, high production values, [and] the presentation of Thainess as a visual attraction," the heritage revival undertakes a particular visual framing of Chineseness that tends toward the upscale, commercial, and ornate, and frequently remains unquestioning of the colonial features of architectural sites.[41] Germane both to this chapter and the next, the heritage revival is opulent, deeply surficial, haptic, and often partakes in Orientalist aesthetics. The embodied sense of history that the patrons of a venue such as Maggie Choo's might experience parallels the lush interiors; portentous, textured exteriors; and sensory-affective properties of *In the Mood for Love*.

At first encounter "the modern Shanghai femme[s] fatale[s]" of Maggie Choo's seem not to be cast in an agentive mode, a role that stands in some contrast to the historical case of women in 1930s Shanghai.[42] Barlow has shown that the relations of femininity and commodity were central to the colonial modernity produced in Shanghai in the first third of the twentieth century. This world of anticipatory and emancipatory "ideation" about the "social experiences to come" was vitally future oriented.[43] The Bangkok club's hostesses may also figure as symbolic of the social experiences to come, but not necessarily in an emancipatory sense. In the visual presentation of the club their relation to a world of commodification is conceived as one in which the women figure as commodities alongside others. Shih details the visual properties of the commodity in early twentieth-century Shanghai: "The commodity fetishism prominent in Shanghai modernism was itself reflective of the semicolonial city as a playground of erotic and decadent desires, consumptive rather than productive in nature. . . . The logic of consumption involves a powerful visual dimension, because the desiring medium of commodity fetishism is triggered by vision: seeing a commodity gives one the illusive promise that one may own it."[44] Stylized and positioned at a remove, the hostesses of Maggie Choo's may be understood to replicate such semicolonial logics of vision, desire, and capitalist exchange. This does not, however, foreclose the agency of the women who work as hostesses. That their personhood and actions in the club always exceed a nonemancipatory feminine historical ideal becomes clear after a show interlude in the club. When some of the hostesses leave their assigned stations, move through the club, and converse, they reassume their everyday personas, engage in conversation as private persons, and abandon their club-assigned function of approximating 1930s Shanghai femininity.[45] While the club may envision them in commoditized roles, their actual praxes break the mold of the semicolonial revival.

Colonial Modernity and Femininity in a Transmaterial Field

How do Bangkok urbanites and visitors occupy the materiality of this re-vivified Chinese colonial modernity, both in the city's edifices and in their own habitus? In what follows I bring the question of architectural texture together with an analysis of the representation of femininity. I begin to work through the double signification of Chinese femininity in Thailand as historically abjected and newly exemplary. Ultimately we find in the re-vival venues a cosmopolitanism against all odds: Here, a historical cosmopolitanism, invoked and inhabited in combination with the materiality of the built environment, lets a contemporary scene of plurality emerge.

While commercial, lifestyle-oriented occupations of colonial heritage and the attendant deployments of femininity demand critique — as in the case of Maggie Choo's — this cannot be a foregone conclusion. Just more than two kilometers north of the club, the Shanghai Mansion Bangkok likewise deploys elements of historical Shanghai. This venue's self-conscious foregrounding of its materiality, its animation of the building's historical signification, the participatory nature of its nightlife, and the engaged disposition of its staff enable it to connect with Shanghai's, Bangkok's, and Hong Kong's colonial material pasts and representations of Chinese femininity in a markedly different fashion.

First opening its doors in a historical Chinatown building in 2008, the hotel initially advertised itself as follows: "Find yourself transported to a bygone golden era, where the old world romance of 1930s Shanghai meets

1.4 Second-floor interior of the Shanghai Mansion Bangkok. Photograph by the author, 2016.

new world Shanghai-chic. In this opulent oasis, each of the seventy-six rooms are indulgently decorated Chinoise-style complete with fine linens, plush textures and rich hues."[46] A first visit to the hotel reveals a colonial-style physical environment and the citation of a commercially available femininity. Thus its furnishings give the guest rooms a boudoir-like ambiance, while the common areas combine luxurious cosmopolitan furniture with images of a distressed Shanghai femininity (figs. 1.4 and 1.5). On my first visit I discounted the hotel's aesthetics as merely a business gimmick.

My second visit to the Shanghai Mansion Bangkok complicates my calibration of the valences of distressed Chinese femininity and urban colonial modernity in its design. When I stayed at the hotel from June 15 to 18 in 2016, the mansion's updated website declared, "Inspired by the building's theatrical roots and original Art Deco flair, Shanghai Mansion reflects the stylish mood of Shanghai, circa 1930, full of rich, vibrant colours, opulent fabrics, imperial furniture and whimsical details."[47]

These details of the hotel's history were infused with nuance during my 2016 stay. On the first rainy evening I was drawn in by the atmosphere at the hotel's ground-floor Red Rose restaurant and I began to experience

1.5 Web publicity for the Shanghai Mansion Bangkok: "Rooms in Bangkok."

the meaning that the hotel's history might hold today. At one end the Red Rose becomes the Shanghai Terrace, a lounge that opens onto busy Yaowarat Road, the core of Bangkok's Samphanthawong district, a district that in its entirety is often called just "Yaowarat." On that night, a traffic policeman sought shelter from the rain. Black-and-white images of women in a past cosmopolitan nightlife graced the wall next to the bar (fig. 1.6). A clothing stand offered Chinese gowns that guests could wear to fully partake in Shanghai colonial modernity; a tall transnational visitor ventured out onto a dark Yaowarat Road in a long red gown.

The hotel's interior architecture also tells the story of a cosmopolitan past. The ground floor's old ceiling beams and flaking paint make palpable the history of a building that housed a Chinese opera as well as a variety of commercial venues: "Shanghai Mansion began life in 1892 as a trading house, and in 1908, it was transformed into Bangkok's first Chinese opera house. . . . By the mid 1900s, the building transformed again, serving as Thailand's stock exchange and a textile trading centre, before becoming Yaowarat Square, a popular department store brimming with restaurants and shops peddling Chinese herbal medicine."[48] I had approached my visit to the hotel with some trepidation, expecting the foreclosure characteristic for heritage ventures of the progressive citation of the urban past. However, during my 2016 stay and follow-up visits until late 2022, the old building with its iron girders, derelict ceilings, opulent new texturing, a staff committed to animating its historicity, as well as its references to a geographically disparate (Shanghai) and a geographically proximate colonial modernity (Bangkok), ultimately engendered a different experience.

1.6 Photographs at the Red Rose restaurant, Shanghai Mansion Bangkok. Photograph by the author, 2020.

I had initially understood the hotel's referencing of colonial modern femininity as part of a masculinist design offering up women as part of the experience of a historical lifestyle. When the writer for the hotel's publicity materials, Rachna Sachasinh, related that the female owner of the Shanghai Mansion Bangkok intends not only to revive the building's history but also to actualize the possibilities for women that the idea of historical Shanghai holds, I reassessed the design.

While the common areas of the building highlight the patina of ceilings, iron girders, art deco glass, leather, and old woods, the "Ying Hua" and "Mu Dan" guest rooms deploy dark red and purple upholstery and curtains, pink pillows, yellow walls, and velvet and brocade fabrics to texture a more explicitly "feminine" space (figs. 1.7 and 1.8). I now understand the guest rooms less as sites that feature women as objects of luxury but rather as spaces that allow (some) women to inhabit a luxurious, "pluritemporal" atmosphere.[49] The rooms' texturing, in combination with the artistic images of "Shanghai" women, thus appear both as accommodating of women and as an enigmatic fetish that lacks immediate intelligibility.

Hotel room interior through parted curtains, Shanghai Mansion Bangkok. Photograph by the author, 2016.

1.8 Hotel room with richly textured wallpaper, curtains, and bed, Shanghai Mansion Bangkok. Photograph by the author, 2016.

On the first evening of my 2016 stay at the hotel, a jazz band played in the Shanghai Terrace and the lounge filled with Bangkok hipsters, some of whom affected a Shanghai look, as well as with Chinese, European, and African tourists: "By night, the spirit of Shanghai is effusive, with a live jazz lineup that beckons folks from around the city."[50] The Czech bartender took cash bets on the outcome of a World Cup game. At the bar Rachna Sachasinh related her history of growing up in Chinatown as someone of South Asian descent, her transnational university education, and current involvement in the hotel's project of self-definition.

In the summer of 2016 the hotel was researching and increasingly incorporating the history of its surroundings. During the next two days of my stay at the hotel, Rachna; the hotel's manager, Woralak Bangprasert; and I explored the neighborhood with the historian Wasana Wongsurawat, ate at the Red Rose, and talked for hours about the hotel's historically grounded vision. The hotel becomes animated in a different way for the observer, especially through the people who run it—from the cheung sam–clad waitress from northeast Thailand, who performs the 1930s and 1960s cosmopolitan look most convincingly, to those who work to integrate the hotel into its surroundings and historical context.

As the jazz lounge filled with people from all corners of the city and the globe on that evening, I realized that I was witnessing a scene that bears the marks of a contemporary cosmopolitanism. To be clear, this cosmopolitanism is not identical with the Shanghai, Hong Kong, and Bangkok colonial modernities referenced in the hotel's branding. Rather than represent a smooth replication of the refined sartorial styles and pastimes cited in the hotel's design, the plural scene that I encountered at the Shanghai Terrace included elements of hyperbole, of the ridiculous (the tall tourist venturing out in a Chinese gown), and of the type of commercialization that turns urban spaces into products. Nonetheless, the Shanghai Terrace produces a kind of urbane plurality. While not identical with them, it relies on the invocation of divergent Chinese histories and colonial modernities to come into being.

The combination of the historical site, its virtual and material referents, and the investment of persons of plural backgrounds animates the Shanghai Mansion Bangkok's ethos and atmosphere. Diverse, multicultural actors work together to give life not exactly to their own histories but to a plurality cognate with these. To be sure, everyone is in the mood for texture, but they are also in the mood for love.

TWO

In the Mood for Texture | Transmedia Revivals of Hong Kong's, Bangkok's, and Shanghai's Chinese Pasts and Colonial Modernities

Marco Wilms's documentary *Durch die Nacht mit Christopher Doyle und Nonzee Nimibutr* (Into the night with Christopher Doyle and Nonzee Nimibutr, 2010) presents a behind-the-scenes account of the making, in Bangkok, of Hong Kong filmmaker Wong Kar-wai's iconic film *In the Mood for Love*. *Durch die Nacht* features Wong's cinematographer, Christopher Doyle, guiding the viewer through relevant locations in the city. In the film's establishing scene Doyle steps onto a Bangkok rooftop. With the city below him, the prominent chronicler of Hong Kong declares: "The only spaces that we really wanted to shoot—which is a Hong Kong that doesn't exist anymore—actually still exist in Bangkok." As Doyle concludes, "So, basically, the Hong Kong of our mind is actually here," *Durch die Nacht* cuts to a scene from *In the Mood for Love*: The 1960s Hong Kong colonial modern interior that is now on display is in fact located in Bangkok's Atlanta Hotel—and Bangkok is where Wong and Doyle filmed all the interior and exterior scenes of colonial Hong Kong.

In Wong's film the materiality of Bangkok's Chinese colonial modernity meets the desire for capacious transregional cultural formations. The film's trope of an unrealized love ideal instantiates the counterfactual temporality of a revisionary gaze on region. The female protagonist's distressed femininity and sartorial style transport historical trans-Asia sociocultural ideals into the present.

2.1 Bangkok's old Customs House. Photograph by the author, 2020.

Ruinous Textures

Doyle's claim that "a Hong Kong that doesn't exist anymore actually still exist[s] in Bangkok" centrally materializes in the fact that the primary outdoor location of *In the Mood for Love* and, to a lesser extent, of its sequel, *2046*, is furnished by Bangkok's Customs House (fig. 2.1). Much of Wilms's documentary focuses on showing how this particular location was made available to the fantasy of an old Hong Kong. The very fact that the Customs House remained in a state of disrepair for years also made it the preeminent film location in Bangkok's Chinatown. Its imminent renovation into a commercial venture (an upscale hotel planned to open in 2026) heightened the edifice's ruinous ephemerality.

The first instantiation of texture that I investigate is thus that of the colonial ruin. In Wong's *In the Mood for Love* the materiality of the ruin provides access not only to the aspirational, alternative history of a relationship but also to the collectivity for which it stands. Ruins also furnish the material link between the cosmopolitanism of 1960s Hong Kong that the film foregrounds and a premodern Southeast Asian cosmopolitanism (that of Angkor Wat). The film draws these two locations into relation so

2.2 Alley by the Customs House. Photograph by the author, 2017.

that they become part of one and the same region. These linkages furnish salient elements of the temporal perspective that the ruin enables, a revisionary gaze that encompasses two conditionals: the "what could have been" and the "what could still be" of history.

The Customs House's patina figures prominently in *In the Mood for Love*'s stylized mise-en-scène of ideal love (fig. 2.2). Countless scenes see the film's protagonists rendezvous before its crumbling walls, the details of cracks and crevices so pronounced that the old building almost takes on the function of a character in its own right (fig. 2.3).

What might the trope of the ruin mean for the imagination of a transregional history and future? At present the ruin occupies a central role in the mediation of Bangkok's, Hong Kong's, and Shanghai's different colonial and postcolonial temporalities. It provides material and virtual linkages between the three cities and the ways in which they double promiscuously across film and hospitality venues. As such the significance of the ruin exceeds the continuity of the colonial.

I neither understand the ruin as situated outside of larger histories— and solely indicative of the personal—nor merely want to read colonial materiality as the wound that keeps on wounding.[1] Rather, I argue that *In*

2.3 Customs House wall in the rain. Film still from Wong Kar-wai, *In the Mood for Love*, 2020.

the Mood for Love's colonial modern spaces and epochs can be drawn into productive relation to the potential of the urban ruin to store vernacular microhistories.

Bradley Garrett examines vernacular, experiential approaches to history that can be accessed through the contemplation of urban decay. This apperception of history is exemplified in a practice he calls urban exploration: "As a practice that temporarily inhabits sites of material history, urban exploration constructs assemblages of complicated emotional and memorial attachments to abandoned places that meld pluritemporal geographic, historical, and experiential imaginations to assay history."[2] In Garrett's theory the ruin thereby acquires an agency of its own with regard to the telling of history. It tells of a different history, however, than that put forth by conventional historical sources.

In *In the Mood for Love* Bangkok's Customs House furnishes the materiality and underwrites the affectivity of a 1960s Hong Kong cosmopolitanism that moreover bears the marks of Shanghai émigré culture.[3] As the two married lovers, Mrs. Chan (Maggie Cheung) and Mr. Chow (Tony Leung), imagine and reenact the affair that their spouses are having with each other, they often meet in the shadowy alley outside their rooming house. In an iconic scene in which Mrs. Chan announces that her husband has returned to Hong Kong, the lovers rehearse their imminent parting in this alley. The derelict wall of the building against which they lean is furnished by the Customs House. The dialogue between the two lovers is as follows:

MRS. CHAN: I didn't think you'd fall in love with me.
MR. CHOW: I didn't either. I was only curious to know how it [their spouses' affair] started. Now I know. Feelings can creep up just like that. I thought I was in control. But I hate to think of your husband coming home. I wish he'd stay away! I'm so bad! ... Will you do me one favor?
MRS. CHAN: What?
MR. CHOW: I want to be prepared.

After a long interval the conversation continues:

MRS. CHAN: You'd better not see me again.
MR. CHOW: Is your husband back?
MRS. CHAN: Yes.... Am I hopeless?[4]

In line with the film's general pacing the scene is slow and the conversation interspersed with long silences and distressed gazes. But this scene of anticipated separation is also unusually long, with exceptional focus on the built environment. Mrs. Chan is caught in the rain on her way home from work and waits, leaning against the wall of the Customs House. The plaster is crumbling and the wall is richly textured, so that it appears inscribed with the etchings of a mundane history. The particularities of weathered wooden shutters and window bars complete the backdrop. Though public, the alley becomes a site of privacy for the lovers, and the rain and darkness provide further seclusion. As this becomes the repeat location for the lovers' meetings and conversations about love, the Customs House's textures become part of the syntax of the film.

In the scene described earlier, the Customs House's features function as "assemblages of complicated emotional and memorial attachments... that meld pluritemporal geographic, historical, and experiential imaginations."[5] For one, this location and its surfaces tell the microhistory of a love that must by necessity remain secret. The ruinous surface supplements the muted emotionality of the scene and of a desire that cannot be expressed fully. In addition this surface indexes a historicity of the relationship that must always be disavowed. If, according to Audrey Yue, the film's slow motion opens up a space of possibility for an emotionality that is otherwise foreclosed, then the urban ruin presents a material counterpart for such potentiality.[6] The ruin's process of decay slows history down even more than slow motion, and the Customs House's wall presents a micromanifestation of the "what could have been" of the affair.

A later scene heightens the intensity of the bond between texture, emotionality, and history. After Mr. Chow moves to Singapore, the newspaper for which he works sends him to Cambodia to report on French president Charles de Gaulle's 1966 visit to the country and historical speech on sovereignty—an event that figures as the powerful symbol of a decolonization that Hong Kong has not yet achieved.

On this trip Mr. Chow also travels to the historical sites of Angkor. In the twelfth-century edifice of Angkor Wat, erected by the Khmer king Suryavarman II (r. 1113–1150), Mr. Chow finds the site to which he can entrust the secret of his enduring, illegitimate love. He whispers the secret into a hole in the temple wall. The scene repeats the unusually long focus on the texture of the built environment and the ruin in Bangkok. It is at Angkor that the ruin is finally ruinous enough, the wall ravaged enough, and history extensive enough to hold the truth of an epochal love.

Angkor Wat represents a high classical style of Khmer architecture, itself a premodern mélange of Khmer and Dravidian styles and a prime exemplar of the "Sanskrit cosmopolis" that in the first millennium of the Common Era extended all the way "from Afghanistan to Java."[7] In the scene in which Mr. Chow whispers the secret into a hole in the temple wall, the premodern cosmopolitanism of Angkor substantiates with monumental gravity the affective charge of a love that could not be realized. This scene of promise and ruination also foregrounds the ruin in order to corroborate the film's vision of a different geopolitical imaginary, however. Together with the scenes at the Customs House the Angkorian scene lays the basis for an alternative, transregional imaginary that spans East and Southeast Asia.

Hong Kong, Shanghai, Bangkok

In addition to supplementing affect and endowing emotion with history, the prominent role of the built environment in Wong's film indexes the complex temporal and semiotic overlay of three cosmopolitan models and colonial eras. Features of the anomalous colonial modernities of Hong Kong, Shanghai, and Bangkok coalesce in *In the Mood for Love*'s design, plot, and production background. First, the film's "classical" backdrop of the Customs House in Bangkok is used to represent an older colonial Hong Kong. This Hong Kong in turn is a location of temporal complexity that, according to Ackbar Abbas, was always already colonial and always already postcolonial.[8] The anomalous specificity of Hong Kong's coloniality moreover lies in its location near or in China. In combination with its status as a majority-Chinese British colony, this made Hong Kong a "world between worlds" and "a prime negotiating space among the contending parties of the Cold War."[9]

Wong's film is further part of the cinema of transition produced around the time of the phased return of Hong Kong to mainland China beginning in 1997—a time in which the question of coloniality is posed anew. According to Audrey Yue, "Hong Kong cinema expresses this temporality of pre-post-1997 as a culture that simultaneously forecasts and recollects."[10] Both Abbas and Yue thus attribute to Hong Kong culture an enhanced mobility within time.

Vivian Lee directly connects *In the Mood for Love*'s temporality with the properties of the city of Hong Kong. She attributes Wong's "fragmentation of time, memory, and narrative structure" to an "urban sensibility nurtured by the experience of growing up in a colonial city which 'is not so much a place as a space of transit.'"[11] Lee further regards the 1960s—that 1990s Hong Kong cinema recuperates and *In the Mood for Love* foregrounds—as pivotal, a blueprint for the city's identity henceforth. She defines this decade as "a time of transition, and the year 1966 . . . saw the beginning of the Cultural Revolution in China and subsequent anti-government riots in Hong Kong in 1967" that occasioned a measure of reform.[12]

Made in the context of turn-of-the-century fears about the disappearance of Hong Kong, *In the Mood for Love* can be understood as the defiant revival of a 1960s Chinese cosmopolitanism—a counterfactual future-present that positions Hong Kong in an unstable temporality and aesthetic that is as future oriented as it is distressed. The unrealized love at the heart of the story marks the film's nostalgia as more complex than merely the retrospective longing for an ideal that never existed. Rather the film's temporality indexes a conditional that reviews the past for indications of what the future could have been, a fragile manifesto for resisting new dependencies imposed on the city-state of Hong Kong before it was even able to actualize its decolonization.[13]

Gina Marchetti and Audrey Yue have stressed the émigré Shanghai milieu in which *In the Mood for Love*'s 1960s story takes place.[14] Shanghai manifests prominently in Hong Kong cinema. Historically Shanghai and Hong Kong cinemas are intimately connected, as "the center of Chinese commercial film and popular music production was transplanted from Shanghai to Hong Kong after the Chinese civil war" (in 1945–1949).[15]

Attached especially to the character of Mrs. Chan is the cosmopolitanism of Shanghai, a colonial entrepôt that flourished both despite and because of its extraterritoriality. In the film Shanghai's high cosmopolitan modernity has recently come to an end with the 1949 communist victory. The melancholy of the émigré characters and their transitory lives in Hong Kong make palpable the gravity of their loss of home. As a Shanghai emigrant himself, Wong prominently foregrounds this migratory trajectory in the stories, dialects, and historical references of his films. What distinguishes Shanghai's from Bangkok's semicolonial situation is that in Shanghai the foreign powers' extraterritorial rights extended to the governance over territory. Abbas recuperates the historical city's ethos as brash, indifferent, and contestatory—its colonial modernity marked by a multilayered cosmopolitanism.[16]

The material base of the distressed, futuristic setting of both *In the Mood for Love* and its sequel, *2046*, is furnished by Bangkok, a location that is marked by the extraterritorial dynamics of a disavowed semicolonial history. Siam's temporality of the "never/yet still" accounts for the elasticity of the colonial imaginary that adheres to Bangkok.[17]

Wong's film combines this Bangkok with Hong Kong and Shanghai to render temporality multiple. Rather than foreclose interpretation of the three cities' colonial modernities, *In the Mood for Love*'s focus on the colonial ruin as a living site that keeps on making history allows historiography to remain open to further intervention. This multiple occupation of time and space is further instantiated in Wong's use of language: Frequently the characters of his films speak to each other in entirely different dialects or languages (such as Shanghainese, Cantonese, Mandarin, and Japanese) without surprise, hesitation, or incomprehension. This is a prominent way in which *In the Mood for Love*'s invocation even of the overdetermined motif of colonial Shanghai retains futuristic-revisionary potential.

Feminine Fetish

Just as the material surfaces of the contemporary city become fetishistically invested as "products," women and the accoutrements of femininity also become part of the texture and fabric of colonial modernity in media and lifestyle venues.[18] The femininity of Mrs. Chan functions as a fetish that allows for renewed access to the past. In the film femininity attains texture in the fetish of the cheung sam, or qipao, a garment closely connected with transnational Chinese modernity. The cheung sam signifies a shoring up of culture and collectivity in the face of a series of historical "falls." I invoke the historical figures of Chiang Kai-shek (1887–1975) and his wife, Soong Mei-ling (1898–2003), and her deployment of the cheung sam as an example. I argue that the fetish of the cheung sam ultimately reanimates latent imaginaries of the region.

The iconic female protagonist of *In the Mood for Love* partakes in the twentieth-century colonial modernities of Shanghai and Hong Kong in a different way than the hostesses of the Bangkok club Maggie Choo's or the women who figure in the décor of the Shanghai Mansion Bangkok (discussed in chapter 1). Mrs. Chan inhabits the Shanghai-influenced colonial modernity of 1960s Hong Kong through her sartorial style, the commodities she uses and trades, and through the time of capital and the work world in which she moves. The fetish of her femininity provides insight into the temporalities of capital and nation, while at the same time exposing manipulations of history.

Laura Mulvey describes the privileged role of femininity in relation to the fetish as follows: "Cinema finds, not its only, but its most perfect fetishistic object in the image of woman. As a signifier of sexuality the image of eroticized femininity . . . has a bridging function [between cinema and market]."[19] Mrs. Chan's carefully curated appearance represents a prime exemplar of the feminine as fetish. This fetish, according to Mulvey, obscures both the labor that produces the cinema and the cinema's status as commodity. At the same time, it presents as beautiful surface a femininity conceived as lack and wound.

The fetish retains a privileged relation to (its own) history, however: "The fetish object fixes and freezes the historic event outside rational memory and individual chronology. But the fetish still stays in touch with its original traumatic real and retains a potential access to its own historical story."[20] This "historic event," in Freudian and Marxian terms, is that of original trauma and of the labor process, respectively. But what of a fetish that indexes a different kind of etiology?

Mulvey's work is also instructive for interpreting the chains of displacement effected by the fetish differently. She stresses that the fetish as "image refers, through displacements of the signifier, to vulnerable or highly charged areas in the social fantasy that produced it."[21] In the contemporary trans-Asia context under consideration, these "highly charged areas" include the obscuration of particular minority histories in Thailand, the violent logic of colonial systems, and the position of women in the global Asian city, both past and present.

As one viewer observes, the role of Mrs. Chan's cheung sams can be understood as follows: "They represent a fetish in the sense that they make you realize that you want something, of which you don't even know what it is (yet)."[22] As an object that harnesses such desires, the cheung sam not only bridges back to original trauma or processes of production but also speaks to the historical displacements that animate *In the Mood for Love*'s regional imaginary. These include the severing of historical memory regarding Southeast and East Asian interconnection, the temporalities of capitalism, the reordering of historical time, and events of political upheaval in twentieth-century Asia, such as the 1960s protests in Hong Kong.

Throughout the film Mrs. Chan appears in dozens of different cheung sams; only once or twice does a repeat appearance of one of their iconic 1960s patterns occur (fig. 2.4).[23] As more and more designs occupy the screen, their patterns become instrumental in structuring a distressed notion of femininity and the high cosmopolitan modernity that it instantiates as textured surface. Yiman Wang has detailed the close connections between femininity and the cheung sam, showing how it serves to mold and constrain women as they are literally "poured into" it.[24] Mrs. Chan wears the cheung sam to work, when she socializes, when she goes downstairs for a bowl of noodles, and when she falls asleep on Mr. Chow's bed. In fact she never wears anything else. Each garment molds itself to her body, and the colorful geometric and floral patterns invite and stand in for the unlimited terrain that fantasy moves in.

2.4 Mrs. Chan and her landlady in characteristic cheung sams. Film still from Wong Kar-wai, *In the Mood for Love*, 2020.

Sartorial Semiotics: The Temporalities of Toil and Love

Yue argues that Mrs. Chan's changing cheung sams help the viewer keep time in the sense of representing the era as a whole and also marking time's progression on a daily level: "Her costumes epitomise the temporality of the film as a form of presentness marked by the new, where the progress of time is ritualised in the changing of her wardrobe. This temporality connotes a dailiness accentuated through the ephemerality of fashion."[25] But while they anchor our attention and move the plot forward, *In the Mood for Love*'s cheung sam patterns also index a relation of femininity to capitalism during this period (fig. 2.5). In Wong's film the cheung sam stands in for the tastes and aspirations of a 1960s cosmopolitan city-state, in and from which a transnational Chinese cosmopolitanism flourished both despite and by way of the colonial routes of trade.

While the garment designs are part and parcel of the construction of an iconic femininity, their energetic patterning also aligns with the industriousness of a period of unprecedented growth. The 1960s saw the expansion of Hong Kong's manufacturing economy, a development largely powered by the textile industry. The floral and geometric patterns in the film are frequently described as lively, matching a zeitgeist that felt up-

2.5 Mrs. Chan at work in a floral-print cheung sam. Film still from Wong Kar-wai, *In the Mood for Love*, 2020.

and-coming, a mass society in which women entered the workforce in unprecedented numbers, and an era that understood itself as combining feminism with a particular performance of femininity.[26]

Mrs. Chan's cheung sams represent a relation to the rhythms of industrial production in an expanding economy. They appear as an integral part of her work persona. She is typically presented in one of the formfitting garments, typing at her desk underneath a large wall clock that signals that, under the temporal regime of the nation and of modern capitalism, all of life is "measured by clock and calendar."[27] Mrs. Chan appears as integral to the capitalist regime of labor and, given the ease with which she operates in it, as more agentive than oppressed by it. This becomes part of the ideal and of the fetish.[28] On the other hand, through techniques such as slow motion, the film stretches the boundaries of the time of capitalist productivity to such an extent that it allows temporalities that exceed it to gain ascendancy.

A case in point are the following two scenes: The exclusive view of a Siemens clock, hung on the wall of Mrs. Chan's office, is underwritten by the diegetic sound of typing. Superimposed on the scene is the soundtrack of an anxious conversation between the two lovers about the imminent return of their respective spouses. The scene references Mrs. Chan's agentive femininity within a capitalist system that relies on the time of "clock and calendar," yet the superimposed conversation directs us to rhythms of feeling not entirely in sync with this temporality.[29]

As the film cuts to a black screen, the mournful strings of its theme song, "Yumeji's Theme," start up. Full-bodied, like a character of its own, the theme enhances psychological intensity and signals deep attachment, profound nostalgia, and pervasive melancholy. Its affective quality is heightened by slow motion in the scene that follows. Opening on the view of a red-curtained hotel corridor, this scene focuses on Mrs. Chan's pensive face turned away from Mr. Chow, who in turn is looking directly at her. She turns to face him slowly, then moves past him as she walks away down the corridor. The scene incorporates the complex affect of a love affair that has, in a sense, never happened. Slow motion catapults the action into the domain of the oneiric and opens the cinematic plot up to counterfactual temporalities. Mrs. Chan's final look back from the end of the corridor instantiates the way in which anticipatory affect merges with melancholy recall. This lends the love affair its ideal form and runs counter to the preceding scene's rhythmic clicking of the typewriter and ticking of the clock, which both spur capitalist exchange.[30]

While love cannot be situated entirely outside capitalism but is incontestably constituted by its logic, the counterfactual temporalities that thread through *In the Mood for Love* exceed at least the time of capitalist production.[31] Inasmuch as the story of the love relation models a temporal schema through which to grasp the world, the film prompts the viewer to ask, over and over again, "What could have been?" and "What could still be?" This utopian mode of questioning pertains as much to sociocultural forms as it does to the relationship. Rather than a reductive trope for colonial or national logics—"domesticating historical complexities to heterosexual romance"—the dynamics of the love story teach a counterfactual mode of thought.[32] In the plurally constituted formations of the Angkorian empire and the Chinese colonial modernities of the twentieth century, the film finds examples of cultural amalgamation and models of collectivity that it invests with great longing.

What is more, the question of how the "homogeneous, empty" time referenced in *In the Mood for Love* relates to the nation is not self-evident, as the film highlights precisely the trans-nation, and the commonalities and simultaneities that it invokes are those of a trans-Asia Chinese modernity (that spans Hong Kong, Phnom Penh, Singapore, Shanghai, and Bangkok).[33] The cheung sam allows us to track the multiple temporalities of this transnational modernity—"the fetish still stays in touch with its

2.6 Mrs. Chan stands against an interior wall. Film still from Wong Kar-wai, *In the Mood for Love*, 2020.

original traumatic real and retains a potential access to its own historical story."[34] As such this feminine garment attains significance also in relation to a series of historical "falls" that occur in twentieth-century transnational China.

In the film the cheung sam must be read in the context of Hong Kong's return to China in 1997. The scene in which Mrs. Chan and Mr. Chow rehearse their imminent parting ends with a close-up of Mrs. Chan standing against a crumbling interior wall (fig. 2.6). This scene's prominent intertextual reference, the 1943 story and 1984 film adaptation of *Love in a Fallen City* (by Eileen Chang [Zhang Ailing]), which chronicles a love relation that moves between Shanghai and a Hong Kong that is falling to the Japanese in the 1940s, further articulates Wong's film with a transnational Chinese history.[35]

If we attribute historical significance to the crumbling wall, the image of perfection that Mrs. Chan furnishes in its foreground lets the meaning of the fetish become clearer.[36] The shot of Mrs. Chan in her high-collared, formfitting cheung sam and flawless makeup in front of the faded wall plastered with notices in Chinese harnesses the desire for Hong Kong's distinctive modernity under a colonial situation that, at the time of the 1997 handover, became invested with retrospective longing.

At the same time, the fetish of the cheung sam references an entire relay of historical events in transnational Chinese history. It is closely associated also with the Shanghai of the 1920s to 1940s, when "the qipao was intended to be worn in public and was an expression of individuality, femininity and women's rising status and assertiveness."[37] Its imprint as the garment of a sophisticated Chinese modernity was further advanced by Chiang Kai-shek's wife, Soong Mei-ling, who owned thousands of qipaos and sported them on official occasions. Across China, Hong Kong, and Southeast Asian treaty port cities, the cheung sam signaled the simultaneity of a cosmopolitan modernity of which women and their sartorial practices were prime harbingers.

Just as we might understand the feminine iconicity of the historical figure of Soong Mei-ling as mourning and masking the Kuomintang's loss of China to communism, the character of Mrs. Chan masks and recovers a number of divergent losses in early to mid-twentieth-century history. In Wong's film femininity is first and foremost fetishistically invested with covering over the wounds of the political and historical loss of Hong Kong to China in 1997 but also bears within it the fall of Shanghai to the Japanese in 1931 and of Shanghai's cosmopolitan modernity to communism in 1949. Mrs. Chan's perfect femininity, foregrounded before the disintegrating edifices of the region's colonial modernities, is tasked with preserving past sociocultural ideals of personhood, belonging, and political order before their respective falls. Rather than merely mask loss and freeze past ideals for a reactionary nostalgia, however, the multiply inscribed textures of femininity in this film reanimate memories of a plural modernity.

Ultimately Bangkok is charged with the material and semiotic embodiment of these past ideals. Though not explicitly the subject of the film, in an extradiegetic context Bangkok is conceptualized outside of the realm of historical loss. Just as the temporality of the love relationship shows the power of counterfactual anticipation, the overdetermined fantasy site of "sovereign Siam" allows for an impossible mobility in time.

De/colonial Fetish

What then of femininity in the context of Bangkok's colonial modernity, which represents the material substratum for the transmedia archive under consideration? An investigation of the Shanghai Mansion Bangkok's online branding reveals that the Chinese femininity invoked in contemporary Bangkok stands in for a coveted past and future cosmopolitan modernity. This analysis also allows for a critique of Thailand's "anticolonial" coloniality. I contrast the hotel's digital presentation of Chinese colonial modernity with the decolonial references of *In the Mood for Love* and then close with speculation about the fetish's counterintuitive potential for historical recovery. Dependent on an element of liveness, both the invocation of femininity and of the ruin in these contexts allows plurality to reemerge in the present.

In the films and hospitality venues under consideration, it is Bangkok's unacknowledged coloniality that bears the most capacious room for fantasy. This is instantiated also in the femininity that the Shanghai Mansion Bangkok's website highlights. Banking on the "heritage" aesthetics of a distressed, futuristic Chinese femininity, the website images intentionally reference *In the Mood for Love* through foregrounding the high modern cuts of the cheung sam that Mrs. Chan sports. Set against worn shutters and opulent market produce and amid the "salt of the earth" inhabitants of Yaowarat, one of the hotel's web pages features models who explore the hotel's surroundings.[38] Mixing referents as it does, the venue's branding creates a mashup of Chinese femininities, drawing on Hong Kong, Shanghai, and Bangkok elements for its mise-en-scène of a gendered form of embodiment that can span eras and national boundaries.

Particularly striking is the highly sexualized image of a model clad in an elegant black cheung sam, sitting in front of the stained wooden doors of a shophouse (fig. 2.7). Surrounded by Yaowarat residents, whose aging, ordinary attire, and mundane activities are accentuated, the Shanghai Mansion Woman represents a fetish that recovers the promise of a colonial modernity that, in the Thai context, is frequently traded as anti- and noncolonial. In such a reading the model's perfect presentation and confident, aggressive pose would signal that nothing has in fact been lost, but that it is within the power of the contemporary feminine actor to provide continuity for the nonthreatening, market-friendly multiculturalism associated with this disavowed colonial modernity.[39]

While the hotel's website may be understood to intensify the deployment of the feminine fetish in this way, *In the Mood for Love* balances the desire for the colonial with decolonial references. Rather than only idealize 1960s Hong Kong, or its colonial modern antecedents (Shanghai), *In the Mood for Love* briefly but prominently features the 1966 Star Ferry protest and the riots of 1967 as symbolic of the desire for decolonization. As John M. Carroll writes, "By 1964 almost 500,000 people, mostly recent refugees, were living in hillside shacks or rooftop huts. Given such poor housing and working conditions, extreme gaps in wealth, and rampant

2.7 Web publicity for the Shanghai Mansion Bangkok: "Explore."

government corruption, the Star Ferry riots of April 1966 should not have come as a surprise. Within days after the young So Sau-chung protested an increase in Star Ferry fares by declaring a hunger strike in front of the Star Ferry pier, one rioter had been killed and more than 1,400 youths had been arrested."[40]

The following year, 1967, was marked by year-long protests against the "poor working conditions and appalling state of welfare provision in Hong Kong during the 1960s": "What began as a strike at an artificial flower factory became a major anti-colonial movement led by local leftists, which was eventually countered by a full range of emergency and security measures instituted by the colonial administration."[41] Wong's citation of the 1960s protests in combination with the invocation of Charles de Gaulle's 1966 speech at Phnom Penh as a decolonial event lets his film diverge from the politics of the Shanghai Mansion Bangkok's online publicity.

As a condensed trope of historical disavowal as well as of historical truth, the fetish plays out its double role of obscuration and recovery across these translocal sites. With regard to transformations of the contemporary city, the fetish obscures not only the workings of labor but also the conjoined operations of finance capital and visual information. The transmedia manifestations of colonial modern Chinese femininity and of the ruin thus frequently support the mechanisms of real estate arbitrage that produce the city as commodity and eviscerate its public foundations. But while the fetish obscures the relays between market and screen or designed surface, in these Bangkok transmedia contexts it always bears traces of the prior, transregional histories that produced it, and its workings are never entirely predetermined. Transporting numerous histories across eras and locations, as it does, the fetish engages these for new forms of apprehending the future-present.

In my analysis the critical potential of such historical recovery has depended on an element of liveness—the live character of the ruin and the animations of femininity of *In the Mood for Love*; the engagement with history of the Shanghai Mansion Bangkok; the constant play with location of the Facebook page "Kratham khwam Wong"; and the emergent character of a new cosmopolitanism at the Shanghai Terrace lounge. These were shown to imbue especially the overdetermined trope of colonial Shanghai with new potential. The materiality of the ruin becomes the vital factor that allows the fetish to perform such critical work. Thus rather than tether it to rigid notions of the past, the ruin's materiality makes it a living site of history. This live quality allows the ruin-as-fetish to bridge back to histories of plurality and make them available for imaginations of a future city and region.

Invocations of colonial modernity in hospitality venues and their attendant deployments of femininity frequently seem to disavow the city as a public site and as a location for living rather than lifestyle. Yet several of the transmedia sites studied in this book bear fragile remnants and portents of the textures of a regional imaginary that is connected to the colonial but exceeds its logics. Across built environments and other visual media the reinhabiting of the textures and temporalities of the colonial thus opens up possibilities for plurality in the present. In a neoliberal present that eviscerates the city's public and historical dimensions, the temporal and spatial transactions of *In the Mood for Love*—as well as Bangkok revelers' desires to inhabit a social formation that is plural in terms of time, ethnicity, and nation—may be some of the few vestiges of urban life that one can at present build on.

In the Mood for a Different Region

In *In the Mood for Love* the implicit and explicit referencing of material Southeast Asia not only provides the semantic and affective texture of the love relationship but also gestures toward a different geopolitical imaginary. In contradistinction to both a mainstream and independent Hong Kong cinema in which representations of Southeast Asia are overdetermined by notions of haunting, criminality, and licentiousness, Wong's film positions Southeast Asia as the terrain of a foundational premodern Asian cosmopolitanism (in its scenes at Angkor) *and* of decolonial futurity (at Phnom Penh), though this latter reference becomes severely burdened by the history of genocide that Cambodia will have undergone.

Wong's imaginary of a trans-Asia Chinese colonial modernity rewrites the histories of both the nation-state and imperial formations. In this imaginary, Bangkok, Hong Kong, Shanghai, Singapore, and Phnom Penh are always already linked by a transnational history—a notable historical configuration that exceeds imperial and national structures. In Wong's films a colonial modernity inhabited by Chinese persons extends across and unites the colonized locations of Singapore and Hong Kong with the formally noncolonized locations of Thailand and China and a Cambodia highlighted as decolonized. Exclusively Chinese (and Japanese) persons inhabit this modernity in Wong's cinematic universe.

How is it that Bangkok becomes the preeminent site for such an imaginary? The temporality of Bangkok's coloniality yields largely troubling ideological results. However, the transregional, transmedia archive that invokes colonial modernity in this location rewrites histories of "area" inventively. Referenced in Bangkok, occupations of the colonial ruin and representations of femininity are historical configurations that also have the potential to contest present-day nationalisms and regional formations.

In the Mood for Love recovers these other historical networks for the imagination of a present in which local and transnational persons in Bangkok desire social, political, and economic forms that diverge from those of an Asia rising under the hegemony of the People's Republic of China as well as from Cold War ideological alignments. Wong's film attributes primacy and prescience to a formation that isn't only colonial or noncolonial but encodes a different notion of space and temporality. His film presents the imagination of a shared Southeast and East Asian history that is not overdetermined by the notion of formal colonization but centrally includes its objects, aesthetics, and economic dynamics. In invoking this modernity, *In the Mood for Love* and other films by Wong also put forth the vision of a transregional present that has not entirely capitulated to the demands of contemporary "reregionalization" and does not rely on Mandarin as the only Chinese language.[42] Texture furnishes the material and virtual substrate and breathes life into this vision.

The different valences of citations of the colonial past discussed in this chapter stem from a difference in medium, form, and commercial intent on the part of Wong's film and the digital branding of the Shanghai Mansion Bangkok. Yet the temporal properties of Bangkok colonial and post-colonial modernities themselves also make possible these highly divergent occupations of the same tropes. Whereas the interpretations of other cities' colonial modernities are more tightly framed by prior critical work, the temporalities of Thailand's modernity are so motile that they are mobilized to bear highly divergent meanings.

In Bangkok, Shanghai's and Hong Kong's colonial modernities attain a kind of elasticity that only Thailand's own historical configuration would allow for. It is here that a tall tourist in a long Chinese gown can enter Yaowarat nightlife without much notice. It is in Bangkok that visitors can wholeheartedly believe in cultural authenticity. It is here that 1960s Hong Kong and 1930s Shanghai can come alive. In Bangkok one can make leaps in time and place, and Chinese cultures from divergent cities can be amalgamated. Against the background of Thailand's disavowed historical dependency *and* colonial engagement, Bangkok can figure, both nationally and internationally, as the paradigmatic site of adaptations of the colonial that frequently remain unconstrained by having to reckon with concrete historical fact. While Bangkok's temporal elasticity can, on the one hand, reinfuse other cities' colonial modernities with mobility, it can, on the other hand, also attenuate any critical potential that they might bear. In both cases it becomes instrumental in the generation of contemporary regional imaginaries.

Viewing *In the Mood for Love* with Wilms's documentary and with the publicity materials for Bangkok leisure venues generates an understanding of Bangkok, Hong Kong, Shanghai, and other former treaty port cities as in principle united not only as Chinese locations but also as territories whose inhabitants still desire a different regional imaginary than one that succumbs to contemporary realpolitik. In these films and in sites like the Shanghai Mansion Bangkok, texture emerges as motif, as an element of design and film syntax, and as a historical material structure—a trace or shadow memory. Breathing life into older transregional forms of exchange, texture constitutes a virtual and material subtext that is able to salvage a plural imaginary for the present.

II   BANGKOK: ORIGINARY CHINESE CITY

THREE

Bangkok | Chinese City of Colonial Modernity

ANECDOTE 1

An international conference in Bangkok hosts a dinner at the upscale Silk Road restaurant. The keynote speaker is from Hong Kong, and her teenage daughter has come along on the trip. The daughter scrutinizes the historical photographs of Chinese Bangkok on the restaurant's walls. Her verdict to her mother at the end of the evening is "They are so much more Chinese than we are!"

ANECDOTE 2

In August 2017 the historian Wasana Wongsurawat and I set out to explore the Chinese revival bars, cafés, and galleries of Bangkok Chinatown's most-frequented leisure alley, Soi Nana. On the way we stop at the Teochew Restaurant for lunch. Teochew are the largest group of historical migrants and largest dialect group in Thailand. In the restaurant the People's Republic's CCTV 4 is showing an imperial drama. To our surprise the restaurant manager speaks little Thai; later we hear him converse in Mandarin with kitchen staff. Thus even the Bangkok Chinatown restaurant bearing the name of a dialect culture may already be owned by investors from mainland China, heralding monumental changes occurring in Bangkok's historically Chinese areas.

Both symbolic and material elements constitute Bangkok as a Chinese city. Chapter 2 weighted discussion toward a textual analysis, in which cinema proffers distressed-utopian visions of the region. But the analysis of Wong Kar-wai's film already showed this cinema's reliance on the material constitution of Bangkok.

The city's recovery of its Chinese pasts is simultaneously representational, material, and experiential. The built environment, sartorial style, and cross-referencing between visual media and leisure venues make up the infrastructure of an imaginary that is regionally based rather than merely local. Fantasy and material history meet in the leisure practices of the Bangkok urbanites who frequent the Chinese-themed hospitality venues; they further coalesce in a second wave of Chinese Thai cultural production; and they coincide in texture. In this context Wong's film *In the Mood for Love* becomes part of a circuit of aesthetic inspiration and consumption. While the film exploits Bangkok's Chinese and colonial modern materiality, the city's hospitality venues in turn draw on Wong's aesthetics for their design. This loop puts questions of origin, identity, and temporality—and notions of the opposition of the material and virtual—into flux.

This chapter investigates Chinatown historical edifices and revival venues, their approaches to history, and the ways that patrons inhabit them. My analysis works through three different registers of the revival: hegemonic, statist revivals; the ambivalent valences of heritage revivals; and a revival that potentially revises a history of disparagement. It moves from the material domain of statist monuments to commercial venues and finally returns to digital representation in the hospitality industry.

Among the three cities referenced, Bangkok currently occupies the position of "the most" Chinese city; however, it is also the city whose Chinese history will be erased most completely. Its Chinese authenticity is largely due to differences in the speed of urban development. At present the city remains more textured by history than Hong Kong or Shanghai; this accounts for its ability to instantiate Chinese pasts with acuity. Bangkok is also able to embody pasts that Shanghai and Hong Kong cannot, due to the ability of its semicolonial temporality to accommodate multiple histories.

Diasporic pasts can moreover be understood as sediments, or temporal hiccups, in national histories. Such sediments are better able than national cultural formations to preserve a particular historical period. This temporal feature is less readily available to Shanghai or Hong Kong, where Chineseness, unless deliberately cultivated as heritage, is always the dominant-contemporary: hence Wong's choice of Bangkok as the filming location for all scenes of 1960s Hong Kong and his cinematographer's remark that "the Hong Kong of our mind is, in fact, here."[1]

If we accept the notion of Chinese immigrants as the main drivers of modernization in Thailand, Bangkok can be understood as a predominantly Chinese city.[2] Even in terms of its demographics Bangkok can be considered a Chinese city. In the 1930s Kuomintang sources calculated the percentage of Chinese persons in Thailand at more than 30 percent of the total population.[3]

Today Bangkok's materiality still retains the textures of Chinese cultural history more accurately and (temporarily) enduringly than the other cities referenced. At the same time, remnants of a semicolonial past materialize strongly in the city. While chapter 4 will investigate manifestations of the Chinese industrial and working-class pasts of the city in more depth, much of this chapter examines the logics of edifices that align with dominant governmental and corporate visions of Chinese Bangkok. Exploring museums, landmarks, and leisure sites that fall under the rubric of the heritage revival, it inquires into styles of revival that are in tendency conservative, statist, royalist, commercial, and upscale. What their invocation of Chinese pasts consistently disavows are histories of racialization, denigration, and the largely Chinese constitution of historical labor forces in Thailand.

Yet this chapter also chronicles histories about to be extinguished: the remnants of Chinese Thai migrations of the nineteenth and twentieth centuries, dialect cultures and neighborhood projects that run counter to the ethos of both the People's Republic of China (PRC) and a populist-authoritarian or military-led Thailand, and ephemeral alternative delineations of trans-Asia collectivity that are emerging in Bangkok's Chinatown.

Modern Translocal Hegemonies and the Built Environment of a Vanishing "Chinatown"

Bangkok's Chinatown extends across the porous area of neighborhoods south of the historical palace, the Pom Prap, Bang Rak, and Samphanthawong districts. The area is often colloquially referred to as "Yaowarat" (also spelled "Yaowaraj") after Yaowarat Road, a main commercial thoroughfare in the Samphanthawong district. That Bangkok possesses such a "Chinatown" area results in part from dynamics of racialization under Thai nationalism.

Wasana Wongsurawat notes that while the Siamese economy depended on a Chinese merchant class and labor force, Siam's elites were wary of the potential transnational allegiances of the Chinese. They therefore instituted the division of this population into "good" and "bad" Chinese.[4] Lawrence Chua writes of the analogous, early twentieth-century bifurcation of Bangkok into a national administrative capital and "a thriving port city populated mostly by 'Chinese' migrants and governed by extraterritorial law."[5]

The individual neighborhoods within Bangkok's Chinatown distinguish themselves by their period of settlement in different waves of migration and by different dialect groups. In addition neighborhoods are structured according to industrial histories: Historical guilds, or occupation groups, and the activities of *ang-yi* secret societies determined their shape.[6] One way of accessing Bangkok's agglomeration of "downtown" central Chinese neighborhoods is via the symbolic Chinatown Gate.

In the middle of the Odeon roundabout in Samphanthawong stands a large decorative monumental edifice, the Chinatown Gate, or the Gate in Celebration of His Majesty's 72nd Birthday, built in 1999 (fig. 3.1). Yaowarat Road extends north from here, and Chinatown's other main thoroughfare, Charoen Krung Road, heads south. No one drives through this gate; rather, it signals a particular set of modern power alliances. The Chinatown Gate and its contemporary mise-en-scène at the Odeon roundabout entexture interlocking national and regional hegemonies, including Thailand's recently intensified alliances with the PRC.[7]

The gate is dominated by the colors red, blue, orange, and gold. It is richly textured with two ornate gables in the style of Chinese *paifang*, or *pailou*, historical gates that marked the entry to different wards or communities. The gate's gables are populated with lively three-dimensional figures. In the middle of a traffic roundabout, in a location in which no other particularly Chinese aesthetics are visible, the gate's plasticity invokes "Chineseness" and signals how it is integrated into the Thai political economy.

I became interested in the ways that the gate was animated by its surroundings and endowed with meaning in August 2017, just prior to Bhumibol Adulyadej's (Rama IX, 1946–2016) cremation in October of that year. During this period, the official and popular cathexis to the father of the nation was particularly strong. On one side of the 1999 gate a Chinese inscription wishes the king a long, boundless life. The other side reads, in Thai, "Gate in Celebration of His Majesty's 72nd Birthday." Beneath the letters a large portrait of the late king adorns the middle of the gate. Topping the gate's upper gable, flanked by two Chinese dragons, are the Brahmin-Buddhist royal insignia of this longest-reigning Thai monarch in history. Looking at the gate from the western side of the roundabout

3.1 Chinatown Gate, Bangkok. Photograph by the author, 2017.

in the summer of 2017, one glimpses behind it to its right another large, gold-framed portrait of Rama IX extending along almost the entire length of a building.

Although richly textured, the Chinatown Gate is static, a monument to the aspirationally stable temporalities of Thailand's populist or royalist-militarist alignment with the PRC. As such the gate promulgates the temporality of the nation in alliance with a regional power. As Benedict Anderson notes, however, "If nation states are widely conceded to be 'new' and 'historical,' the nations to which they give political expression always loom out of an immemorial past, and, still more important, glide into a limitless future."[8] The late monarch Bhumibol was the figure who best embodied the nation's reach back into "an immemorial past," lending legitimacy and sanctity to its present-day order. Rama IX stood in for the Brahmin-Buddhist-secular notion of kingship that undergirded governmental rationale since the late 1950s.[9] As a Devaraja god-king and Dhammaraja righteous Buddhist king, Bhumibol was supposed to tie the nation to transhistorical, trans-Asia moral and political principles and, as a modern Renaissance king (excelling in pursuits ranging from science to the arts), to its developmentalist present-futures. The citizen experiencing the staging of the Chinatown Gate is thus interpellated into the time of the continually modernizing nation-in-regional-alliance and simultaneously into a sacred "immemorial" community. The setup at the Odeon roundabout in 2017 moreover works magic with temporality by suggesting the congruence of the current Thai-PRC alliance with the entire seventy-year reign of Rama IX.

Curating Chinese History

Viewed from the West, Buddhist elements also become part of the mise-en-scène at the Odeon roundabout, the golden spires that overlook the area bestowing upon contemporary geopolitical allegiances the sanctity of the country's de facto national religion of Buddhism.

The spires are those of the temple just north of the roundabout, Wat Traimitr, which also houses the Samphanthawong Museum, or Yaowarat Heritage Center. Vividly entextured in holograms, installations, photography, and other media, this museum presents a particular teleology of the history of Chinese migration to Thailand that is congruent with the ethos of the gate. The museum reshapes the fraught histories of Chinese migrants' convergence with and divergence from dominant Thai national ideology into a coherent narrative of harmonious integration.[10] As Wongsurawat adjudges, "Students of modern history, exploring Bangkok Chinatown's celebrated museum . . . will find among the museum's exhibits no memory of state violence toward Thailand's ethnic Chinese."[11]

What is more, the Yaowarat Heritage Center's entry and exit rooms espouse a counterfactual, symbiotic relation of the Chinese community in Thailand with the royal family. In this the center underwrites the temporality embodied by the Chinatown Gate, presenting Chinese Thai history as always already connected and culminating in relations to today's PRC, a polity only established in 1949. Without question this curation of migration history in Bangkok's most important Chinese museum obfuscates its many divergent trajectories.

What further remains unaddressed in the center's presentation is the fact of racialization that created "Chinese" as a category of difference in Siam. Early twentieth-century Thai nationalism forged this identity out of what had hitherto been discrete dialect groups such as Teochew, Hokkien, or Hakka. Chua describes this process as follows: "The term *Chinese* was deployed as a rhetorical device by the nascent state to mask a variety of class, linguistic, and social differences among the migrant population of Bangkok, but it also served to mark them, and the spaces that they built and occupied, as a race within the Siamese capital that was necessary for the economy of the city but needed to be disciplined."[12]

The discursive framing of this racial order through Rama VI, Vaji-ravudh, in *Jews of the Orient*, first serialized in a Thai newspaper in 1914, is well known.[13] "Wichitwathakan's public statement [under Phibun Songkhram] that the Thai government might need to consider dealing with the 'Chinese problem' in the same way the German Nazi government was dealing with the 'Jewish problem'" extended this line of thinking, though it was decidedly not put into practice in any manner resembling the National Socialist genocide.[14] The midcentury, however, saw the large-scale application of anti-Chinese measures under Phibun Song-khram (1938–1944; 1948–1957). Though not expunged entirely from national memory, these histories are elided from the center's triumphalist accounts of economic ascension and social integration.[15]

Hegemonic, statist invocations of Chinese migration to Thailand also disavow certain histories of labor. Lisa Lowe has tracked a global history in which the Chinese "coolie" is tasked with fulfilling labor demands while occupying ambiguous positions within racialized colonial orders.[16] In mid-nineteenth-century Siam, too, Chinese wage labor began to sup-plant a corvée system through which the state had conscripted Siamese men into (unpaid) labor.[17] Enormous Chinese labor contingents con-tinued to provide the conditions of possibility for infrastructural mod-ernization throughout the twentieth century.[18] Although this remains undertheorized, Chinese labor history in Thailand thus parallels global histories of Chinese labor—while also diverging from these, due to Siam/Thailand's complex position within a colonial world.

Dominant Thai representations elide the foundational role of Chi-nese labor contingents in nineteenth- and twentieth-century moderniza-tion and the fact that migrants were deployed as what Ari Heinrich has termed "Chinese surplus" for hard labor while racialized as the other of the nation.[19] Instead dominant accounts subsume such histories of labor into narratives of social ascension, such as the so-called *suea phuen mon bai*, or "Mat and Pillow" legend.[20]

Histories of Modernization

A kilometer from the Yaowarat Heritage Center, on Charoen Krung Road, to the northwest of the Roundabout of July 22, stands a different monument to Chinese Thai history that highlights the role of the Chinese in economic and scientific modernization. Emblematic of Siam's colonial modernity in architectural form, usage, and educational history, the Berlin Dispensary Co. Ltd. and Pharmaceutical Museum is situated at the crossroads of the Suea Pa and Charoen Krung roads (fig. 3.2). The museum occupies a Singapore-type shophouse built in the reign of Rama IV (1851–1868) in the neoclassical Renaissance and Palladian styles associated with the British empire.[21] It has been refurbished and currently has white trim and is painted yellow, the birth color of both Rama IX and his successor, Rama X. The building was bestowed on Rama IV's (1804–1868) daughter and son, who were to use it for revenue purposes. In the seventh reign (1925–1935) it was under the ownership of Queen Rambai Barni.[22] Since its early history the building thereby exemplified the tendency for Chinatown real estate to be under the control of the Crown.

The Berlin Pharmaceutical Museum opened in 2016 to commemorate the eighty-fourth anniversary of both the building and the life of the Chinese Thai doctor Chai Chainuvati (Tsai Yen-Kiang), who had worked in it. From Bangkok, Chai had gone to study medicine at the Tongji German Medical School in Shanghai. The medical student's lecture notes in German, English, and Chinese exemplify the multilingual practices of a Chinese cosmopolitan knowledge class. In the museum's narrative Chai's biography coheres around Chinese Thai values of filial piety, national service, and dedication to education: "Poverty was the driving force of his struggle, diligence, and studiousness until he received a scholarship and completed his degree at a German university in Shanghai. Subsequently, due to his desire to repay the generosity of his father, mother, and country, he returned to Siam to use his knowledge to treat the population."[23]

Returning to Siam in 1932, Chai opened the Berlin clinic "as one of the first private clinics of the communities in the Charoen Krung-Yaowarat area."[24] He also sought licensure for the dispensary and later pharmaceutical company, which weathered World War II and other economic and political obstacles. Designing and producing his own medicines, he managed to take care of patients even during periods of economic difficulty and medical-supply shortages. In the museum's presentation Chai thus exemplifies Chinese social mobility as well as migrants' roles in Thailand's

3.2 Berlin Dispensary Co. Ltd. and Pharmaceutical Museum, Bangkok. Photograph by the author, 2017.

modernization, development, and knowledge industries. The temporality that the Berlin Museum invokes is that of the integrative nation, in which Chinese Thais occupy a firm position in the teleology of development; but, unlike the Yaowarat Heritage Center or the Chinatown Gate, the museum does not emphasize the nation's "immemorial past." Though the history of its building is closely tied to the Chakri dynasty, the museum's narrative emphasizes the social mobility, education, and entrepreneurship of a Chinese Thai historical figure rather than primarily highlighting royalist affiliations. Having reviewed three sites that diverge in their embodiment of dominant perspectives on Chinese Thai history, I now turn to larger infrastructural changes underway in Chinatown.

The Berlin Museum is located approximately one city block away from a site of recent infrastructural expansion, the Metropolitan Rapid Transit underground train station that opened in 2019 in the heart of Chinatown on Charoen Krung Road, named after the nearby temple Wat Mangkorn. The extension of the subway is part of Bangkok Metropolitan Authority (BMA) zoning plans that aim to use transportation nodes to increase urban density in Chinatown.

Urban planning scholar Napong Tao Rugkhapan evaluates the BMA zoning plans negatively. Urban density is deployed in this case as a generic "best practice" that does not take into account the specific density that Bangkok's Chinatown already possesses. Condemning the BMA's technocratic rationality and blindness to historical urban specificity, Napong argues that in this plan "zoning [becomes] a technology of unseeing."[25] He describes "how the particularities of Chinatown are being unseen and risk being unmade" by such planning rationales.[26] In response Charoen Chai residents have formed the Charoen Chai Conservation and Rehabilitation Group to meticulously "re-see" their neighborhood as one in which the built environment materializes a complex history of Chinese migration, labor, and collectivity.[27]

By contrast, Bangkok's oldest Chinese neighborhood, Talad Noi, a subdistrict of Samphanthawong, has taken a different approach to countering urban development.[28] Talad Noi dates from the Thonburi period (1767–1782) — from before the Bangkok period. Typical for the neighborhood today are its numerous auto-parts shops lining small alleys that can almost be navigated only on foot. Housing Bangkok's oldest Chinese edifices, Talad Noi is the most fetishistically invested grounds of the revival. The neighborhood also represents the most vulnerable grounds of urban transformation, as a high percentage of its real estate belongs to the Crown Property Bureau (CPB), whose actions cannot be contested. Residents of Talad Noi have chosen to embrace the reevaluation of their neighborhood community style. They are attempting to redirect the current reappraisal of Talad Noi by initiating archival and hospitality projects, such as a neighborhood museum and guesthouses.[29]

Talad Noi is the neighborhood in which the revival of nineteenth- and twentieth-century as well as pre(semi)colonial histories is most visible. Two commercial ventures restored buildings that are respectively more than one hundred and approximately two hundred years old, Tai Guan Café and Patina Café.[30] While much local expertise went into their sensitive restoration, both venues consciously deployed the patina of colonial modernity and Chinese history as a business strategy.[31]

Talad Noi's most iconic marker of early nineteenth-century, pre–Bowring Treaty Chinese life, however, is the classical Sou Heng Tai Mansion (fig. 3.3). In contrast to Tai Guan and Patina, the courtyard house instantiates rather than deploys history, disrupting the fetishization of Chinese histories in this location. The small compound was open and free to visitors (in a subsequent period Sou Heng Tai asked for a token drinks order or

3.3 A swimming pool in the courtyard of Sou Heng Tai Mansion, Bangkok. Photograph by the author, 2017.

entry fee); upon entry the visitor is surprised to find a diving school in the middle of its courtyard as well as a small café. For a while, the compound also housed a beagle farm. Sou Heng Tai exemplifies continuous evolution rather than cultural recovery. Still in the possession of and inhabited by the descendants (with the current Thai surname Posayachinda) of the Sou family who built it, the mansion represents living testimony to Chinese history and creates freewheeling cross-century contemporaneities.[32]

Material Yaowarat

The greatest factor in urban transformation is that Bangkok's Chinatown, long left relatively undeveloped, has recently come to represent a prime real estate location. Only 50 percent of the land is freehold, while the remaining land and real estate, especially in Talad Noi, is owned by the CPB and members of the royal family.[33] The CPB is evicting current occupants and raising rents to levels that force residents out of homes and businesses, with corporations, mainland Chinese investors, and wealthy individuals subsequently buying or renting these historical properties. In addition infrastructural projects, such as those of the BMA, will continue to complicate life for the majority of the current residents of Samphanthawong, Pom Prap, and Bang Rak districts and cause their eventual eviction.

The lifestyle-oriented gentrification that we see in entertainment venues, coffee shops, and hotels across Chinatown must be understood against the background of these developments. Yet the mostly small-scale revival venues popular since the 2010s do not represent a significant threat to the preservation of Chinese Thai heritage and livelihoods. Several of the trendy new venues are owned or co-owned by local residents, who use a family business or an adjacent shophouse to open a café, gallery, bar, or restaurant.

In order to situate the revival historically, one must distinguish between two phases of Chinese cultural recovery in a country in which Chineseness was, for divergent reasons, disavowed for decades.[34] The first phase of cultural recovery consisted of a period beginning in the 1980s, in which, as one commentator writes, "Suddenly, it's cool to be Chinese."[35] In this phase the material remnants of Teochew and other dialect cultures remained intact, even though much linguistic heritage had been lost. Reinvoked as the culture of dialect groups, in clan associations and other organizations, this new consciousness of Chinese culture mixed with a general turn toward all things Chinese. For many young Thais of Chinese descent, this took the form of enrolling in Mandarin-language classes, rather than learning the dialects their grandparents spoke. Beyond language learning, Sittithep Eaksittipong investigates a broader affective regime related to the recovery of lost Chinese identities and knowledge. From the late 1980s on, he documents the flourishing of Thai-language radio and print media that respond to "desires to consume media that assuage feelings of lack and [desires] for a Chinese Thai cultural identity" and an attendant rise in expert authors (not conversant in Chinese).[36]

The refurbished Chinese culture of the past decades is thus always already an explicitly hybrid form of cultural recovery. The second phase of cultural recovery in the 2000s consisted of a period in which the material remnants of dialect culture were about to be erased—and in which remembrance transfers to "prosthetic memory," or to the visual and literary spheres as well as to transgenerational and transethnic memory.[37] These first and second phases correspond to two periods of the PRC's cultural, political, and economic activity in the region. In the early days of China's opening to increased global interactivity the country was still dependent on transnational Chinese networks. Only in the early to mid-2000s did

China take a more assertive role in economic expansion, contributing to an obscuring of local Chinese cultures and giving rise to a retroactively PRC-aligned historical narrative in Thailand.[38]

Thus the distinctive cultural and linguistic roots of Chinese Thais that were thoroughly suppressed by Thai nationalism—and since the late 1980s found a cautious, hybrid revival in public consciousness—are under threat of erasure. Some visual and material evidence will remain. Filmmaker Salee Every (Waraluck Hiransrettawat) states that when confronted with the destruction of the Bangkok Chinese cemetery in which her ancestors were buried, she began to ask herself, "Who were these people?," "Who am I?," and "How am I connected to them?"[39] Salee's film *Kith and Kin* transfers practices of remembering from the material location of the cemetery—in which the family performed rituals of ancestor worship—to the prosthetic realm of cinema: *Kith and Kin* records the splitting of the family into opposing factions regarding the question of how to deal with the remains of their oldest ancestor, Koh Bien Tiet. After explosive confrontations, family members develop divergent theories of memory, cultural belonging, belief, and politics. As Salee describes it, "We had to ask ourselves—who are we? Are we Buddhist? Chinese? Thai? Democratic? Populist? Or ... fascist?"

Salee's film is part of a second wave of Chinese cultural revival—one in which the materiality of heritage is transferred to the domain of cinema and other art forms. This shift is reminiscent of the ways in which Hong Kong's Kowloon Walled City—the quintessential document of a Chinese city that remained beyond both British imperial and mainland Chinese control—was given texture in films and other visual media after colonial authorities demolished it in 1984. In many cases a visual culture that foregrounds the textures of history is all that will remain of pre–Belt and Road cities, cultures, and collectivities. However, in Bangkok's leisure culture visual invocations of the past still mix with the material remnants of Chinese history. The experiential dimension of patrons' visits to the revival venues also plays a significant role in renegotiating identity and region.

Material Mood

Leisure scenes at venues across Yaowarat, such as the bar and restaurant FooJohn Building; the Shanghai Mansion Bangkok; the bars Ba Hao, Tep Bar, Rabbit Hill, and Opium; the nostalgia restaurants Baan Phad

Thai and Hong Sieng Kong; the speakeasy-style bar Honest Mistake; Amdaeng Hotel; and the cafés As Is, Sarnies, and Vahap, cohere axiomatically around texture and affect.[40] In these locations customers can touch (on) the material properties of the past. The collective affect swirling through these venues is connected to both space and time, materializing longing for a different present and a kind of belonging that exceeds the local. As Michael Lucey and Tom McEnaney write, "Texture . . . is the felt sense of the indexical relations that always potentially exist between the work, the world from which it emerged, and the world in which it is circulating."[41] While Lucey and McEnaney write about literature, the Bangkok venues also possess such indexical properties.

A section of the patrons who gather here is wary of the new regional hegemony of China while also resisting the politics of Thailand's populist and military-dominated governments of the past two decades. Such patrons seek to inhabit historical Chinese sites that have turned into leisure venues as platforms for oppositional plurality.[42] Thus Salee Every, who frequents FooJohn Bar, links her recovery of her Chinese roots to her disaffection with contemporary Thai governance and society. She expresses her enthusiasm for Hong Kong (pre-2019) and describes her identification with its cosmopolitan Chinese culture.[43] The novelist Veeraporn Nitiprapha, who is a customer of Rabbit Hill and Honest Mistake, is singularly concerned with imagining social and political possibilities beyond those dictated by a resurgent Thai military and populist governments. Their goals, and those of many other oppositional artists, include democratization, the redressing of political massacres from the 1970s onward, feminist and queer agendas, and migrants' rights.

Bangkok's elastic temporality and the textured nature of the environments in which these artists congregate make such alternative political imaginaries possible. But an additional horizon now defines the temporality of Bangkok as a Chinese city: Chineseness was just barely able to resurface into public view as a culture reclaimed by descendants of migrants to Thailand. Their current reinhabiting of the city as a Chinese city in design and leisure practices is also now in danger of erasure. Against the background of real estate developments and government collaboration with PRC regional expansion, Chinatown is witnessing the all-too-brief revival of a history that "will not have been." Thus while Bangkok will have been "the most Chinese" in terms of a still-enduring material history, it is also the city in which vernacular Chinese pasts are most endangered.

In this in-between moment, lifestyle venues rely on texture to make the city's pasts available to consumptive ideological practices and preferences. But such commercial projects are also invested in providing inventive indexical links to a material heritage set to disappear with urban transformation and the dominant renarrativization of Chinese Thai history.

A little to the west of Bangkok's imposing neo-Renaissance Hua Lampong train station (1916), across Krung Kasem Canal, lies Chinatown's most popular leisure alley. Extending between Rama IV Road and Maitrichit Road, Soi Nana is lined with bars, cafés, galleries, and small hotels that draw on the material remnants of Chinese migration, business histories, classical Thai performance traditions, and contemporary hipster culture. Tep Bar (Angels Bar, from "Krung Thep"—City of Angels, or Bangkok) is housed in a restored heritage shophouse and serves whimsical Thai liquor cocktails while featuring live classical Thai music.[44] Wallflowers Café packs the narrow floors of a corner shophouse with extravagant cake and coffee creations, plants, and lifestyle connoisseurs.[45] The bars (Pijiu, Teens of Thailand), cafés (Nahim), and galleries (Cho Why) in Soi Nana draw middle- and upper-middle-class Bangkokians, tourists, and a small, diverse intellectual-artistic crowd.

Viranjini Munasinghe details how even the transgenerational immigrant body has to bear the burden of functioning as a "culture bearer."[46] Thus migrants are frequently tasked with standing in as the custodians of a culture thought to have disappeared in the location of origin but to have persisted in the diaspora. This then is the predicament of not only persons but also locations in the case of Bangkok's embodiment of Chinese history. The popular nighttime haunt Ba Hao near the northern end of Soi Nana is a good example. This venue presents a condensed formula for the revival of both a period and a culture, approximating a colonial modernity similar to that of *In the Mood for Love* but inflecting it with local flavor and highlighting a marginally different era, the 1970s. The first two floors of the (much older) historical shophouse consist of a bar and restaurant, while the third features a communal living room and the fourth houses two luxurious colonial modern–style Airbnb accommodations (fig. 3.4). Ba Hao promises its customers a "Chinese era experience." Its stylized bar occupies the high-ceilinged ground floor of the original shophouse, a space that would in the past have been used for storage or commercial activities. In an ambiance of low red lighting, customers consume small inventive fusion dishes ("Drunken Chicken," "Ginger Mayo Taro Ball," "Coriander

3.4 The interior of the Ba Hao restaurant and bar, Bangkok. Photograph by the author, 2019.

Ice Cream") accompanied by a themed drinks menu ("Opium," "Five Rivers," "Forbidden Gold," "Mandarin Tonic," "Drunken Mistress").

C. Nadia Seremetakis has investigated the ways that artifacts, including foods, store history—and how our senses together with such artifacts are able to recover history: "The sensory landscape and its meaning-endowing objects bear within them historical and emotional sedimentation."[47] She explains that "the ability to replicate cultural identity is a material practice embedded in the reciprocities, aesthetics, and sensory strata of material objects."[48] Ba Hao's menu intimates the luxurious, risqué, and Orientalist. As such it is firmly connected to the revival of a colonial modern imaginary. The period in Bangkok that Ba Hao foregrounds in its narrative and reconstructs in its "sensory landscape" is that of the 1970s, which is inexorably linked with the Cold War. During this time Thailand represented the main ally of the United States in that country's deleterious wars against communism in Southeast Asia. Inasmuch as this period is part of the venue's self-definition ("Bring back Bangkok's Chinatown to the 70s"), one would expect Taiwan and Hong Kong to furnish its trans-regional Chinese references.[49] However, rather than celebrate Thailand's historical membership in a "free world" alliance that excluded the PRC, Ba Hao surprises by invoking connection precisely with China. Promising its customers "Chinese/Yaowaraj-inspired comfort bar food . . . [and] combining our old-time favorite snacks with China's popular street food to re-create our own dishes both savory and sweet," Ba Hao both lays claim to a rooting in local heritage and plugs into transnational repertoires.

With the provenance of its culinary culture a mashup, Ba Hao's "Chinese era experience" is curated as a transregional haptic, olfactory, and gustatory affair. Texture is evident in the phenomenology through which the bar connects its customers with a distinct 1970s trans-Asia semicolonial modernity and with a cross-bloc culinary alliance—in the decade in which Thailand first established diplomatic relations with the PRC.[50] If Ba Hao's food and ambiance—and patrons' experiences of them—"bear within them historical and emotional sedimentation," they may well evoke the memory both of a disastrous Cold War geopolitics and of the transregional cultural phenomena that transcended it.

Approximately one kilometer to the southwest of the Soi Nana leisure alley on the Thonburi side of the Chao Phraya River lies the largest and visually most striking Chinese heritage venue, Lhong 1919 (fig. 3.5). Incorporating multiple temporalities, the venue centrally embodies both the semicoloniality of the treaty port culture of Bangkok and also the temporality of the maverick migrant tycoon, whose comfortable descendants can now turn to lifestyle and consumption. Lhong 1919 is a mixed-use leisure destination that houses shops, restaurants, performances, musealhistorical preservation, and an elaborate shrine to the goddess Ma Zhou (fig. 3.6). Lhong 1919 uses the site and structures of a major wharf complex built in 1850. The venue's name is adapted from the Chinese name, Huai Jung Long (Steamboat Port), of the port that was vital for trade with transnational China and Southeast Asian countries. Acquired in 1919 by the Wang Lee business family, whose residence is adjacent to the site, the former port and warehouses were transformed into the upmarket leisure venue in 2017.

A November 2017 article in the daily *Matichon* heralds Lhong 1919 as the "port that looks back in time to Thai Chinese history. . . . Treading the path to greater familiarity with one's ancestry is of no small interest: Lhong 1919 performs that task for the descendants of the overseas Chinese." Owner-descendant Ruchiraporn Wang Lee describes the entire project as a "heritage renovation."[51] Occupying a site of six *rai*, or nearly one hectare, most of the complex's buildings are two-story Chinese ware-

3.5 Ground-floor shops at Lhong 1919's historical warehouses, Bangkok. Photograph by the author, 2018.

houses that surround a large courtyard. The ground floors house mostly shops and restaurants. The second-floor rooms of the renovated warehouses, however, contain museal heritage. Their presentation of exquisitely carved old furniture and woodwork as well as the restored mural paintings on the walls seem almost uncurated and contrast with the design of the commercial venues on the ground floor (fig. 3.7).

The mode of Lhong 1919's heritage renovation interpellates the visitor into the embodied experience of a "history"—whether accurate or not. The renovation intentionally preserves the patina of the structures, highlighting the flaking warehouse walls, under which were discovered the mural paintings chronicling port life. Lhong 1919 animates the historical site as one of treaty port culture. This is significant, as the referencing of colonial modernity across Bangkok leisure venues relies precisely on the culture of treaty port cities—as the quintessential fuel of colonial modern cosmopolitanisms. Sited at a port that was operational for the majority of the period of Siam's extraterritoriality (1855–1938), Lhong 1919 is also factually synonymous with semicoloniality and treaty port culture.[52]

3.6 The Ma Zhou shrine in the middle of the Lhong 1919 courtyard. Photograph by the author, 2018.

3.7 Second-floor museal display at Lhong 1919. Photograph by the author, 2018.

Lhong 1919's attempt to invoke treaty port culture as material mood proves successful in the ways that its sensitive renovation style showcases the port's history. The warehouses themselves, the patina of the structures, and the museal displays and wall painting restoration, as well as the prominent inclusion of the Ma Zhou shrine for Teochew and Hokkien seafarers, all represent conscious, informed relations to history. However, the fact that Lhong 1919 is so commercially upscale has been deplored by Bangkok patrons. Critics have stressed that the affluent Wang Lee family had the means to make the site more of a commons, rather than a private, commercial "theme park." Thus while the venue's "sensory landscape" in part links directly to treaty port culture, it also significantly diverts the visitor's sensorial mnemonic capacities through its predominantly commercial framing. As of December 2023 Lhong 1919 was awaiting redevelopment.

Material-Virtual Girl(s)

A further domain of urban transformation is found in cyberspace. The digital functions as a terrain of primitive accumulation in the city—a mode of opening up ever-new frontiers for capital. Conversely, the digital sphere also allows for critical intervention into overdetermined modes of approaching the urban. Within this domain the figure of femininity occupies a central role in delineating the shape of the city and re-presencing Chinese history. It is femininity that is malleable and generative enough to take on the task of facilitating optimization in the neoliberal order. In this context it is worth recalling the general threefold function of Chinese femininity in the contemporary city (first advanced in the introduction): (1) This figure embodies the leap from the historical denigration of Chineseness into present-day desirability in Thailand (a local phenomenon); (2) she denotes a particular continental past and holds the key to a transregional future (a regional phenomenon); and (3) she encodes the changing forms of value in the city under finance capitalism (a global phenomenon).

In chapter 2 I understood femininity in the Shanghai Mansion Bangkok's web publicity to be cognate with the very grounds of urban transformation. By contrast, in this chapter I examine Chinese femininity as a vector that also revises the terms of its own historical deployment. While one could argue that the hotel's digital branding deploys femininity as a contemporary kind of "Chinese surplus," a second review of the website will show the ways that this figure exceeds its designated commercial function and historical overdetermination.

Chapter 2 demonstrated how the Shanghai Mansion Bangkok's website sets distressed, futuristic femininities in relation to Bangkok's colonial materiality. In December 2024 the majority of images on the website's "Explore" page show an individual woman in distinctive cheung sams exploring cultural and culinary offerings in and around the hotel ("Chinatown Beckons")—in "Food & Drink: Food Stories from Bangkok's Chinatown," "Culture & Events: Festivals, Temples & Community Stories," and "Markets & Shops: A Shopper's Dream Come True." The double valence of a Chinese femininity set against textured backgrounds indexing authentic cultural life becomes salient in these images. Setting this figure against the opulence of produce and goods in "Hidden Yaowaraj" positions her as a consumable entity among others and touches on the history of Chinese women's sexualization in Thailand (as well as Thai women's and Asian women's sexualization in a multiplicity of locations).[53] On the other hand, this Shanghai Mansion Woman is also the consumer—a moneyed, independent woman roaming Chinatown to eat and shop. This is where the third function of femininity in the city, that of encoding the changing forms of value, becomes apparent.

Even in the scene of conviviality featured on the banner of the website's "Dining" page, the model diner essentially remains alone, her individual consumptive agency accented (fig. 3.8).[54] Men and women are gathered around a glass table. The lighting focuses on the model, throwing into relief her pale skin, red lipstick, and red lace cheung sam. Seated on a leather couch, she is flanked by a white man and a South Asian man, who are looking away from her. Only she gazes directly at the camera. Rather than "dining," she is smoking and drinking, lending to this nightlife scene the nefarious glamour of a speakeasy with its connotations of illicit business dealings. In scenes such as these the model's sartorial style incarnates personal distinction and consumer preferences, foregrounding the elevated tastes to which the Shanghai Mansion Bangkok caters.

A more convivial setting makes up the "Explore" page's cover image for "Food & Drink" (fig. 3.9). Together with an older woman, the Shanghai Mansion Woman is engaged in the pleasurable activity of scrutinizing dishes on a tray over a clay stove. She is seated but depicted at equal height with the shopkeeper, evoking an egalitarian sphere of agentive female business actors.

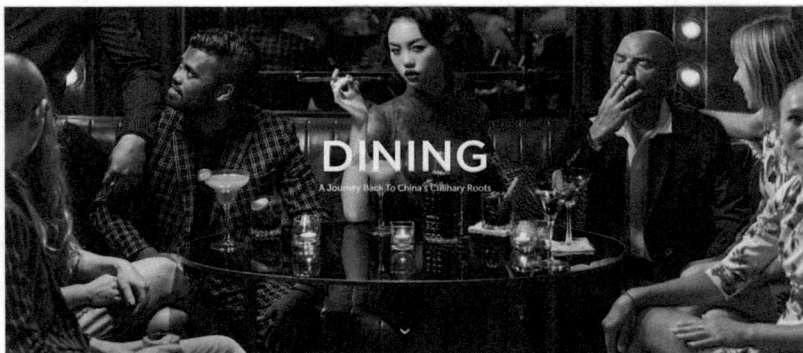

3.8 Web publicity for the Shanghai Mansion Bangkok: "Dining."

3.9 Web publicity for the Shanghai Mansion Bangkok: "Food & Drink."

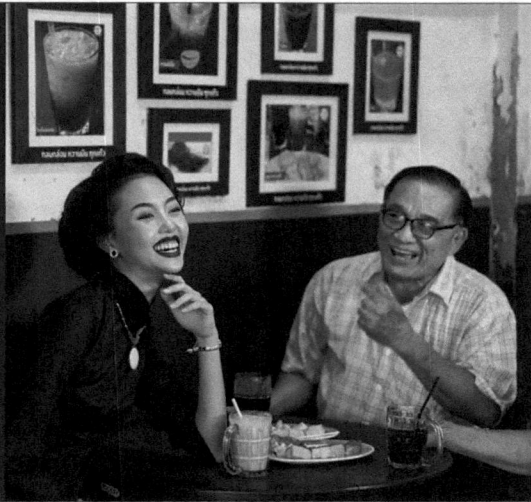

3.10 Web publicity for the Shanghai Mansion Bangkok featuring cross-generational conviviality: "Hidden Yaowaraj."

Her sociability with men, too, can be marked by comradeship (fig. 3.10). In a previous configuration of the "Explore" page, the Shanghai Mansion Woman appeared in the "century old Elah [sic] Sae Coffee Shop, a favorite spot to share a traditional Chinese cup of coffee in the company of the area's old-timers, many of whom come here each day to conduct business or to catch up on neighborhood gossip."[55] In the image accompanying the vignette "Hidden Yaowaraj," the model shares coffee and snacks with two men. She is laughing, with her gaze directed beyond her small party toward a broader audience; an older man in his sixties or seventies laughs, too, his gaze directed toward her. Only the arm of the third man is visible. The scene performs a conviviality in which the Shanghai Mansion Woman is distinct due to her 1960s-style black cheung sam but integrated into a wider, transgenerational community. The image suggests that she is of this culture, too: a stylish daughter of Chinatown, a successful upper-middle-class woman who is as connected to her heritage as to a wider world.

The accoutrements of class are important. In chapter 2 I examined a previous banner of the "Explore" page that shows the Shanghai Mansion Woman in refined evening attire (black cheung sam, jewelry, and small purse), sitting at a slight elevation among male workers eating on the street

3.11 Web publicity for the Shanghai Mansion Bangkok: "Explore."

(fig. 3.11). The heavily stained doors of a shophouse and the ordinary embodiment of the denizens of Yaowarat accentuate her distinction and aver
this location's ability to give shape to history.

Reading this image in the context of urban transformation, I suggested
in chapter 2 that Chinese femininity may serve to recuperate a market-
friendly multiculturalism and represent a ploy in the service of urban
development. In such a reading the Shanghai Mansion Woman would
represent the updated instantiation of a laboring body that produces surplus.[56] Heinrich writes about Chinese bodies as surplus, "a source of profit
whose humanity is qualified or conditioned by its availability as a kind of
global corporeal surplus."[57] How is such a relation between economy and
ethnicity configured in contemporary Bangkok?

What is distinct in Thai representations of this sort is that today's Chinese femininity supersedes a Thai national history in which Chinese persons explicitly represented such "corporeal surplus." Chinese femininity in
the contemporary city of Bangkok labors in the tracks of such a history—
however, this labor reveals itself to be of a different quality. The difference to the historical case is that in this image a Chinese woman would
be laboring as a national/ized body—no longer racialized but ethnicized
in alignment with logics of optimization and a revaluation of region. She
could thus be understood to instantiate a contemporary "Chinese surplus," in which a newly valorized form of ethnic personhood encodes surplus value or, rather, compound value.

Tani Barlow has examined the dynamics of late twentieth-century
Asian economies in which femininity represents "a singular economic sub-

jectivity predicated as labor power" and becomes virtually synonymous with surplus value.[58] Femininity's role remains similar in the twenty-first century, yet its potential to produce value sees some transformation. This would be where a trans-Asia history of racialized labor meets with the logic of the contemporary city. David Harvey has outlined the ways that the city historically both absorbed and produced surplus value. In times of electronic capitalism the relation of city and capital is transformed further, as the city must now absorb and produce the compound value derived from interest on interest.[59] In Bangkok investors seek to maximize the profits that can be derived from distinctive historical areas precisely through the imaginative surplus that design adds to mundane real estate. In this context figurations of the feminine align with complex new forms of value produced by finance capitalism (rather than only surplus value). Femininity, both in embodied and representational form, is thus called on to perform the labor of lending historical depth and fantastically enhanced value to urban "lifestyle" projects.

Distinction or Dignity?

I want to take a second look at the Shanghai Mansion Bangkok's image and speculate on what else the invocation of this femininity in this location might accomplish, especially with regard to the first function of Chinese femininity in the contemporary city: thinking through the leap from the historical denigration of Chineseness into present-day desirability in Thailand. When I first encountered a visual culture (digital and otherwise) that references Chinese femininity in Bangkok, I was quick to discount these images as commercial gimmicks at best and at worst misogynist. Indeed, in figure 3.11 the caption pasted across the model's upper body reads "Travel Back in Time and Uncover the Hidden Secrets of Vibrant Chinatown," suggesting that she might be among the secrets to be uncovered.

The caption links uncomfortably to Bangkok Chinatown's intricate connection with the past sexualization of Chinese women in Thailand. The sex trade was historically linked to Chinese culture. Brothels were frequently located in the Chinese neighborhoods and called *rong nam cha* (teahouses) and sex workers labeled *i kwang tung* (roughly, vulgarly, "Cantonese woman").[60] The situating of a commercial publicity that foregrounds Chinese femininity in this location ultimately works to disrupt this history, however. If this figure's embodiment denotes a shift from denigration into desirability, she also allows us to track such a history of abjection back.

Jean Ma has argued that the task of telling histories that center on traumatic events has in recent decades devolved onto women in several national contexts in Asia.[61] We may thus understand the Shanghai Mansion Woman as also addressing the embodiment and spatial grounds of a gendered historical grievance. The image foregrounds a feminine physique that was denigrated but since the 1990s saw ascendancy into desirability.[62] She thus reasserts Chinese femininity precisely in a location in which it was previously disparaged.

In the present a figure such as the Shanghai Mansion Woman can be understood as freely choosing Chineseness—in addition to her inalienable Thainess. Thus her appearance in this setting both reanimates her historical racial exploitation and the fact that her Chineseness today represents "added value" in processes of urban gentrification. However, as a placeholder for distinction, she adds value to the surficial city but also subverts this process.

I suggest that it is possible to read her image as referencing both the denigration and sexualization of Chinese women *as well as* the possibility of inhabiting this history differently in the present. Thus it is not consumerist distinction alone but a certain dignity that the Shanghai Mansion Woman puts forth in this image. We can understand her pose and sartorial style not merely as a way to encapsulate differentiated consumer choice but rather as an informed assertion of Chinese personhood in all its past and present complexity.

Rather than disavowing the losses that come with moving from disparagement to cultural ascendancy, the scene in which the Shanghai Mansion Woman appears encompasses both traumatic memory and a repossessing of ethnicity in this location. What is more, it intervenes in the commercial function of femininity in the contemporary city by throwing a wrench in the attempt to market the Chinese city of Bangkok as a site in which an ahistorical, market-friendly multiculturalism reigns supreme. One can on the contrary argue that a critical repositioning of minoritized identities finds great traction in the terrain of fantasy that Bangkok enables.

In the Mood for a Different Region II

I learned to read the revivals of Chinese pasts in the city's hospitality venues in more capacious ways as I began to grasp the context of their emergence. As I immersed myself in these leisure practices, I began to understand that Bangkok urbanites are creatively "sheathing" themselves in the fabric of local and regional imaginaries that connect to diverse pasts that are about to be erased.[63] At the same time, they are protesting restrictive power alliances, such as those of Thai governments with the PRC.

While monuments such as the Chinatown Gate or institutions such as the Yaowarat Heritage Center strive to curate stable alignments between migrant history and contemporary governance, leisure venues — even those in the vein of the heritage revival — generate more ambivalent temporalities. The textures of migrant histories remain strong in such locations, enabling a different experience for the visitor. Visitors' affective engagement with venues like Ba Hao, Lhong 1919, or the Shanghai Mansion Bangkok becomes decisive for how historical revival is understood in each case. Finally digital representation is instrumental in urban gentrification yet can also intervene into nonemancipatory recuperations of history.

A site like the Shanghai Mansion Bangkok scrambles notions of region and identity both through the potentially radical signification of its digital representation and patrons' use of its material site. I recounted in chapter 1 how in the evenings the hotel's Shanghai Terrace jazz lounge becomes populated with a diverse crowd. These patrons actualize some of the possibility intimated by the hotel's website. As they reinhabit prior transregional cosmopolitanisms, Bangkok's, Hong Kong's, and Shanghai's histories are not necessarily invoked in accurate form, nor does the venue stop short of a mashup of time and place in this endeavor. Nevertheless, as design, performance, and desire come together on these evenings, the live quality of this scene opens it up to novel encodings of Chineseness. Most notably in the Shanghai Terrace the revival of the past is invested with the potential for broad experimentation. One cannot yet know what new paradigms for identity and collectivity might be born there.

As part of the citational and consumptive circuits of a colonial modernity inhabited by Chinese persons, the hotel is neither only originary nor merely derivative. In its invocation of Bangkok's, Hong Kong's, and Shanghai's colonial modernities, the hotel dislocates identity in a Thai present in which Chineseness is pervasive and ubiquitous, though it cannot be recuperated in true historical form. It invokes Chineseness at a time when its double valence of assimilation (as either an obscuration or as a refusal of identity) is being revoked in Thailand but also cannot be undone entirely.

The Shanghai Mansion Bangkok then does not solely recover the history of Chineseness's position as Thainess's other; it also does not purport to restore cultural affiliations in original form. It neither merely highlights the singularity of Southeast Asian Chineseness nor avers the notion of this diaspora's realignment with China. Prominently foregrounding Bangkok's Chinese materiality and emphasizing its regional connectedness, the Shanghai Mansion Bangkok also opens this history up to fantasy. Suggesting overlapping spatial and temporal dimensions to its diverse customers, the venue becomes a platform for exploring plural social formations in the present— be they antinationalist, feminist, or cosmopolitan, such as the critical transregional identifications of the filmmaker Salee Every or of the novelist Veeraporn Nitiprapha.

FOUR

How to Dump | Radical Revitalization in Thai Cinema and Hospitality Venues

In the 2019 film *Happy Old Year*—released with the Thai title *How to Ting . . . Ting yang rai mai hai luea thoe* (How to dump? . . . How to dump so that there will be nothing left of you)—interior designer Jean has newly returned to her home in Bangkok after working in Sweden. Director Nawapol Thamrongrattanarit tells the story of a home renovation in conjunction with a meditation on the impossibility of a hygienic psychological minimalism. At the same time, the film allegorizes a present in which the Chinese histories of Bangkok are at once being revived and forever erased by the exigencies of real estate arbitrage.

When Jean returns to Bangkok she seeks to apply her minimalist design philosophy to her parents' cluttered shophouse. Her aesthetic preference stands in close connection with attempts to rid herself of lingering feelings from past relationships. In the language of home optimization, *How to Ting . . .* (hereafter *How to Dump*) constructs a psycho-aesthetic portrait of loss that one might understand as also applying to current transformations of city, nation, and region. Jean desires to get rid of the messy residues of emotional attachment—especially to her ex-boyfriend Am and to her father—through a very thorough home renovation. This project begins, against the wishes of Jean's mother, with a Marie Kondo–style purge in the family's "maximalist" shophouse home and former music school in Bangkok. Critic Kong Rithdee writes that Jean's renovation aims for the "sparse, sub-Arctic, Zen-like detachment of [a] European home."[1]

In its foregrounding of surface and texture Nawapol's film parallels the aesthetics and sociopolitical significance of a particular set of cafés, clubs, hotels, and other leisure projects that are revitalizing the Chinese pasts of Bangkok neighborhoods.[2] As it fuses affect, body, and built environment, the digital format of *How to Dump* moreover makes palpable an updated understanding of memory. Nawapol's film thereby puts forth a prosthetic-postmigrant theory of cultural survival.

Transformation Beyond Yaowarat

While the downtown Chinese districts of Bang Rak, Pom Prap, and Sam-phanthawong are falling victim to Crown Property Bureau (CPB) real es-tate politics and Bangkok Metropolitan Authority planning rationales, many other areas of the city are also experiencing restructuring. Much of the constantly expanding "Greater Bangkok" metropolis is marked by rows of four-story shophouses lining wide arterial roads. The shophouse, or *hong thaeo* (in Thai; *thong lao* in Cantonese), takes on significance as a quintessential transregional element uniting Southeast and East Asia. Often labeled vernacular architecture, the shophouse is seeing revivals in cities such as Singapore, Penang, Hong Kong, and Bangkok.[3] In South-east Asia the shophouse is always already Chinese and connotes migrant trajectories within national economies. While increasingly musealized in Hong Kong, the Bangkok shophouse is a living, functioning part of urban economies—though it is beginning to see stylized renovation as well.[4] In places the shophouse-lined streets and *sois* (alleys) that branch off Bang-kok's generic arterial roads still lead to neighborhoods that have not yet been eviscerated by corporate investment. As Jean in *How to Dump* says of her neighborhood, which seems to be located in a less-trafficked, southern part of the city, "There is daytime parking here!"

How to Dump's references to Bangkok as a Chinese city are subtle if not inadvertent. Chapter 3 noted that in the 1990s "suddenly [it became] cool to be Chinese."[5] There was a new consciousness of Chinese culture mixed with a general turn toward all things Chinese, paralleling the open-ing of the People's Republic of China (PRC). For many Thais of Chinese descent, this took the form of learning Mandarin rather than the dialects of their grandparents, yet local clan associations also saw invigoration. In *How to Dump* no explicit cultural recovery of this kind takes place. Nei-ther does the film invoke PRC-aligned historical narratives or other re-gional connections. Instead we can situate the occurrences in the film in the second phase of Chinese cultural recovery in Thailand, in which Chineseness has become a taken-for-granted feature of the mainstream everyday, while the material remnants of dialect culture are about to be erased. At this time remembrance transfers to prosthetic memory, including that of the visual and literary spheres as well as embodied transgenerational and transethnic memory.[6]

How to Dump instantiates such prosthetic memory and thematizes the transfer of historical knowledge through reflection on the analog and the digital. Significantly the film indicates that the prosthetic captures *as* material "that which (already) isn't anymore." It remains deplorable that many of the cultural and linguistic roots of Chinese Thais that were thoroughly suppressed by midcentury Thai nationalism are in danger of being extinguished. At the same time, they are finding new materiality in films such as Nawapol's, which uses the alteration of a building to probe the history of a Chinese Thai family and the transformation of Bangkok. *How to Dump* further dwells at length on a contemporary Chinese Thai person: The film is driven by a focus on Jean's interiority as well as her embodiment and sartorial style.

Two Modes of Revival

We can roughly divide the revivals of Bangkok's Chinese pasts into two types: The first is the heritage revival reviewed in previous chapters. These chapters investigated the divergent shapes that heritage revivals take—from the high-concept Shanghai-themed club Maggie Choo's to the Shanghai Mansion Bangkok's combination of Hong Kong, Shanghai, and Bangkok influences, and the mixed-use consumer compound Lhong 1919's authentic yet commercial renovation of a historical port. In tendency this type of revival is upscale, relies to a greater degree on colonial aesthetics, and binds these into commercialized accounts of Chinese history. It is associated with high-production images and publicity. Many heritage revivals make salient the degree to which the city must materialize spiraling forms of surplus value.

But not only the logics of surplus and surface under electronic capitalism become prominent in Bangkok's heritage revivals; several projects underwrite state and transnational agendas. Thus the Yaowarat Heritage Center museum espoused a counterfactual, nearly symbiotic relation of the Chinese community in Thailand with the royal family and a version of Chinese Thai history overdetermined by relations to today's PRC.

Rather than dismiss all heritage revival projects merely as compromised, however, I argued that several venues also militate against dominant geopolitical imaginaries. The citational-consumptive loop between the leisure locations in Bangkok and a transnationally circulating cinema, of which Wong Kar-wai's *In the Mood for Love* is the preeminent example, facilitates such proliferation of meaning. Between Bangkok's materialization of transregional colonial modernity and the importation of Hong Kong and Shanghai aesthetics into Bangkok lifestyle venues, colonial modern aesthetics and Chinese pasts become motile texts that both uphold the status quo of hegemonic visions of region and bear the potential to undermine it.

A second kind of revival project does not reference the colonial or transregional in the same manner. Rather this type of revival relies on highlighting the working-class and modest entrepreneurial pasts of the various Bangkok neighborhoods. Thus in *How to Dump*, Jean and her family live in a modernist shophouse from the 1960s or 1970s.

In Bangkok the history and aesthetics of the shophouse provide a counterpoint to what a popular Thai magazine calls the "Chinese Dream" or the *suea phuen mon bai* legend—the "Mat and Pillow" legend (fig. 4.1).[7] In the January 27, 2020, issue of *A Day Bulletin* titled "Chinese Dream," novelist Veeraporn Nitiprapha references the "rags to riches fairytales" under which "the Chinese came to prosper under the auspices of benevolent Thai kings." Veeraporn, however, debunks anti-Chinese notions of capital drain and stresses that it was the Chinese migrants who *brought* capital to Thailand. According to the novelist migrants achieved success relatively independently and at great cost to themselves. Against the notion of a rapid rise to wealth and transhistorical royalist allegiance, she holds that if migrants experienced social mobility at all, such mobility was and remains much more modest: "Those that came as laborers—as coolies, rikshaw pedalers, or to dig canals—at most, these families today run a grocery store, a noodle shop, or other kind of small business."[8]

How to Dump chronicles the past of just such a family. In Jean's family's mixed-use modernist shophouse, living spaces and workspaces blend seamlessly. The downstairs office of the former music school and instrument repair business doubles as a place to have dinner and a place where the mother sleeps in a chair or sings karaoke. Although we do not encounter a first generation, we can imagine Jean's family as having made the leap from the hardships of migrant labor to middle-class entrepreneurship. Finally the piano left behind by an absent father is a strong symbol of this

4.1 Cover of *A Day Bulletin*, January 27, 2020.

middle class's further shift into expanding educational and cultural sectors and Chinese Thais' central roles in the intellectual life of the country.

The Psychology of *Long*

If revitalization is an enhancing of certain attributes of a space's pasts, its psychological parallel is shown to have to do with both remembering and forgetting. In *How to Dump* the characters often use the Thai term *long*, which can mean both "spacious" as well as "relieved." This is what Jean longs for in her life: an expanse of space and of mind. However, as she makes space both physically and affectively, memory and desire come rushing back.

Against the resistance of her mother and the skepticism of her brother Jay, she begins to discard everything that constitutes the history of a middle-class Chinese family in Thailand. It is only through remembering, however, that we can ultimately forget.[9] So what begins as a mass discarding of objects forces Jean, first of all, to recollect and work through old conflicts in her relationships. The film culminates in the family's coming to blows over how to approach memory when Jean proposes to sell the long-gone father's piano.

The film's theme of psycho-aesthetic renovation lends itself to a counterintuitive analysis of forgetting and remembering and thereby to an understanding of Bangkok's Chinese revitalization as something that does not merely parallel dynamics of erasure under reregionalization and the politics of the Thai state. With Adam Phillips (and Freud) we can understand memory to make copies of copies, only. *How to Dump* teaches us that the recovery of buried histories relies on screen memories—that is, on the kind of remembrance that always only reworks a prior memory.[10] It is not that an original does not exist, but that it cannot be recovered in true form.[11]

Phillips further understands the notion of forgetting as operating as "a certain kind of storage."[12] It stores things such as "desires, thoughts, histories, traumas, parts of the self."[13] Such a notion of forgetting facilitates an understanding of the hybrid and partial recoveries that occur in *How to Dump* as animating valuable information. In particular, forgetting-as-storage transmits information about nonelite histories hitherto secreted in the unconscious of a Thai national narrative that disavows much of Chinese labor and dissident history.

Although Jean's finished renovation is an instance of extreme minimalism, the reductionist makeover does not erase all markers of Chinese history but rather enhances some. The renovation now separates the formerly fluid, overlapping living and working spaces of the family's business-domicile, but the sparse design nevertheless gestures toward the functionalism of the original shophouse. In this Jean's renovation resonates vitally with the citational character of the revival espoused by several Chinese-themed hospitality venues across Bangkok.

FooJohn Building

Much of Jean's renovation is cognate with the design of FooJohn Building (now FooJohn Jazz Club), a bar, restaurant, and performance space in the neighborhood of Talad Noi. Like Jean's home, the bar and restaurant is housed in a generic multistory edifice, the former commercial building Akhan Foo Yon. The venue took pains to preserve functionalist features of the original 1960s Foo Yon motor business's headquarters that it occupies. Its retention of historical markers of the modernist business/domicile recalls the customary multifunctional character of the Southeast Asian shophouse or commercial building: In the living and working space, family members and employees conduct business, do schoolwork, watch television, or rest in the ground-floor area designated for commercial use. In contemporary Bangkok, ground-floor shops frequently extend onto busy multifunctional sidewalks, positioning tables, vitrines, magazine stands, or other objects in these expanded semipublic domains.[14]

FooJohn Building implements a different commercial-residential formula than that of the original Foo Yon company but, like Jean's renovation, vitally draws on characteristic features of the shophouse, its historical materiality enhanced by atmospheric design (figs. 4.2, 4.3, and 4.4). At its entrance, on the roof terrace, and in the second-floor bar space where patrons relax living-room style on sofas, the leisure venue blends (semi)public and private, a commercial structure with an intimate, homely atmosphere.

At the same time, FooJohn Building retains the historical façade of the Foo Yon motor business, with the company's sign prominently ensconced on top of the building. Co-owner Supattra Vimonsuknopparat points out the venue's conscious preservation of the original features of the building and retention of its original name, albeit in slightly modified form.[15] "FooJohn" sounds more like a Hong Kong name than the Chinese-Sanskritic

4.2 Historical image of FooJohn Building, Bangkok. Courtesy of FooJohn Building.

4.3 FooJohn Building on a rainy night. Photograph by the author, 2021.

4.4 FooJohn Building historical signage. Photograph by the author, 2021.

4.5 Entrance of FooJohn Building. Photograph: *BKK Menu*, January 19, 2018.

Thai business name "Foo Yon," in which Foo (or Fu) is a family name and the Sanskritic "yon" means vehicle. The venue thereby prominently foregrounds its historical linkage to the Foo Yon company and to the Talad Noi neighborhood's trademark automobile-related character, but it also intimates a transregional Chinese connection (fig. 4.4). Unlike Ba Hao in Soi Nana, FooJohn Building occupies one in a row of commercial buildings, at the head of a soi that is still lined by the neighborhood's characteristic auto-part businesses. A further living commercial reference is found in the venue's neon sign that the owners aimed to make "like that of the [traditional Chinatown] gold shops" on Yaowarat Road (fig. 4.5).

In *How to Dump* one of the only sinotropic and sinographic references is the trilingual business sign of Jean's family's music school (fig. 4.6). Jean's radical renovation leaves not even this reference to her family's provenance and occupation intact (fig. 4.7). Instead the finished renovation's engagement with Bangkok as a Chinese city is even more minimalist: In *How to Dump*, the pattern that Jean chooses for the redesign of the ground-level exterior of her home echoes 1960s modernist features of buildings across Bangkok. After the renovation is complete, the lattice ironwork in front of the large ground-floor windows of the former music school mirrors the original "breeze-block" style of the lattice casing around the top part of the building. As co-owner Supattra notes, the FooJohn building also invested especially into preserving the lattice breeze-block wall as a central feature of its bar space (fig. 4.8). The breeze-block

4.6 Exterior of the music school with its trilingual business sign. Film still from Nawapol Thamrongrattanarit, *How to Dump*, 2019.

4.7 The former music school after Jean's renovation, its sign gone. Film still from Nawapol Thamrongrattanarit, *How to Dump*, 2019.

4.8 Second-floor breeze-block wall at FooJohn Building. Photograph by the author, 2020.

wall on one side of the second-floor bar was filled with specially made glass bricks to close it off, rather than removing or cementing over this mid-twentieth-century industrial-design detail.

FooJohn Building presents a provocative, hybrid mode of revival. Like many of the projects that I have classified as heritage renovations, the venue derives information from *In the Mood for Love*. On my first visit in July 2017 Supattra recounted, "The week we opened [in early 2017], I heard that Wong Kar-wai was in town. 'Oh, if only we could get him to come,' I thought!" She references the director again when she details the aesthetics of the building. Wong's 1960s Hong Kong aesthetic thus emerges again as the language of a design that is combined with elements of local history to carry a cosmopolitan Chineseness into the future-present. However, FooJohn Building's historically informed refurbishing diverts colonial modern elements to other ends than mere nostalgia, integrating this aesthetic with an industrial history—and deploying it toward the creation of a progressive vibe, as the venue continues to draw a critical intellectual and artistic crowd.

4.9 Business sign for the As Is café, Bangkok. Photograph by the author, 2017.

As Is Café

About 650 meters north of FooJohn Building, on Rama IV Road, in close proximity to the popular Chinatown leisure alley Soi Nana, sits a stylish coffee shop, As Is, that opened in 2017. The owner refurbished the bottom of the shophouse next to his parents' seed and small animal business into a hip café, in which he crafts espresso drinks and select French and Italian sweets.[16] Outside, the shop retains the old family business name in Chinese and Thai. In Teochew, transliterated into Thai, the sign reads "Khou Ia Hong" (fig. 4.9). The name's rendition in classical Chinese characters, rather than in the simplified characters used in mainland China, signals that Thailand is part of an alternative Chinese cultural formation that includes Taiwan and Hong Kong rather than the PRC.

Paying homage to the industrial histories of its location, the café traces a line from working-class to modest entrepreneurial pasts, rather than invoking the rags-to-riches myth of Thailand's plenitude and Chinese integration. Like FooJohn Building it thereby stands in opposition to the heritage invocation of Chinese courtly, Thai royalist, and bourgeois aspects of the past.

4.10 Interior of the As Is café. Photograph by the author, 2018.

As Is's linkage to a local, nonelite Chinese history manifests in the 1960s or 1970s shophouse that the café inhabits. But with its exposed brick walls, metal staircase, and the bales of denim fabric suspended from its walls, As Is also recuperates the industrial character of Chinatown—those elements of Chinese Thai modernity that allowed a section of working-class migrants to move from labor into small entrepreneurship (fig. 4.10). Chinese migrants to Thailand are credited with bringing about the country's modernity—as laborers, small business owners, and always-already transnational actors in the global markets of the nineteenth and twentieth centuries. A fact that is muted in contemporary discourse is that this labor history is also always a political history.

Yet it is not far from the café's location that race riots took place in 1945 and 1974. The invocation of the racial otherness of the Chinese was prominent already in early twentieth-century Thai nationalist rhetoric but was applied most perniciously in midcentury policy under Phibun Songkhram (1938–1944; 1948–1957).[17] Anti-Chinese sentiment lingered long into the postwar era, however. The Yaowarat incident in September 1945 is "the first race riot to take place in Bangkok in the modern history of Thailand." On this occasion, both the military and general public perpetrated violence against the area's Chinese residents. As Wasana Wong-surawat explains, "That event is known today among only a tiny segment of the general public in Thailand, and it has been virtually invisible in Thai academia."[18] Almost three decades later the 1974 Phlapphla Chai riot, or "Chinatown riots," began with protests against police extortion in Chinatown in front of the Phlapphla Chai police station, approximately one kilometer from As Is café, and culminated in an uprising that spread to neighboring districts. The protest was violently suppressed by state forces over several days.[19] Together these incidents represent repressed strains of history in the postwar era.[20] Consistently associating the Chinese working class with dissent and revolution, the Thai state persecuted this class with unprecedented brutality.

Rather than reference this history through more literal forms of local production, the café chooses a defamiliarizing mode of citation when it foregrounds the texture of denim as connotative of an industrial working-class past. The metal that likewise defines the As Is design relates directly to the history of metal businesses in Chinatown. Yuwadi Tonsakulrun-gruang's bilingual novel *Roi Wasan* (2010; the English version is *A Walk Through Spring* by Judy Chan) is centrally set in a lathe factory. It recounts the story of four female Cantonese-speaking adolescent migrants from southern China, two of whom begin working in a lathe factory near Talad Noi in the 1940s. Yuwadi's novel chronicles the progression from the harsh labor of the initial migrants to their white-collar present-day offspring, staging provocative encounters between first- and third-generation Chinese Thais. In parallel As Is sutures disparate, transgenerational histories in an experiential-consumptive experience. The industrial reference of the steel décor is moreover echoed in the handcraftedness of the café's drinks and foods, their texture and materiality potentially bridging the gap between lifestyle business and labor history (fig. 4.11).

Mother Roaster

An entirely different relation to the materiality of history is furnished by the café Mother Roaster, which unapologetically incorporates the gritty textures of an auto-body shop. Mother Roaster eclipses the other projects in that it does not attempt to make over a working-class past. Its uncompromising incorporation of industrial detritus is not merely citational but a literal instantiation of ongoing neighborhood development. As the visi-

4.11 Web publicity for the As Is café. As Is Facebook page, October 6, 2019.

tor steps through the café's ground-floor entrance, she is disoriented (figs. 4.12 and 4.13). Dimly lit and littered with auto-shop debris, the ground floor makes the visitor think that it must be the wrong entrance. But it *is* the café's entrance, and the visitor is forced to inhabit the materiality of urban transformation while navigating around oily metal scraps to ascend to the second-floor coffee shop.

Mother Roaster's "as is" scaffolding provides an almost real-time snapshot of Talad Noi's predicament, a neighborhood that has been transforming into a lifestyle destination but is still defined by labor with small auto shops lining its narrow alleys. In comparison with other venues this café goes to another extreme, however. As one observer puts it, as the hippest of all revival cafés, "Mother Roaster wins" in the game of flippant irony of venues engaged in the revivification of Chinese pasts (fig. 4.14).

4.12 Entrance of Mother Roaster coffee shop, Bangkok. Photograph by the author, 2020.

4.13 Ground floor of Mother Roaster. Photograph by the author, 2020.

4.14 Second floor of Mother Roaster. Photograph by the author, 2020.

On the other hand, upon entry to Mother Roaster one is confronted with a large graffito, "Jek," a derogatory term for "Chinese," sprayed in large red letters on a pillar in the room, which does not let the visitor forget the still-recent histories of both formal legal and social discrimination faced by Chinese Thais (fig. 4.15). It remains unclear whether this graffiti represents a discriminatory, abusive declaration, or whether "Jek" is here recuperated in the same assertive manner as the term "queer." Suspended between a traumatic history, the critical occupation of derogation, and the transformation of minoritized cultures into cutting-edge lifestyle markers, Mother Roaster's big red "Jek" is apposite to the temporality of the Chinese revival.

In their design FooJohn Building, As Is, and Mother Roaster make the past and present concomitant and concurrent. All three venues rely on the materiality of commercial-use Chinatown buildings but diverge in their mode of citation and the degree of defamiliarization of historical referents. These different dynamics of engaging urban materiality teach us about the complicated traces left in the present by the histories of simultaneous economic centrality and social and political marginality of Chinese persons in Thailand. These design mnemonics make palpable the history

4.15 The graffito "Jek" in Mother Roaster, ground floor. Photograph by the author, 2020.

of a laboring, entrepreneurial, and later professional class responsible for modernization that was for much of the twentieth century also relegated to the margins of the nation as its racial other.

Symptom or Oblivion

The constitution of the venues, stories, and discourses under consideration in this chapter points to what Phillips usefully characterizes as the dilemma of remembering: "Either the most significant bits of one's past are unconscious, and only available in the compromised form of symptoms or dreams; or the past is released through interpretation, into oblivion."[21] I want to argue, however, that the examples of cultural and historical recovery discussed in this chapter find a balance between the two extremes of unconscious symptom and oblivion.

Thus what Jean's renovation in *How to Dump* accomplishes through its symbolic, partial enhancing of features of the entrepreneurial past of Bangkok is the suspension of history between its "compromised form of symptom"—half-buried, not entirely available to consciousness—and its "release into oblivion" through a too-literal reinstantiation. Jean's renovation distinguishes itself precisely through being "merely" citational, perhaps even defamiliarizing, of an unacknowledged history. It thereby manages to make something about a Chinese Thai history of the masses intelligible without overtypifying, as the heritage revivals do at times.

Jean's design must be understood against the background of a national history that has struggled to situate Chinese migration, which it frequently defined as entirely outside the Thai nation—as either a capitalist or communist threat; or as completely inside—as assimilated into disappearance. The suspension of the past between disturbing symptom and all-too-literal reworking that we find in Jean's renovation and in the citational character of leisure venues that draw on Chinese industrial and labor histories is a precarious undertaking. But if such citation bears enough historical and affective legibility, it may represent a viable strategy: a surficial consumptive-citational practice that possesses depth. In the leisure venues the recovery of this history takes the form of praxis. Patrons not only ingest foods and imbibe drinks that are in part associated with a transregional Chinese past but also breathe in atmospheres conjured through design and citation.

If remembering and forgetting are concomitant and need to be concurrent to have a transformative effect for consciousness, then the revival venues, the explicit discussions occurring in Thailand today, such as those worked through in *A Day Bulletin* and films such as *How to Dump*, are able to hold the present-past of ordinary and working-class Thai Chineseness in sway for a moment, before urban transformation and reregionalization remove it entirely from the corporatized city.

As Jean remembers, she attempts to make forgetting possible. But even her most radical efforts to abolish memory fail, and the residues of attachment rematerialize. An hour and twenty minutes into the film the family comes to blows over the most contentious item to be purged, when Jean tells her mother that she wants to discard the old piano of her father, who had long left the family. Jean states, "I don't want to see you going in circles anymore." The mother yells back, "If you want to forget, go ahead!" Jean retorts, "Then you remember, alone. Jay and I don't want to remember anymore" (figs. 4.16 and 4.17).

The removal is precipitated by a reliving of feelings around the father and his departure. A photograph of Jean's birthday, in which the father is playing the piano and a young Jean sings, crystallizes the residual attachment that Jean still holds. Finally she calls her father to announce her

All of these cluttered rooms

4.16 Jean in an unrenovated room of the former music school. Film still from Nawapol Thamrongrattanarit, *How to Dump*, 2019.

4.17 Jean's family disagrees on the removal of the piano. Film still from Nawapol Thamrongrattanarit, *How to Dump*, 2019.

becoming more open space to use.

4.18 Jean's home office after the renovation. Film still from Nawapol Thamrongrattanarit, *How to Dump*, 2019.

intention to sell the piano. The nearly silent, monosyllabic conversation appears cathartic as Jean puts down her phone and cries in this climax of psycho-aesthetic clearance.

She subsequently sends her mother off with Jay and proceeds to have the piano removed. A collector who has been in regular contact appreciates the many old items in the possession of Jean's family, thereby appearing as a custodian of Chinese Thai history. The physical removal of the piano culminates Jean's decluttering process. As the last item that the collector removes, it is given due honor as a central memento of the family's (affective) history. From the perspective of Thai history the centrality of the piano to the story symbolizes the combination of entrepreneurship and the particular Bildungsbürgertum that marks Chinese families' histories in Thailand and the country's trajectory of modernization.

Finally Jean succeeds in taking out every last superfluous item, or nearly every item altogether, from the family home. The result is the comically minimalist aesthetic that she presents to her new employer's "global team" on their visit to her office (fig. 4.18). At the end of the film everything and everyone has been discarded, leaving the former music school, as her contractor friend Pink comments, *long*, empty and ready for remodeling. Pink's assessment is that Jean must also feel *long*—relieved.

Jean concurs but, as the camera slowly closes in, her carefully controlled expression turns distraught as tears stream down her face.

A close-up on face and eyes signals the concentration on a character's interiority. In *How to Dump*'s denouement the focus on Jean's contorting face is intercut with views of the empty front of the music school that had housed the piano, as the nostalgic tune "Klap pai thi kao" (literally, "returning to the old place"; its official English title is "Revoke") starts up. Cross-cutting in film indicates simultaneity, but this juxtaposition of Jean's interior state with the empty space of the built environment also signals the impossibility of a hygienic psychological minimalism—or of the forgetting for which Jean had aimed. Instead the painful clutter of feelings of loss that persists in her consciousness is reinforced.

What *How to Dump* has thereby impressed on its audience is a series of material and affective personal and collective histories. Even if one eradicates their material traces and attempts to annihilate their affective residues, such histories will continue to exist as shadow memories. In order to convey this logic, the film has not only synced psychological interiority and the built environment but also provided this dynamic with certain temporal characteristics. Phillips's, and Freud's, theory of memory does not allow for the existence of a primary, foundational memory event, leaving memory with no definable beginning; but in Nawapol's formulation memory also has no end: It merely proliferates in a series of open-ended screenings and rescreenings. This is important to the project of preserving minoritized histories. In *How to Dump* and in Bangkok's revival cafés and bars, memory screenings and rescreenings appear in the form of moods, atmospheres, and affects, rather than figuring only as products of the storytelling capacity of consciousness. It is to such sensate and material residues of Chinese histories that the Bangkok leisure venues and new cultural production give texture.

Revival Temporalities

All the revival projects hold open a space for imagining buried histories. They do so in different ways. We saw temporality frequently invoked as elastic in the postcolonial location of Bangkok and most fetishistically expanded in some of the heritage revivals. In this context Bangkok appears as the quintessential Chinese and colonial city. The city's semicolonial temporality allows different actors to invest a material past with divergent meanings. Against this background the projects that cite labor and industrial pasts are allowing Bangkokians to witness the brief recovery of a history that "will not have been." These revivals seem most successful in the difficult task of harnessing fantasy to the project of a progressive invocation of ethnicity, collectivity, and alternate futures. They are able to keep the past ghostly, haunting a present bent on erasure. It is in the multiply occupied fantasy space of Bangkok that such a repositioning of buried histories and minoritized identities becomes practicable.

To think about Chineseness from a site of heterogeneity—Bangkok, rather than cities that are assumed to be more self-evidently Chinese— allows for the revision of rigid notions of identity. Several Bangkok invocations of Chineseness proffer understandings of ethnic personhood that neither invoke only histories of Chinese minoritization nor solely oppose Chineseness in Thailand to a center that is China—nor do they posit a convergence of diaspora and center. Rather contemporary designers and cultural producers retain links to specific histories of migration while inventing platforms for personhood that model future collectivities, convivialities, and identifications.

As historical actors die, memory becomes prosthetic, according to Alison Landsberg.[22] Prosthetic memory is borne by media as well as by populations at various degrees of remove from the historical actors—some not at all related to those who experienced the history in question. We can understand *How to Dump*—and the audience who views it—as forms of prosthetic memory: The film makes present those material remnants of a Chinese past that still exist in Bangkok. At the same time, its audience members are part of new, embodied publics who desire to inhabit historical ground through a particular aesthetics, lifestyle, and relation to city and region. In its diegesis as well *How to Dump*'s engagement with retaining the memory of Bangkok as a Chinese city considers both the built environment and the people who inhabit it. The film suggests how urban pasts might be retained in citational, affective-aesthetic form, its defamiliarizing invocation of industrial history one effective mode of preserving Bangkok's Chinese heritage.

With regard to the ways that people remember urban histories *How to Dump* shows memory to be shifting away from the embodied memory of the first and second generations of Chinese migrants to Thailand. It moreover highlights the digital's capacity to give shape to texture and affect and avers the material properties of prosthetic memory. Nawapol's film debates the shift to the prosthetic through several scenes that thematize the analog and digital. The photograph of a happy childhood memory, in which Jean is enveloped in the warmth of her family on a birthday, represents an indexical artifact of memory. For Jean it represents evidence of a better past but also the remnants of painful attachment. Singularly connotative of the long-gone father and the loss at the heart of Jean's psyche, the photograph is recovered by Jay and pinned to an old corkboard. Jean eventually discards the photograph, leaving its place on the board empty before the board, too, is disposed of. The photograph and the film's focus on its loss — the empty space it leaves — are visible. By contrast, digital storage at first appears invisible and immaterial, though it will be shown to bear its own material effects.

Jean, who is bent on eradicating all trace of clutter, is not averse to digital storage. Rather than buy a design book that appeals to her, she photographs relevant pages. She even keeps large storage boxes full of CDs with digital images. When her friends ask for an old photo, she conducts an arduous search through her digital archives. She is triumphantly happy when she manages to find the photo and presents it to the two friends. This process of searching for a valued past and then finding and remembering it animates Jean and seems to provide resolution. It is not clear, however, whether she is remembering to forget more permanently or whether she is working through past attachment in order not to have to forget or repress. It often seems as though she is intending to rekindle old friendships. Yet it remains Jean's stated goal to get rid of the emotions of the past. The assignation of storage to the seemingly immaterial realm of the digital does not stave off pain, however.

Rather than mourn the shift from analog to digital, *How to Dump* manifests a high consciousness of the properties of digital remediation. Film theorist Iggy Cortez does not set the digital in opposition to the analog but rather shows it to bear a different relation to materiality, affect, and legibility. For the viewer of digital cinema, he describes a "reconfigured sensory threshold."[23] In this he relies also on Simon Rothöhler, who stresses "the distinct perceptual affordances of digitally recorded images, such as the precision of details and the receptivity to light in conditions of darkness" that "generate distinct sensory configurations."[24] Rothöhler provides the following example that is pertinent for this book's consideration of representations of the urban: "The highly light-sensitive or light-receptive HD [high-definition] image develops almost encyclopedic traits; as an expanded, hyper-photographic device for storing light it collects numerous forms and colors of artificial, urban illumination: rays of headlights and streetlights, neon lights, spotlights, private and public lighting systems."[25]

Further detailing the ontology of the digital, Cortez speaks of "a turn within digitally produced cinema towards the primacy of bodily affect over the semantic transparency of its poses and gestures."[26] *How to Dump* uses the propensity of the digital to foreground bodily affect, materiality, and atmosphere to make salient the link between psychological interiority and built environment. It masterfully links Jean's melancholy minimalist disposition to the textures of both her maximalist shophouse home and the minimalist structures that she desires and designs.

The digital's close connection to affect, the senses, and the material further complicates conventional timelines of memory; it renders intergenerational or prosthetic memory not derivative or secondary but rather as primary as forms of memory considered immediate and directly embodied.

The ability of the digital to foreground materiality is pertinent for the kind of memory generated by the encounter with texture.[27] "The atmospheric textures digital aesthetics conjure" are thus of particular interest for the memory work that the Bangkok revival performs.[28] In contemporary Bangkok, affective-consumptive practices blend with material histories, and bodies fuse with the built environment, so that an updated version of prosthetic memory takes shape. It is the nature of prosthetic memory, as outlined by Landsberg, to travel between different bodies as well as between bodies and media. In the (digital) revival cinema and Bangkok patrons' leisure practices, ontological distinctions between virtuality and materiality are obliterated further as body, media, fantasy, and material history blend ever more intimately.

What is more, Cortez avers that digital cinema's "reconfigured sensory threshold co-emerges with our attunement toward forms of minoritarian being that are revisited and reframed by digital formats." Digital cinema thereby "evokes the sensory conditions for alternative forms of social collectivity."[29] Such a propensity to reconfigure attunement to the minoritarian is of great pertinence to the uncovering of obscured Chinese histories.

In examples of cultural production such as *How to Dump* as well as in Bangkok's leisure venues we encounter Chinese Thai history at a particular moment in time. Minor Chinese histories are revived in affect and texture at the very moment of their disappearance—at a time when linguistic loss is a fait accompli and material disappearance either already concluded or imminent. What does it mean when cultural revival and disappearance become concomitant and concurrent?

Veeraporn Nitiprapha's understanding of cultural recovery addresses the reviving of that which has disappeared or is about to be lost. In her role as public intellectual the novelist speaks out against assumed cultural consensus as well as commonplaces regarding Chinese Thai heritage. Doing away with the notion of an original, Veeraporn elaborates on her understanding of heritage in her interview with *A Day Bulletin*. She displaces the notion of Chinese roots to an ethical grounding in humanism, rather than advocating for authentic belonging. At one point the interviewer asks, "Roots are not necessary for our lives in the present anymore, are they?" Veeraporn lays out her skepticism regarding notions of roots and origin:

> Let me ask you this. At present what is left of your Chinese Lunar New Year ritual? It's either duck or chicken, right? The rest isn't there anymore. You don't even know how to set up the food properly—or, even if you do, do you know its meaning? If you want to have roots, let me ask you—are they real roots or fake roots? And how far back do you want to go for your roots? ... [To the Altai mountain region as the presumed origin of the Thais? To Africa as the origin of humanity?] ... In the present it is rather our humanness that propels us.[30]

Sittithep Eaksittipong likewise cautions against the belief in a *saratha*, "an unchangeable core that Thais of Chinese descent have inherited from the ancestors who left China," and urges readers instead to recognize the specificities of *Thai* Chineseness.[31]

How to Dump also puts origins in question. The only location outside of Thailand that Jean explicitly references is Sweden. Yet one can find in the transregional ideal of Chinese femininity that she embodies, and in the 1960s industrial resonances of her renovation, a link to Chinese Thai cultural production's quest for the kind of collectivity that exceeds the nation but also counters a PRC hegemony that is proving oppressive for Southeast Asia. One can further observe in Jean's deployment of Buddhism a way of putting heritage into motion, rather than tying it to fixed notions of place, embodiment, and ownership or to linear histories.

Buddhist (Renovation) Psychoanalysis

Jean's statements about Buddhism as well as her repeated use of the vernacular concept *long* (spacious and relieved) are closely aligned with Theravada Buddhist notions of detaching. Buddhism provides fine-honed

4.19 Jean interviews at the design agency. Film still from Nawapol Thamrongrattanarit, *How to Dump*, 2019.

frameworks for thinking about the logics of desire and attachment—and especially for how to get rid of them. In these frameworks a person has to contemplate an object of desire and pass through a phase of heightened attachment in order to ultimately detach.[32] Jean's aesthetic and psychological process can moreover be aligned with the Mahayana Buddhist concept of emptiness, or *śūnyatā*.

The fact that detachment never occurs in *How to Dump* makes possible a technology of memory that is otherwise unavailable for history writing in the current political moment. The story of the Buddhist-inspired renovation is thus able to perform the work of intimating other aspects of Chinese history than those condoned by current dominant discourses.

How to Dump appears at first to relate a linear therapeutic story. Jean is consistently prompted to narrativize her artistic-psychological process, her interiority externalized through Socratic questioning. Not only her friend Pink and brother Jay but also her colleagues continuously elicit information in this manner. A work interview delineates the degree to which minimalism bears both professional and embodied signification for Jean (fig. 4.19). In this scene person, feeling, style, and materiality converge. The conversation is amiable, as the interviewer is "already a fan" of

Jean's design. The hyperminimalist style of the agency—and the American English spoken by the interviewer while Jean answers in Thai—lends this event hyperbolic and comical overtones. In order to telegraph Jean's aesthetic-existential ethos, the scene further fuses materiality and affect: In the triangular courtyard of the gray-and-black, steel-and-glass office of the agency, Jean, clad in black-and-white attire with simple lines, appears to feel at home and experience pleasurable recognition.

Jean labels the entire process of her redesign a Buddhist one. As she seeks to turn a home that her contractor calls "fucking maximal" (*khot maximal*) into a minimalist space, Buddhism functions as the local and global idiom designating the feat that she is attempting to pull off. This information is first elicited by the design agency's "global team" when they appear at Jean's house for an office visit. The camera's survey of the impossibly minimalist spaces of the renovated shophouse is underwritten by Jean's design philosophy: "Minimalism is, kind of, Buddhist [*phut phut*]" is the first sentence spoken in the film. As Jean continues, "It is about a letting go [*kan ploi wang*]. I liked this style when I was working in Sweden. After I returned, I wanted to apply it to this place." Kong Rithdee also classifies the style that Jean aspires to as "Zen-like detachment."[33]

The anchoring in Buddhism of the Swedish design that Jean reconfigures to apply (*prap chai*) to her house roots her minimalism in something supposedly local and incontrovertibly worthwhile, yet also transnational. The space that may now be considered contemplative, no longer diverting attention to the guitar poster and old Christmas tree in the cluttered home office or other memorabilia of a life struggled through by each of the family members—and Jean's repeated use of the concept *long* (spacious, bare, clear, relieved)—can easily be aligned with a Mahayana Buddhist concept of emptiness. For Jean *khwam long*, spaciousness, is not surficial: It is as much the paradigmatic ethos of her design as it is existential.

The Buddhism that Kong explicitly associates with the renovation is an East Asian Buddhism, Zen. Jean's narrativization of her concept for the finished hyperminimalist rooms, denuded of any trace of a personal history, also implies a Mahayana or Vajrayana Buddhism. In Thailand, where Theravada Buddhism is the dominant, official orientation, Mahayana Buddhism can at times perform the work of undergirding counternormative political endeavors. Thus at a time when official Theravada Buddhism was occupied by Cold War political ideologies, artists who invoked Mahayana Buddhist elements were able to reach beyond the damaging "free world" heritage of the Thai official political public sphere.[34] It is against the background of such a history that we can understand the film's deployment of Mahayana concepts. The Buddhist-inspired, multiorigin minimalism of Jean's renovation is thus able to perform the work of intimating other temporalities of the history of Chinese migration than those condoned by the nationalist center.

For this to happen, the counterintuitive operation of a Buddhist concept must come into play. The act of "letting go," as Jean describes it, frames the renovation as Buddhist. Yet the process that Jean undergoes doesn't quite arrive at that end. While she fully intends to reach detachment, the renovation sets in motion a counterdoctrinal process. Even as the old music school is gutted, and Jean spells out to Pink the changes that have taken place in her hitherto-unresolved relationship with her exboyfriend, she remains haunted by the artifacts and people she has discarded, rather than experiencing release.

As remembering and forgetting become concomitant and concurrent in the Swedish-informed minimalist makeover of the Chinese shophouse, it initially appears as though Jean is embarking on a Buddhist process (undertaking remembering—or the intensified focus on an object of desire—in order to detach). However, such a soteriological teleology is arrested midway. In Buddhist philosophy as in Phillips's theorization the simultaneity of forgetting and remembering still entails further development; but in *How to Dump* the process simply stops at intensified remembrance.

As much as Jean adheres strictly to her program of "letting go," memory and attachment persist in stronger form than ever. But while a linear process of detachment that conforms to doctrinal exigencies has gone thoroughly wrong, Buddhism has performed other kinds of work in *How to Dump*. The invocation in modern cultural production of Mahayana Buddhist concepts such as emptiness frequently functions as a switch point that makes possible the figuration of seemingly incommensurable elements—a "both . . . and" (or "neither . . . nor") rather than only an "either . . . or."[35]

In *How to Dump* remembering and the attempt to forget become concomitant and concurrent, but remembering leads neither to permanent forgetting nor to renewed repression. Rather Jean's process leads to a constant conscious remembering and rematerialization of the past. If a Mahayana Buddhist propensity to hold seemingly incommensurable concepts in sway is operative here, it underwrites a particular historical temporality.

Fusing psychology and built environment, *How to Dump* exemplifies a temporality in which the past lingers in the present with a new materiality. Aspects of Jean's personal history—and by extension of Chinese Thai history—are irrevocably lost, yet they cannot be forgotten, expunged, or repressed. With regard to the Chinese city of Bangkok the film's story of psycho-aesthetic renovation indicates that this urban history is entering a stage in which it can only be given a home in prosthetic memory. Yet this kind of prosthesis, in media and in the psyches and bodies of postmigrant persons, proves to possess astounding persistence.

That the past cannot be extirpated but persists in the present with new obduracy is a result of current configurations of the political in city, nation, and region and of medial developments (the propensity of the digital to give shape to affect and materiality).[36] This particular contemporaneity of the past is not automatically progressive or historically revisionary, yet it can entail salutary effects in specific cases.

We can thus find in contemporary Bangkok a parallel in the workings of the digital, the temporal contours of memory, and a Mahayana Buddhist logic. Allegorized in the third-generation figure of Jean, a complex temporal portrait emerges for both the city and Chinese Thai history. *How to Dump* prominently investigates remembering and forgetting through the theme of generations. In this context the figure of Jean might at first appear as a failed original, a third-generation figure of loss fully interpellated by Thai nationalism, who through her irreverent disposal of the past will destroy her family's history and by extension a Chinese Thai history. This is dramatized especially through Jean's conflict with her mother, who comes out on the side of (absolute) preservation. Upon closer inspection, however, we can recognize the designer as the agentive figure of a present in which Chinese Thai histories have to be mined and take material shape in new ways. While "original" memory is no longer extant or never was, the prosthetic memory that both Jean and her citational renovation embody represents merely a different form of storage. For better or worse prosthesis is not any less material or enduring than "first-generation" embodied analog witnessing and testimony.

Chinese Thainess thus emerges neither merely as a historically disparaged form of difference nor as "diversity," the difference valorized by regimes of optimization. Rather in its most provocative form it emerges as a technology of memory in the present—a technology that relies on embodied historical testimony but also exceeds it through the digital's

4.20 Chinese film poster for *How to Dump*. Facebook, May 10, 2021.

alternative foci, through new affective forms of inhabiting history, and through refusals of the dictates of neoliberal productivity.

Region remains only implicit, yet transregional Chineseness is a strong component of the form of personhood that *How to Dump* showcases. Anticipating its resonance for trans-Asia audiences, the film was released in early 2021 in the PRC as well as various other East and Southeast Asian locations. Thus the design and femininity highlighted in the Thai production subsidiary GDH's Chinese film poster foregrounds actor Chutimon Chuengcharoensukying's potential transregional compatibility—in this film publicity, she could just as well figure as the protagonist of a PRC, Hong Kong, or Taiwanese production (fig. 4.20).

III THINKING REGION FROM SOUTHEAST ASIA

Memories of the Memories of the Black Rose Cat | Thai Literature as Contemporary Chinese Literature

The work of the Thai novelist Veeraporn Nitiprapha exemplifies some of the ways that contemporary Southeast Asian texts reformulate notions of region, identity, and kinship. In her 2019 keynote speech at a literary festival in Kunming, China, the two-time Southeast Asian Write awardee tells the story of an uncle from China who appeared in her home in Bangkok one afternoon in 1985 but was subsequently not heard from again. In close connection Veeraporn tells the story of an Asia in which both persons and cultural texts follow complex routes of migration:

> After Uncle Qiang left, we went back to being busy with our lives and forgot we never heard from him since, and later on we forgot about him too. "Have you ever written Uncle Qiang, Mom?" I asked my mother years later. "No, never," she replied. "You see, he is not quite . . . family although he is very much . . . family."
>
> I am telling you the story because that was how I felt too when I first visited China months ago—not quite . . . family but very much . . . family, not quite a homecoming but very much like one. Having to tell this story of a lost child of China, which is, in a way, a story of both of us, you and me, in English, [a] language that isn't yours or mine, also makes me feel like both a relative and a stranger at the same time.
>
> But, yes, I am glad, more than glad, to have this opportunity to share the story with you in whatever language. To tell the story of the people who left China to travel the world and never returned was my ambition

when I wrote my second novel about Chinese immigrants in Thailand. The ambition was to humanize the people from one of the most complicated times in our history, who left behind nothing more than their stories.

And when the book—*The Twilight Era and the Memory of the Memory of the Black-Rose-Cat*—comes out in English next year, I wish that it, too, will find its road home back to China.[1]

Veeraporn's speech indicates the ways that Southeast Asian texts put minority histories into conversation with novel understandings of region. The previous chapters analyzed visual media and leisure venues that invoke a trans-Asia Chinese modernity, rather than only local pasts, in order to recalibrate notions of region. In this chapter, I argue that a seemingly marginal, sinotropic Thai literature also makes effective interventions into understandings of region. Cheow Thia Chan's work on Malaysian Chinese (Mahua) literature supports this idea. Chan argues that Mahua literature represents a "vital site for forging strategic regionalism" and shows it as "[embedded] in different geographical scales of cultural production, ranging from the subnational to the national, as well as to the translocal and global."[2] Veeraporn's work undertakes rescaling especially on the national and regional levels.

The materials analyzed in this book dislocate identity in a Thai present in which Chineseness is constantly referenced, though it cannot be recovered in originary form. Veeraporn addresses this latter conundrum by inserting Chineseness into historical contexts that loop back and forth between China and Thailand. In her keynote address she speaks of homecomings that are not quite homecomings, relatives who are "not quite" but also "very much" family, and languages that are not one's own yet bring into being new kinds of relationality: "Having to tell this story of a lost child of China, which is, in a way, a story of both of us, you and me, in English, [a] language that isn't yours or mine, also makes me feel like both a relative and a stranger at the same time."

Somewhat surprisingly the "lost child of China" of Veeraporn's keynote is the "story of both of us, you and me," referring not only to the diasporic Chinese Thai novelist herself but also to her listeners in mainland China. In her speech to this Chinese audience Chineseness is not given a taken-for-granted location in places or persons. China moreover appears as both a home and not a home. Only Veeraporn's novel will have an unqualified homecoming to China. The story itself, however, inserts literature into a chain of historical exchanges between China and Thailand. The author thereby propels into motion received understandings of the origins and derivations of culture. Titled *Phutthasakarat atsadong kab song jam khong song jam khong maeo kulab dum* (Dusk of the Buddhist era and the memories of the memories of the black rose cat, 2016) in Thai and published as *Memories of the Memories of the Black Rose Cat* (2022) in English, Veeraporn's second novel retells Chinese and Thai history from the early twentieth century until the 1970s.[3] I rely mostly on the Thai version of the novel but also consider Kong Rithdee's masterful translation.

Toh Wen Li introduces *Memories of the Memories of the Black Rose Cat* as follows: "The story begins in the early decades of the 20th century, when Great-Grandpa Tong arrives in Siam from Guangdong, China, to help his uncle in the rice trade. He marries Great-Grandma Sangiem, a palace cook, and they have five children together [Jarungsilp, Jerdsri, Jitsawai, Jarassang, and the adopted Jongsawang]. The narrator tells of the family's trials and tribulations against the turbulent backdrop of the Siamese Revolution of 1932, World War II, various rebellions and coups, and the Vietnam War. Memory is a slippery, untrustworthy thing, and memories of memories even more so. Events of the past are loosely framed by Dao, a mysterious boy in an old house who contemplates the memories of Grandma Sri, one of Tong's daughters."[4] The story is told in a nonlinear fashion and partially fantastic idiom. Max Crosbie-Jones characterizes *Memories* as a "a curlicued family saga," while Li notes that its "chapters—ringed with foreshadowings—meld like ripples of rain in water."[5] The translator of the novel, Kong Rithdee, emphasizes that Veeraporn's mode of storytelling thereby "tests the limits of how far a novel can fictionalise history and how much a novelist can historicise her imagination."[6]

Weaving deftly between imaginative invocation and concrete history telling, Veeraporn is exemplary of cultural producers who reoccupy Asia as a site in which the "not quite . . . although very much" of relation outlined in her keynote speech takes center stage. As Thai literature and media ask new questions about the temporality and location of Chineseness, their recasting of history, materiality, and representation offers glimpses into "that which will not have been" to produce a "what might still be." Supplementing embodied memory, film and print media furnish vital remnants of histories, cultural and linguistic practices, and material environments on the brink of disappearance. Chinese Thai history thus continues to exist in virtual, revived form—as a prosthetic memory that possesses an anticipatory dimension.

While many of the revivals aim for nostalgic, colonial modern performances of Chineseness that do not challenge the political status quo, I have argued that even commercial, mainstream efforts to recuperate the past or align with a contemporary hegemony must always fail—and that this failure is a productive one. Thus even the Bangkok club Maggie Choo's rigorous curation of semicolonial Shanghai is interrupted by the actual performance of the women hired to perform it. In both the Chinese revival venues and cultural production, the interstices between the virtual and material bear the freeing property of the no-longer and the not-quite-yet, a counterfactual oriented toward possibility. Veeraporn's keynote speech likewise turns counterfactuals into future possibilities.

While previous chapters detailed the textured, transtemporal circulations of *In the Mood for Love* and other visual materials, Veeraporn's novel reworks notions of Chinese identity through a dynamic of circulation, in which literary work takes on life and agency in travels across eras, countries, and systems of governance. It is women and other feminized characters who renegotiate Thailand-China relations in recent literary works. It is also women cultural producers, such as author Veeraporn Nitiprapha and filmmaker Salee Every, who tell history and deploy memory, fantasy, and even forms such as gossip to do so.

Sending certainties about the spatial and temporal properties of identity and region into a spin becomes habitual in the novel and films under consideration in these final chapters. The degree to which the Southeast Asian present is refracted by both China's political and economic ascension and the policies of the member-states of the Association of Southeast Asian Nations makes these alternative medial and literary perspectives especially valuable. In their virtual and material effervescence they are fragile reminders that the region is not merely fated endlessly to replicate its neoliberal presents.

Trans-Asia Cycles

Veeraporn's work thinks region differently—*from* the location of Thailand and *in relation* to China, as well as *through* gender. As one of the most recent writers to take on the fraught histories of the Chinese in Thailand the novelist puts a different spin on understandings of heritage than the accounts of hard (male) labor and gradual social ascent that have dominated this discourse.[7] Thorn Pitidol asserts that "transmitting memories of loss and of feeling other makes *Phutthasakarat* a novel that diverges from literary convention regarding the overseas Chinese in Thailand."[8] Brian Bernards concurs with this assessment as regards Thai-language literary production but underlines the difference of Sinophone literary output: "Thai-language popular novels span the entire arc of modern Sino-Thai history with archetypal, soap-operatic domestic sagas of Sino-Thai immigration, assimilation, upward mobility, and national influence. By contrast, the Sinophone sequential novel addresses the disenfranchisement of the migrant working class that accompanied national development during the Cold War."[9]

Thak Chaloemtiarana's comprehensive analysis of twentieth-century Thai-language literature traces the transformation of the Chinese from "outsiders within" to a position integral to Thai society. In so doing, his analysis also presents works that diverge from the formulaic invocation of Chinese immigrant gratitude to a royal Thai nation. Thak investigates authors and historians in the 1980s and 1990s who critically "[wrote] the Chinese back into Thai historiography" and addressed the position of the Chinese from a subaltern point of view.[10]

In addition to highlighting histories of displacement and loss across four generations of a Chinese family in Thailand, Veeraporn's novel distinguishes itself by animating understandings of the migration of culture, identity, and collectivity in new ways. A first foundational way in which *Phutthasakarat* rethinks region is through questioning the terms of belonging, or being housed, in both the place of origin and the (post)migratory location. In Thailand the novel takes place in both Bangkok and the central province of Chachoengsao. The house originally bought by the family patriarch Tong in the small river town of Paed Riu in Chachoengsao after World War II plays a significant role in the story. The novel's cover by collagist Nakrob Moonmanas features a black-and-white photographic family portrait that is superimposed on the brown, black, gray, and blue background of a landscape (fig. 5.1). Each person's face is obscured by a flower bud, which can be understood as representing the titular black rose. Folded out, the book's front and back covers together show the expanse of the landscape. In the middle of the back cover stands a lone wooden house. However, the house is far in the distance, invoking the question of shelter in the material and psychic senses. Is the family housed, were they ever housed, and will they ever be housed—and in which national context? And if yes, why is their house separate from other human abodes? The cover's design intimates that the novel will centrally address displace-

5.1 Front and back cover of Veeraporn Nitiprapha, *Phutthasakarat atsadong* (Dusk of the Buddhist era), 1st edition, 2016.

ment. It will moreover use the circulation of writing between Southeast and East Asia to put forth an alternate proposal for imagining the linkages of region.

Phutthasakarat tells of the manifold, cruel displacements of the twentieth century in China and Thailand. As Veeraporn describes the purpose of her novel, "The ambition was to humanize the people from one of the most complicated times in our history, who left behind nothing more than their stories."[11] Chapter 12, "Refuge [or, Residence] of the Soul" (or "Sanctuary of Souls" in Kong's translation), tells the story of the PRC-born son, Hong, who never meets his father, Tong, who had left before Hong's birth to return to his other, first family in Thailand.[12] Drawing on her own family history, Veeraporn tells the story of China's Cultural Revolution (1966–1976). Hong and his mother become victims of the violence and the young boy finds himself orphaned. All that sustains him—his "refuge of the soul"—are a family photograph from Thailand, a hand-drawn map of the family's immediate surroundings, and a sixteen-page letter describing the family's life from "his" Thai mother, written in literary Chinese by a commercial writer in the market in Paed Riu: "It was this luminous, ethereal, untouchable vision that prevented Hong from getting lost inside the collective oblivion that was the radiant fantasy of Mao Zedong."[13] Hong is drawn to the imaginative language of the letter, studies literature, and becomes a university lecturer and writer. When China opens, he sets out to find his father in Thailand.

When Hong finally finds the house that was his family's residence in Thailand, its inhabitants are long gone and he never finds them again. Upon his return to China, he writes out the until-then-secret story of "the refuge of his soul." His novel, *The Lone Refuge of the Soul*, earns him fame and nominations for the Nobel Prize. The cover image of the first edition of *Phutthasakarat* can be understood as referencing the photograph that sustained the orphan Hong through his hard childhood and youth during the Cultural Revolution. But the image also intimates that Hong's family in Thailand remained unknown (their faces are obscured) and history remains unatoned. There is no resolution to the multiple traumatic displacements that haunt the adult Hong's small China-based family — except in his partner's conception of a son. This trope of continuity through generationality is spun out in yet another way by the story of Chinese literature as Veeraporn tells it.

In "Refuge of the Soul" Veeraporn redresses some of the violence of the Cultural Revolution, under which the fantastic *wuxia* writer Wang Dulu is killed in China (he dies in a labor camp). She does so by letting another piece of literature — the novel produced by Hong decades later — continue the work of the type of literary imagination that the Cultural Revolution sought to eliminate. Crucially Chinese literature in "Refuge of the Soul" circulates through the space of Thailand, as we read of the market scribe who writes letters in Chinese for a fee. This scribe in the town of Paed Riu composed the literary-style account of daily life that *yai thuat* (Great-Grandmother) Sangiam had sent to her husband's second wife, Hong's mother, in China. "Like hundreds of millions of his compatriots, Hong never had the chance to read Wang Dulu's forbidden stories. He didn't know that the writer's celebrated series even existed, or that there was a scribe in Siam who could write such beautiful letters."[14] The way in which forbidden Chinese literature is transmitted to the son, Hong, is thus by way of the Thai market scribe, who "honed his literary skills by reading the *Crane-Iron* pentalogy [by Wang Dulu] repeatedly over ten years" and composed the long letter from the Thailand-based first wife to the Chinese second wife.[15]

China does not appear as a default home in *Phutthasakarat* but in fact represents an alienating space for the boy Hong. He can find a home only in the fictional space that the letter and photograph from Thailand create for him. It is literary language that is invested with the capacity to produce belonging in this story. Several relays of translation occur in the production of such a home in literature. Its languages include, first of all, Chinese and Thai as well as English in Veeraporn's keynote speech. But this trans-Asia Chinese literature also traverses different social spaces—the literary language deemed bourgeois during China's Cultural Revolution, the writer of which is killed, is taken up by the scribe in the commercial space of the Paed Riu market and in turn transposed by Hong into a contemporary literature in post–Cultural Revolution China. In this it becomes translation in Naoki Sakai's sense, a practice that has a profound revisionary impact on the violence that the "process of bordering" engenders.[16]

In her keynote speech, too, Veeraporn envisions the Thai-produced literary text's "homecoming" to China. But neither her novel nor her speech runs the risk of declaring the diaspora the repository of a tradition that is then repatriated. Rather Veeraporn's work defamiliarizes the origins of Chinese literature through outlining this literature's transnational Thai detour. *Phutthasakarat* even renders a putatively bourgeois literature nonbourgeois through the figure of the market scribe. In the story it is through the commissioned letter from Thailand, and later Hong's novel, that a Chinese literary tradition survives. Finally, Veeraporn's novel itself also continues the tasks of writing a Chinese literature and history that succumbs neither to the dictates of PRC cultural policy nor to those of Thailand's governing regimes and ruling classes. Like works by the writer Wang Dulu and the market scribe, Veeraporn's work deploys fantastic elements. *Phutthasakarat* avoids the potentially revisionist connotation of resuscitating a fantasy genre deemed bourgeois, however. With regard to her critical representation of PRC history, the author states that she intends to represent standard Thai perspectives rather than to put forth an anti-communist stance.[17]

Toward the end of the novel Veeraporn further recounts the 1970s events of pro-democratic uprisings in Thailand—in particular the still largely unaddressable massacre of October 6, 1976. Through the story of third-generation family member Rapin, who documents on camera the military, police, and right-wing groups' killing of students in Bangkok's Thammasat University grounds on that day, Veeraporn performs left critique in the Thai context. The story of Rapin's shooting and drowning in the Chao Phraya River bordering the university, too, includes elements of the imaginary. In the novel as a whole, genre or register can thus be said to be deployed in a revisionary, rather than revisionist, manner, allowing for the occupation of the fantastic as nonbourgeois as well as adding critical force to a Thai left imaginary.

In this Chinese Thai author's conception, literature can salvage lives torn from homes, persons torn from other persons, and dreams rendered void by historical upheaval. On a primary level this literature is written in Thai. However, its Sinophone, sinographic, and sinotropic instantiations in the long letter written in a Thai market are of marked importance. Here the sinographic does not manifest in concretely visible, embodied form. Rather, to the contemporary reader of Veeraporn's novel, it appears in the form of a trope, representing a vehicle that transports crucial intellectual and affective content across territories, eras, and political systems. Yet its nonliteral appearance signifies the difference of Southeast Asia, where Chineseness surpasses visibility, language, and patronym.

A Double Loss of Home

While text lives a life of plenitude in Veeraporn's framework, the circulation of persons and possessions between Thailand and China is rife with losses. These losses are concretely historical ones, but the novel mobilizes a geontological imaginary to work through the trauma engendered by political upheaval. Through the imaginative space furnished by Thailand's geophysical plenitude, Veeraporn broadens the ontological grounding of region. History takes place not only in the national spaces of China or Thailand but also in the psycho-affective space furnished by the tropical environment of the migrants' new home. The addition of geontological strata to the locations of the novel provokes a rescaling that makes the relation between China and Thailand not merely one of domination but rather of interchange: of intellectual content and cultural production and also of hope, kinship, and notions of futurity.

The cover of *Phutthasakarat*'s second edition superimposes the graphics of a small Chinese sailboat in orange on a black background (fig. 5.2). Plants grow out of the boat and there are also animals on it—most notably the novel's titular black cat. The cover references the family's life on a boat as they wait out World War II. The prominence of the overgrowth stands in for the degree to which the geocultural landscape of Thailand has become part of the younger individuals' psyches—their "growing into" the country. This stands in contrast to the enduring hope of Great-

5.2 Front cover of Veeraporn Nitiprapha, *Phutthasakarat atsadong* (Dusk of the Buddhist era), 2nd edition, 2018.

Grandfather Tong for the family's return to China. The end to the dream of this sojourner comes with the end of the Chinese civil war in 1949 and subsequent expropriation of Tong's land, house, and assets in China.[18]

Phutthasakarat thereby tells of the mourning of a double loss of home on the part of "the people who left China to travel the world and never returned."[19] This loss is figured most strongly in the first-generation character of Tong, who is explicitly never at home in Thailand but can also not return to the now-lost home of China. His story stands in for that of numerous waves of migrants to Thailand. Each time Tong returns from travel to China, this hardship overcomes him and is figured as psychological and physical oppression. Tong is thus doubly unhoused. He turns to work to stave off depression. After the 1949 victory of the communists, which engenders his final loss of home, Tong sequesters himself in his room. This room later becomes the so-called rain room, a space filled with unknown noises and unspoken memories that the novel's young narrator Dao encounters in chapter 14 ("The Rain Room"). The rain room figures the crushed dreams of millions of so-called sojourners, who had always hoped to return with wealth to their homes in the mainland. Just as the evocative letter from Thailand becomes the "refuge" of his PRC-born son's soul, China had always remained the refuge of Tong's soul.

Thailand and China are intimately, and tragically, connected in *Phutthasakarat* and their histories told in parallel. A passage in "Refuge of the Soul" recounts how, as Mao Zedong traversed the expanse of China on the Long March, he "brought the hope for a better life—just like the hope that he [Tong] had once had—to every tuft of grass that he traversed, while sowing the seeds of revolution in the heart of every person he met along the way."[20] However, on the Long March Mao also brings with him the revolutionary fervor that eventually leads to the 1949 communist victory—and the dashing of Tong's hope for a return home. The passages that detail Tong's depression in chapter 12 tell the story of the involuntary diasporic existence of sojourners in Thailand as a parallel Long March. However, the Long March of the sojourners lacks as clear a "victory"—at least in the story of Tong's family. China's history is thus also always Thailand's. In *Phutthasakarat* this becomes palpable in the forfeited dreams of its characters.

Rather than invoke the triumphalist accounts of the rags-to-riches "Mat and Pillow" legends of Chinese migration to Thailand, the novel conceives of migration in terms of involuntary displacement, nonredemptive life trajectories, and unredressed losses. Thorn Pitidol writes, "*Phutthasakarat*'s breaking of convention also prompts us to review once again which angles of the past of the overseas Chinese we have forgotten. This diverges from the belief of the descendants of the Chinese in Thailand, who often believe, simplistically, that their ancestors' leaving of home constitutes good luck as they came to a country that provided them with opportunity. But, in reality, the path of the Chinese who migrated to Siam, especially of the laborers that arrived in great numbers during the time of Rama V. [1868–1910], was not at all an easy one."[21]

An As-Yet-Unwritten (Transnational) History

The intertwined histories of China and Thailand culminate in *Phutthasakarat*'s boy narrator, Dao, a figure who is feminized through his status as a young child. What is more, the footing of Dao's role as the repository of memory is also put in question. At the end of the novel the question of whether the boy Dao actually exists remains unresolved. The novel also leaves open whose memories have been recorded—grandmother Sri's, Dao's, the black rose cat's, or anyone's at all?

Throughout the main body of the narrative Chinese history is condensed in the expansive imagination of Dao. A joyful child who is figured in close proximity to his grandmother Sri (Jerdsri), Dao grows up loved, with rich experience of the characters and events that his grandmother tells him about. This is underwritten by Dao's vivid sensory experience in his childhood home. There are sounds and smells and, again and again, the impression of the plant life surrounding his house. For Veeraporn, as for many contemporary film directors, the properties of Thailand's geophysical landscape merge with her characters' minds—a tropics of post-migrant psyches that conveys to the reader a specific affective history of transregional life throughout the displacements of the twentieth century in Asia.[22]

Through the stories that Dao's grandmother tells him, *Phutthasakarat* transmits the long family history to the reader. The losses over generations of the family, however, inform Dao's personhood as plenitude. He is frequently amused by the stories, laughing at the idiosyncrasies and concerns of his ancestors. This contrasts the relative ease of the present with the hardships of the past. But it also breaks the sanctity and masculinist cast of the rags-to-riches fairytales of Chinese migration to Thailand. The novel thereby diversifies the telling of this history beyond its stereotypical accounts of arduous labor and ascent, through paternalistic genealogies, into the middle and upper echelons of Thai society.[23]

The cover of the novel's second edition is significant in this respect, too. Each child and adult figured is represented through a black-and-white photograph superimposed on the graphics of the boat with its plant overgrowth. Unlike in the first edition's family portrait, the people on the boat are sitting at a distance from each other, implying that, though they may be related, their lives each bear different trajectories that the novel will follow. The cover image intimates that, rather than being reducible to hard work and social ascent, the story of Chinese migration to Thailand is highly variegated.

Chapters 14 and 19 of *Phutthasakarat* tell Chinese history in such a divergent way, figuring it as an empty room with inexplicable noises and smells. The room in which Dao's Great-Grandfather Tong sequestered himself during times of depression over his permanent exile from China is called the rain room. In chapter 14 Dao hears noises from the uninhabited room each time he passes. Upon entry he encounters in the room's rose-wood mirror from Shanghai a girl not much older than himself. As Dao begins to decode his experiences in the rain room, the chapter loosely connects the apparition with the unknown fate of two child-bride minor-wife sisters who either were killed or had committed suicide. Chapter 19, "Song of the Yellow Oriole," puts forth the story of another young woman's potential rape and possible suicide.

What Great-Grandfather Tong has lost appears to Dao in the form of dense histories frequently propelled by female individuals. The rosewood mirror represents a portal into the tragic histories of the family and of their two countries. At times Dao is able to enter the mirror and attain a clarity of memory otherwise unachievable.

Phutthasakarat tells history in part through the unknown fate of young women, marginalized in virtually all historical accounts yet central to the story of the Chinese in Thailand. Cognate with the novel's covers' obscuration of faces and figuration of multiplicity, Chinese Thai history is thus presented as in part still entirely unnamed, its origins unpinpointed, its trajectories not uplifting, its paths meandering and productive of lingering, complex psychological effects. Kong considers the novel's approach to the past "a subtextual wrist-slapping to the way history is told, repeated and sanctified—the history of modern Thailand that often overlooks and dispenses with the millions of faceless people, immigrants or otherwise, whose destinies congeal like spilled blood to make up the real story of this land."[24]

In much of the novel the family is moreover held together by its female and marginalized members—from Great-Grandmother Sangiem to her daughter Jerdsri, to the adopted son, Jongsawang. The industriousness, imagination, and perseverance of these characters assure the family's survival. However, none of them are able to lead the family into a redemptive present. Rather, "the stream of fortune continually separates them until each person disappears in a different direction" and each meets a tragic, cruel end.[25] I understand this as part of Veeraporn's feminist, historical critique.

Throughout *Phutthasakarat* contemporary Chineseness is instantiated in the figure of the imaginative child Dao. He grows into a life that is very much his own but also contains the multitudes of stories of those who came before him. The novel ends with a surprising twist, however, leaving open whether Dao is an actual child or the mere materialization of memory and desire. It also poses the question of whether the girl Dao saw in the rosewood mirror is his mother: "Dao might have been a child that hadn't been born and would never be born, a child that existed only in the solitary ruminations of a girl who was robbed of her chance to become a mother."[26] Dao thus also appears as the "what if" of the story, productively haunting Chinese Thai memory politics.

Finally the novel further speculates, "Or maybe he was just a memory — deranged and ill-defined, like the memory of the memory of a cat." However, *Phutthasakarat*'s last sentence dispels even this notion of memory's perdurance when it continues: "a cat that was sitting camouflaged within a pool of ash-colored shadows, watching the coming of a storm and the desolate arrival of yellow pollen that was being blown across the sky and that would wipe out everything and bury the memories of the memories into oblivion."[27]

Phutthasakarat successively de-individualizes and ultimately radically questions any conception of memory at all. In so doing the novel presents a capacity of capturing history at once more ephemeral and more enduring than any conventional notion of memory. With the delineation of this contemporary mode of remembering, Veeraporn does not abstract from or disregard Chineseness — rather her novel de-essentializes identity without disavowing the traumata of migrant lives and racialized injury. *Phutthasakarat* does not shy away from centering the failures of love, betrayals of family, and the cruelly intertwined histories of China and Thailand. At the same time, the novel as a whole playfully propels Asia into motion in a way that counters the assumption of the reconvergence of center and diaspora and that undermines the unequal distribution of power among different regional players.

Conclusion

Veeraporn's novel, speech, and interview (referenced in chapter 4) leave readers with little to grasp with regard to the "thereness" of a Chinese identity. The author has put Ien Ang's injunction to question "the very validity and usefulness of the spatial matrix of center and periphery that is so constitutive of the conventional thinking about the Chinese diaspora" to a radical test.[28] In Veeraporn's novel, no roots, origins, or home remain. Family ties are lost, loosened, or disputed. Writers have been killed and languages disappeared. But in the world imagined by this Southeast Asian writer, Chineseness has also embarked on travels that keep it constantly in motion and compelled to make new homes, roots, and alliances.

The register of fantasy enables a rescaling of the relations of base and superstructure (or of history and psyche) as well as of geopolitics. In this literature the Southeast Asian location of Thailand does not merely reproduce China's centrality. *Phutthasakarat*'s imaginative access to location and history makes Thailand determinative of history, rather than merely secondary or solely the site of a loss of identity. And yet, while "Southeast Asia" decenters China, it also does not vilify it. Rather, it produces a new perspective on a minority identity as well as on the hegemonic nature of a new regionality. As "not quite . . . although very much family" Southeast Asia's relation to China as a geopolitical entity or as fantasy is never entirely predetermined. A Southeast Asian point of departure thus deconstructs and reconstructs understandings of Chineseness—reconfiguring notions of centrality and marginality as well as fidelity to neoliberal trans-Asia projects. Nation, diaspora, and region become fissured, opening up opportunity for imagining belonging, embodiment, and relationality anew.

SIX

Southeast Asia as Question | Thinking
Region from Bangkok

Does the location of Southeast Asia allow for privileged access to transformative understandings of city and region? After working through critical scholarship on region, this chapter turns to the analysis of women as figures of optimization in city and region. In Bangkok femininity stands at the heart of the revitalization of local Chinese pasts. As such it operates closely with transformations of the city, the expansion of capital, and shifts in regional power formations—as well as with their undoing. The 2017 heist thriller *Bad Genius* (Nattawut Poonpiriya, director) exemplifies the ways that a contemporary Chinese femininity, situated in the new urban economies at the heart of reregionalization, invokes historical phenomena and redirects trajectories of optimization.

Tani Barlow has shown the critical difference that Asia scholarship produces for concepts of region and gender, in which neither variable exists without the other.[1] Building on her critique I inquire into the conceptual difference that the location of Southeast Asia yields in this context. East Asia remains the predominant point of departure in recent efforts to rethink region.[2]

Aspirationally progressive projects thinking about Asia run up against the heterogeneous formation called Southeast Asia. Scholars frequently base their conceptualization of this region on the fact that Southeast Asia was part of Chinese premodern networks of trade and tribute, later subject to European and Japanese colonization, and that, as a regional formation, it bears World War II and Cold War legacies. Southeast Asia scholarship assigns unity to the region by privileging histories of imperial expansion or of the Cold War, foregrounding indigenous premodern patterns of rule, or recurring to the region's distinct, heterogeneous geo-physical, linguistic, or ethnic makeup.[3] However, the bulk of this scholarship does not prioritize the theorization of Southeast Asia's role in a wider Asian context. Meanwhile, in East Asia scholarship, a strand of work is emerging that recuperates premodern Chinese transregional networks as benign precedents for contemporary China–Southeast Asia relations.

By contrast, my analysis has addressed region through an archive of digital materials, films, print media, and sites that activate a switch point between the virtual and material. In these texts long histories, colonial logics, and local Chinese pasts are tasked with neither recuperation nor vituperation of China. Rather than advance a blanket declaration regarding the impact that the reimagination of region from the perspective of Southeast Asia might have, I foreground the potential of cultural and intellectual efforts undertaken in this location for a significantly different understanding of the present in Asia. My analysis does not solely rely on precolonial, colonial, or postcolonial periodization; neither does it fetishize a supposed quintessential Southeast Asian heterogeneity or recuperate the notion of benign historical regional orders. Rather, it highlights the differential occupation of all such frameworks by current Bangkok cultural producers and leisure venues.

China in the Region

The assessment of the role of the People's Republic of China (PRC) is crucial in the contemporary Southeast Asian context. Calibrations of this role must neither merely decry China's hegemony nor, conversely, refute its dominant role.[4] Evaluations of China's regional impact must also not disavow Chinese expansionary aspirations or rely on formulations that define China's translocal influence as "soft" because, historically, it did not seek dominion over territory.

Several of the new East Asian policies toward Southeast Asia, including the Belt and Road Initiative (BRI), invoke prior forms of transregional engagement (such as the Silk Road) that did not explicitly set out to occupy territory and are therefore advanced as more benign than other forms of empire.[5] Leo Ching, quoting Martin Jacques, references the revival of frameworks that characterized early relations between China and Southeast Asia: "The region's [Asia's] realignment toward China bears some of the hallmarks of the tributary system, a sinocentric hierarchical and concentric structure of relations that marked the Middle Kingdom's dominance in the era of world empires."[6] However, desires to recuperate premodern forms of regionality do not consider altered modes of governance or facts of expansion in the present.

Prasenjit Duara traces the forms through which China interlinked with Southeast Asia throughout imperial history and the Cold War but emphasizes that current PRC transnational projects are different in kind. He diagnoses "unexpected convergences between the imperial Chinese order and BRI. But each mode of dominance also generates novel realms of power."[7] Uncovering parallels between the historical Tribute Order and China's contemporary use of soft power, Duara stresses China's two-pronged strategy utilizing soft and hard power. He cautions, "Traditional soft power, including infrastructural development and economic diplomacy, will proceed even while military flexing and threats will be undertaken in some zones."[8] He is especially critical of the damage to community and environment engendered by Chinese infrastructural projects in Southeast Asia.

Perspectives that look beyond the PRC to the notion of the Sinophone or the newly minted Milk Tea Alliance do not in all cases provide progressive alternatives. Neither do Taiwan-based perspectives necessarily represent an opposite to the PRC's. Alan Yang argues that the 2016 New Southbound Policy under Ing-Wen Tsai shifted Taiwan's "instrumentalist attitude" to a more collaborative, "people-centered" approach.[9] However, Taiwan's "Go South" policy has since 1993 also cast an extractionary gaze on Southeast Asia.[10]

Remaking Region

Naoki Sakai's work aims for a comprehensive deconstruction of area, especially that of the nation: "The concept of transnationality must be invigorated. It must be rejuvenated in order both to undermine the apparent naturalness of nationality and internationality."[11] Sakai deploys "transnationality" as a translational concept that breaks up the notion of discrete units of the national existing in theoretically comparative format (internationality) — "the space of commensurability in which all the units of sovereignty are 'countable' and 'comparable.'"[12] What upholds notions of area and nation is "the undercurrent or substratum of the territorial grounding of the population through techniques of unification and semiotic effects such as 'culture,' 'language,' 'ethnicity,' and so forth that are de-manded by the system of the international world."[13] Language is accorded a privileged position in Sakai's theory, and he deploys translation to break up the seeming unity of nation, national language, and (post)colonial world order. His conceptualization allows for a thorough reframing of dif-ference and sameness across regions through "the locale of translation that opens up the place of comparison. While internationality operates within the logical economy of *species* and *genus*, transnationality undermines and reconfigures the schemata of nationality and internationality. It is in this sense that translation deterritorializes."[14]

Diverging from these analyses in scale, Leo Ching and Andrea Bach-ner direct attention to the ways that specific medial and literary trends in-flect region and identity. In his investigation of mainstream transnational Asian media, Ching describes the reorientations of countries in Asia to-ward other locations in Asia—as opposed to a sole focus on the West.[15] Especially Korea and China proffer new frameworks of reference for Asia. Ching is adamant, however, that this change does not include a paradigm shift with regard to global capitalism. While acknowledging that popu-lar media from Asia speak centrally of the struggle with neoliberalism, he stresses that there is no indication that they are producing a different framework of reference or living.

Andrea Bachner's theorization of "allography" in Southeast Asian Chinese literature perceptively outlines what identity might look like in a Southeast Asia–generated framework of difference.[16] Her careful analysis of graphesis in the works of Chinese Malaysian writer Kim-chew Ng, Tai-wanese author Wuhe, and others concludes that the proposition that these works are making about identity primarily has to do with internal differ-ence. The central object of Bachner's analysis are two graphemes in the story "Allah's Command" by Kim-chew Ng. The graphemes in question are part of the protagonist's efforts to recover a Chinese identity forcibly wrested from him under Malay ethnonationalism. While the graphemes recover Chineseness as vitally counterposed to the ethnonational ideology that holds sway in Malaysia, they do not reproduce it as "sameness"—the recovery does not succeed in producing a universally legible version of Chinese: "'Allah's Command' is less interested in pitting alphabetic Malay and logo-graphic Chinese against each other. Rather, graphic difference is shown at work in the Chinese script itself: Chinese writing becomes other to itself, as the sinograph becomes its own allograph."[17] The graph-emes thus produce Chinese writing as internally differentiated, as a difference to itself.[18] What the story's protagonist "produce[s] in this attempt at scriptural loyalism is in fact a hybridization of the Chinese script. His crypto-Chinese—both encrypted and unviable—reverses rather than endorses an identity politics connected to writing."[19]

In the Thai materials that I examine, a similar logic obtains. Chineseness emerges as neither the other of Thainess nor a uniform identity. It exceeds also the figuration of a different kind of Chineseness. Instead, Chineseness is recuperated as a historical platform for difference as such. What is more, the examples from Thailand largely transcend the Sinophone and the sinographic and thereby further complicate understandings of Chineseness.

City, Region, and Gender

How can the location of Bangkok make a difference for understandings of Asia under Chinese hegemony? Bangkok encapsulates what Gayatri Spivak describes as a secessionary urban culture under electronic capitalism: Large cities, productive and absorbent of capital, resources, and infrastructure, are intimately connected to other global cities but secede from their national contexts and immediate—often rural—surroundings.[20] Other theorists, too, understand the city as the epitome of the logics of finance capitalism and the site in which the localization of the global takes place.[21] Contemporary Bangkok embodies an updated version of national(ist) "development" with regional and transnational characteristics: The city has a monopoly on resources, and planning rationales are both conceptualized and most prominently visible here. It is moreover a regional metropole as well as the seat of royalist-militarist or populist governments who broker Thailand's relations with the PRC.

What does the deterritorialization through gender of dominant notions of region in the Chinese city of Bangkok look like? In media and leisure practices Bangkok also becomes the site for the undoing of capture by capital and governance. This is enabled by the *difference* of Southeast Asia, the changing valences of Chineseness in this location, and the figuration of urban Chinese femininities. It is women, in collaboration with other women, who reconfigure history for the present. Female protagonists in contemporary Thai films such as *How to Dump* and *Bad Genius* reshape region not as the hegemonic mediator between the national and the global but as the site of lived, newly invented aspirational politics.[22]

If Chinese Thai cultural production is instrumental in the deterritori-alization and reterritorialization of region, *How to Dump* and *Bad Genius* negotiate region through attention to women's embodiment, capabilities, and senses.[23] As Barlow writes, "Reregionalization of Asia into a multilay-ered and multipolar social, economic, and ideological formation occurs in part through the work of gender."[24] Global governance paradigms are responsible for the near fusion of understandings of gender and region; yet they do not overdetermine notions of gender or of region or preclude feminist reinterpretation.[25]

Two conceptualizations of Chineseness in Southeast Asia become in-structive for examining how the current notions of femininity in Chinese Thai cultural production intervene into dominant formulations of region and identity. The first dominant assumption is that a convergence of cen-ter and diaspora is taking place in Thailand, in which Chinese-descent persons' sentiments, cultural orientations, and aspirations would fuse with those of a presumed center or motherland. The second is the notion of disappearance-into-assimilation.

Analyzing a Chinese cinema that extends across Southeast and East Asia, Elizabeth Wijaya poses a provocative question: "Could we imagine a diaspora without the desire to return, since even the land of return is imagined, and consequently, could we imagine a Chinese cinema without Chineseness?"[26] Without refuting the effects of national, racial, and re-gional interpellation, Wijaya aims to decenter China as well as to propel analysis beyond the domain of the Sinophone. What she terms the "provi-sional frame of the trans-Chinese" seeks at once to transcend area studies models and universalizing interpretations.[27]

Ien Ang's work traces a multiply situated Chineseness in conjunction with a biography that spans Indonesia, the Netherlands, and Australia. Her analysis of a diasporic and, by implication, always-female Chineseness is instructive for understanding the spatial reach of a gendered, racialized embodiment that questions the conditions that produce identity instead of solidifying it. Ang writes, "What we must start to question is the very validity and usefulness of the spatial matrix of center and periphery that is so constitutive of the conventional thinking about the Chinese diaspora; we must give the living tree a good shake."[28]

The Thai films *Bad Genius* and *How to Dump* shake up the central-izing notion of a living tree of Chinese descent through the taken-for-granted ethnic and gendered embodiment of their female protagonists. Chutimon "Aokbab" Chuengcharoensukying, who plays the character of

6.1 Lynn refracted in mirrors. Film still from Nattawut Poonpiriya, *Bad Genius*, 2017.

Jean in *How to Dump*, also stars in *Bad Genius*, "the most internationally successful Thai film ever," available through Netflix and the iTunes store.[29] Both films foreground a female agency defined by efficacious decisiveness (fig. 6.1). Tall and light-complexioned, Chutimon plays supremely capable female characters in both films (as well as in the 2023 Netflix feature film *Hunger* by Sitisiri Mongkolsiri). Neither film explicitly thematizes Chineseness, but each film's treatment of Chineseness is precisely what furnishes its revisionary potential.

In chapter 4 we encountered the protagonist of *How to Dump*, who bears as a nickname the English name Jean—but "jeen" is also a homonym of the adjective *jeen*, or Chinese, in Thai. As a third- or fourth-generation Chinese Thai person, Jean might for some exemplify cultural loss, a generation fully interpellated by Thai nationalism and no longer conversant in the Chinese dialects of their grand- or great-grandparents. At the same time, Jean represents a generation that inhabits Chineseness in an entirely taken-for-granted way.[30] For one, this is instantiated in Jean's look: She embodies a transregional ideal of Chinese femininity. Once disparaged in Thailand, this femininity at present exemplifies a mainstream look to which many aspire.[31]

In *Bad Genius* Chutimon plays lightning-sharp teenager Lynn, who heads a grand exam-cheating scheme. When Lynn is accepted to a private school, filial piety and friendship prompt her to invent a variety of modalities for cheating. Remembering childhood piano lessons, she develops methods such as tapping out exam answers with her fingers on her desk.

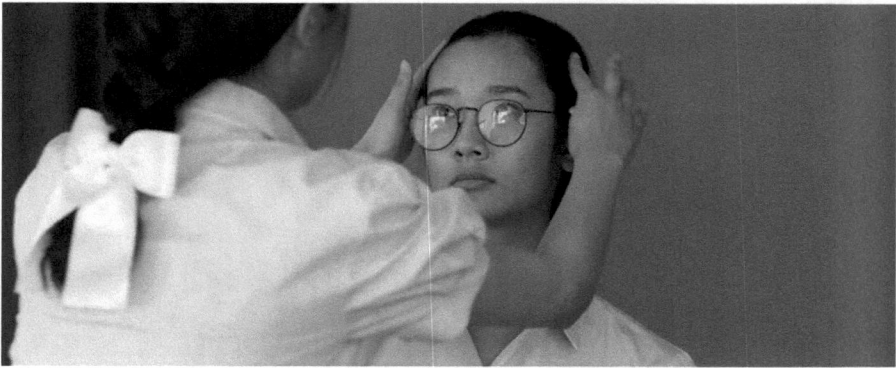

6.2 Grace shows tenderness toward Lynn at her new school. Film still from Nattawut Poonpiriya, *Bad Genius*, 2017.

With new friends, she expands this enterprise to an elaborate scheme to game a transnational university entrance exam. The students are caught and from this moment on Lynn's intellectual pursuits take a different turn, as she develops an idealistic philosophy of education instead.

The film plays out a drama between a regionally legible ideal of trans-Asia embodiment and personhood and a local subversion of this ideal. In this fast-paced story Lynn initially appears as a reserved youngster who lives in a lower-middle-class, financially challenged, single-parent household with her father, a teacher. When she transfers to the prestigious new school, Lynn at first tutors a new friend, Grace, who approaches Lynn with tenderness from day one (fig. 6.2). She subsequently expands her tutoring to the for-profit cheating schemes.

Lynn's sartorial style underwrites her capacitation; dressed in an understated manner, she embodies a pared-down, intellectual beauty and supremely enabled, upwardly mobile feminine potential. At the same time, her family's negligible purchasing power in combination with structural problems such as her school's corruption hamper her progress. Lynn's quest is not only a deceitful one—of fraudulence and for money—but also a doomed fight against unequally weighted odds. *Bad Genius* thus enacts a systemic critique of class and educational institutions, one that centrally reflects Chinese Thai postmigration histories.[32]

Lynn's feminine glamor is contrasted with her male counterpart Bank's sincere, slightly naïve masculinity. Bank is working class and gifted and also comes from a single-parent household. Despite initial misgivings, the

6.3 Lynn cries on her father's shoulder after confessing to fraud. Film still from Nattawut Poonpiriya, *Bad Genius*, 2017.

two friends go through with the transnational cheating scheme, which will earn them millions of baht. They travel to Sydney, Australia, from where they transmit to their friends in Bangkok the answers to a US university entrance exam, the "STIC." Bank is caught but, upon returning to Thailand, Lynn, with the support of her father, rises to the full height of her integrity and claims sole responsibility (fig. 6.3). At the university she applies to the education faculty to become a teacher like her father, relinquishing her dreams of studying at a prestigious university abroad.

The film seems to do something contradictory by centering a transregionally legible, upwardly mobile feminine ideal while proffering an ending that forgoes exactly that mobility. It thereby produces an instructive quandary, however, and questions notions of educational progress in contemporary Thailand. It also shows that great intellectual potential is furnished by students who come from the financially modest households from which Lynn and Bank hail. Students like Lynn and Bank have the prerequisites for becoming government scholars, that class of persons from which many Southeast Asian countries draw their university faculty and civil servants. That many gifted scholars in Thailand come from lower-middle-class, small entrepreneurial, or even working-class Chinese backgrounds does not even have to be explicitly stated in *Bad Genius*. We can thus understand the film implicitly to make a claim about the class of knowledge workers as being composed to a great extent of Chinese-heritage persons.

In chapter 4, *How to Dump* steered us away from the focus on ethnicized identities and bodies as the sole bearers of historical memory. Instead Nawapol's film gestures toward a prosthetic, postmigrant approach to minority histories, the disappearance of which is imminent. In this perspective, memory becomes the purview of a plurality of persons, bodies, and ethnicities. *Bad Genius* puts yet another spin on postmigrant personhood when it questions capacitation in the knowledge economy and the role that ethnic, female bodies assume in this context.

Rey Chow has outlined the extent to which ethnic personhood is subject to difference's capture by capitalism.[33] The Thai media that I examine situate the ethnic body in yet another history of understandings of race and social plurality. At present, Chinese-heritage persons' distinction in Thailand is determined by factors other than visible difference, linguistic competency, or cultural practice. How are we to imagine an identity that exceeds such taxonomies?

While lightly referencing historical trajectory and social role, *Bad Genius*'s invocation of Chineseness does not reify identity. Viranjini Munasinghe has argued that the migrant body is—more clearly than a national body—able to epitomize a specific period.[34] This claim becomes particularly intriguing in the Thai context. The ability to somatize history is in part due to the fact that the migrant body is marked and hypervisible.[35] The conditions that obtain for Chineseness in Thailand in the present have undergone a significant shift, however. Chinese femininity, both off-screen and in visual representation, occupies a complex position that exceeds questions of visibility and invisibility: In many contexts today— economic, cultural, and educational—Chineseness appears as visibly outstanding yet unremarkable in its exceptionality.

What is more, the transnationality that was at times negatively attributed to Chinese persons in the past has in the present been reoccupied as desirable. With regard to Chinese femininity in Thailand the purported disappearance effected by the notion of assimilation has been transformed into the desirable ubiquity of this personhood, a taken-for-granted (re)appearance.

Both *How to Dump* and *Bad Genius* thus foreground an embodiment not necessarily labeled; no explicit designation of ethnicity *needs* to be put forth. These films are moreover non-Sinophone—except where they make brief sinographic references and show Chinese-language business signs, they present a Chineseness without (much) Chinese language. Instead they showcase a Chinese-descent, postmigrant feminine centrality.

This then is the difference that Southeast Asia can make: It detemporalizes and deterritorializes identity and thereby intervenes into new hegemonies. Southeast Asia militates against any presumed reconvergence of center and diaspora; rather, it makes possible their disaggregation. This location moreover allows cultural producers touching on Chinese thematics to surpass even the invocation of the Sinophone, the established critical conception designating heterogeneous languages and locations of origin beyond China.[36] Both decentering China and stretching beyond the Sinophone, the location of Southeast Asia opens up the descriptor "Chinese" to newer meaning. It is women who primarily negotiate this domain, embodying both ideal neoliberal optimization as well as its undoing.

Women in the City

In *Bad Genius* and *How to Dump* the question of region is negotiated almost entirely within the space of Bangkok, as that location where the subnational, national, regional, and global coincide. Bangkok, as a "primate city, a type of city which is exponentially larger than the country's other cities and more influential," represents the center of national and regional knowledge industries.[37] Much of the salience of the urban to the regional, of Bangkok to "Asia," is negotiated through the trope of women's expertise.

Lynn and Jean struggle as women in the neoliberal urban order, yet they are also supremely prepared to take it on. In both films the feminine senses for knowing the (urban) world and grasping essential features of the future represent the primary mode of apperceiving the present. In *How to Dump* Jean attempts to tame the ravages of urban capitalism and her psyche through the strict aesthetics of her design. In *Bad Genius* Lynn approaches contemporary urban life by imposing numerical grids on space to produce pertinent schemas for grasping the complexities of education in a neoliberal age. Both women also "go international."

In *How to Dump* we never see the characters leave Bangkok, while a part of *Bad Genius* takes place in Sydney. However, the largest part of the action is set in the middle-class and small entrepreneurial spaces of Bangkok, implicitly coded as the homes of working- and lower-middle-class Chinese Thai families. Lynn's middle-class home and Bank's home, which is also his mother's laundry business, both potentially figure as Chinese. An additional location provides historical anchoring for the story as a story of Chinese Bangkok: Grace's family's decommissioned printing house named Sue Trong Phanit (Honest Commerce). Marked as Chinese, the former printing house serves to ground the action of *Bad Genius* in an entrepreneurial ethos and migrant history. The printing house's name points to a history of Thai bias toward Chinese migrants. Chinese business and family names that include terms such as *sue trong* (honest) or *phak di* (loyal) may in part have been chosen to counter such bias.[38]

Sue Trong Phanit extends over several floors of a shophouse. A large workroom on the second floor bears the slogan "Perform to Produce Results"; elsewhere a sign in English reads "Safety First." Both point to Thailand's developmentalist history, technocratic orientation, and efforts to standardize in order to participate in global networks of industry. The business's large Heidelberg printing presses invoke the extensive networks of a colonial modernity that traded in European goods and centered precisely on Chinese entrepreneurs in Southeast Asia. The camera repeatedly focuses on the shophouse entrance of the press and the sign with the business's name, which takes on ironic significance in light of the students' cheating scheme. The location then also poses the charge that Lynn, Bank, and Grace are betraying the ethical grounding of a heritage based on "honest commerce."

Mobile / Motile Bodies

The degree of mobility that the female characters possess—Lynn travels to Sydney overnight while in *How to Dump* Jean has just returned from Sweden—stands out. Within the city, too, the women's mobility is foregrounded. Lynn is always out and about in Bangkok, appearing at night at Bank's house, in a restaurant with Grace, and various other locations. Li Shaohong's film *Baober in Love* (China, 2004) provides a salient comparison regarding the interrelation of women's mobility, economy, and urban space in Asia. Its protagonist Baober ("Doll")—an adaptation of the figure of "Amélie"—traverses with ease private and public space, socialist and postsocialist space, and upscale and working-class locations in Beijing.[39] The one place that she cannot inhabit without damage to her body and psyche, however, is the stylized factory loft that is supposed to become her marital home. Very much at home in the industrial, working-class, and lower-middle-class spaces of the city, and adept at crashing upper-class spaces, Baober becomes immunocompromised when it comes to living in the refurbished factory loft. In this we can understand her also to be allergic to upper-middle-class, neoliberal heteronormativity in postsocialist Beijing. As a panacea to this socioeconomic order Baober fantasizes a psychosomatic doubling and imagines that she has given birth to a child.

In her analysis of *Baober in Love* Erin Huang argues that body and city are not separate but represent interdependent domains in the contemporary PRC. In the Thai films I have discussed, the female characters somatize their relation to the urban neoliberal order differently, yet the comparison with the role of female bodies in Chinese cities is instructive. Huang understands "cinema as a record of post-socialist gender negotiations where bourgeois heteronormativity reemerges as the field of recoding gender identities. In making a post-socialist woman's body, the 'post' becomes a complex site of geopolitical imaginary, where bodies are infinitely experimented on, transposed, and superimposed."[40] Huang defines "post-socialist" as denoting a generalized concept of the neoliberal present across territories. Thus her conception of postsocialism also encompasses locations such as Taiwan and Hong Kong and, by implication, Thailand.

According to Huang, urban space in *Baober* and other films by director Li is always already feminine. She contends that "the gendered body seeps into urban imaginaries of Chinese metropolises, creating expanded spaces of consumption in a continuum of bodies and cities—an embodied landscape."[41] For the female protagonists of Li's films this is a dystopian urban landscape, in which Baober's body is seized by embourgeoisement. At the same time, the female body becomes the site for resignification, when Baober creates her own version of space through the doubling of the fantasized pregnancy that she somatizes.

In her conceptualization of postsocialist urban femininity, Huang relies also on Barlow's argument that "what is occurring in China now is an obsessive recoding of femininity as money."[42] In Bangkok, too, femininity, economic transformation, and urban space encode each other. The protagonists of *How to Dump* and *Bad Genius* also have to deal with the classed losses of urban transformation but, in contradistinction to Baober, whose imagined pregnancy is diagnosed as a mental disorder, Lynn's and Jean's states of mind are not labeled aberrant. Yet, while they are not abjected, they are likewise required to mobilize extraordinary mental energies to traverse changing urban societies. Jean attempts to control the space of the transforming city very tightly: Returning to an increasingly neoliberal, gentrifying Bangkok from Sweden, she attempts to get a hold on things by stratifying her domestic space. She redesigns the family shophouse's interiors in almost comically minimalist style and signals these disciplined aesthetics also through her own sartorial style—so much so that a minimalist motility of the female body emerges.

Rather than "doubled," as Baober's body, Jean's body appears as pared down, yet we can determine a parallel of body and built environment in the film. Jean's clean, streamlined attire becomes nearly indistinct from the aesthetics of the minimalist built environment. In this she fully, corporeally inhabits a functionalist neoliberal order. At the same time, her embodiment exceeds mere functionalism. The ideal prototype of the built environment in *How to Dump* is made of concrete, glass, and steel; these materials furnish the building blocks of creative spaces (design offices). We may, with Audrey Yue, understand these spaces to exemplify the ways that "creativity" is harnessed to the goals of neoliberal economies.[43] Yet the vast spaces of the artful, generous structures Jean designs and desires leave boundless room for the mind to wander, for the psyche to fill up with memory, and for fantasy to take hold. Thus creativity does not remain limited to utility but ultimately throws a wrench in the updated developmentalist dream of optimal productivity.

In *Bad Genius* Lynn likewise learns new forms of navigating a transforming urban space and society in the playing field in which she reigns supreme: knowledge and its commodification. Women are compelled to stretch, modify, and manipulate their bodies in new urban economies, yet they also apply their own discipline on their environment. Women figure as the agentive drivers of reregionalization but also impose their own grids on space and use their apperception of the present for superior navigation of the neoliberal city.

Genius in the City

Education codes as urban like almost no other domain. Bangkok, where the majority of Thai educational and professional resources are concentrated, is virtually synonymous with this sector. Much of *Bad Genius*'s action takes place in educational spaces. In addition Lynn's sartorial style and modes of inhabiting space encode the genius of the film's protagonist.

When she is not dressed in her school uniform, Lynn wears jeans with simple, commercial-print t-shirts. These signal her prowess in hacking into the transnational—and making something out of the commercial-entrepreneurial cheap, or free, ordinary (fig. 6.4). They also gesture toward her hipsterish superiority over those classmates who are merely rich, merely greedy, or merely skilled and dutiful but lacking Lynn's ingenuity.

6.4 Lynn in casual clothing. Film still from Nattawut Poonpiriya, *Bad Genius*, 2017.

Her skill in traversing contemporary knowledge orders also becomes encoded in Lynn's movement through spaces other than those of educational institutions. Her arrival at the Sydney airport is a case in point (fig. 6.5). As Lynn glides along the walkway in slow motion, we see her from the side: tall, urbane, full of confidence, with flowing hair and sunglasses. She is going global, arriving as a conqueror, who is well positioned to ace the transnational test.

In the Thai political and cultural present, women's agency is often figured through the economic sphere. In *Bad Genius* this motif is tweaked further, as the protagonist attempts to gain mastery over an intellectual and economic terrain. This is a highly symbolic act, as Thailand increasingly has to shift its economic pursuits to a knowledge economy—be it in higher education services or expanding IT sectors. *Bad Genius* negotiates this shift by coming out on the side of an idealistic educational philosophy, rather than on that of neoliberal knowledge optimization. As the film works through the quandary of the futures of education, it relies on particular uses of color and lighting.

One of the dominant colors in *Bad Genius* is brown—whether in the venerable brown of the wood paneling at Lynn's new private school, the browns of her lower-middle-class home, or Bank's working-class home. These shades contrast with the expansive, bright, and symmetrical spaces of higher education into which Lynn transitions. Brown signals the comfort of a home and privacy, but the dark spaces of Lynn's school are also full of shadows that obscure. Here brown evokes the double valence of privacy as both protective and potentially abusive. Bright neon-

6.5 Lynn arrives in Sydney. Film still from Nattawut Poonpiriya, *Bad Genius*, 2017.

lit spaces, by contrast, suggest transparency but also signal the violence of surveillance.

Although the darkened interiors of childhood are in part confining for her, Lynn gains a foothold against the powers that be from within the new school. Her mode of mastery consists of applying intellectual skills to the spaces in question. We frequently witness Lynn taking control of a space through her mathematical skills. These skills are showcased in the initial conversation that Lynn and her father have with the prestigious school's principal in her dark wood-paneled office. As Lynn worries about and calculates the cost of attendance in her head, she speaks out the equations. At the same time, her mental calculations are superimposed on the screen in numbers. This computational prowess henceforth encodes the protagonist's personhood. It is consistently reinvoked in large exam halls that are symbolic of the transition to higher education. Here Lynn taps out answers with her fingers on her desk for her friends to see. Finally she exerts her spatial and numerical abilities on the transnational test and the symmetrically laid-out STIC exam building in Sydney.

While Huang discerns a "continuum of bodies and cities" in which women's bodies double and split under new social and economic demands in postsocialist Beijing, a different body-city continuum predominates in *Bad Genius*. In the Thai blockbuster, the female body and mind enact the analytics that overdetermine the present. As her body and brain move like machines in national and transnational space, Lynn also mobilizes the mathematical and spatial engineering required for mastery in the contemporary city. Her body and mind approximate the speed of electronic capital and instant media transactions—she works like an algorithm, a "step-by-step procedure for calculating the answer to a problem from a given set of inputs."[44] Malte Ziewitz argues that, in the common imagination, the algorithm—understood as "recursively applied decision rules"—is fixed, scripted, and automated; it appears as a "mysterious and seemingly complete figure."[45]

In line with her algorithmic identity Lynn's sartorial style is unembellished rather than ornate like that of *In the Mood for Love*'s protagonist. She is further often refracted in mirrors, underlining the notion of her multiplicatory potential but also pointing to the fact that Lynn is still forming an identity.

Denouement

In these contemporary films, Chinese female bodies labor as bodies that have become national and whose historical racialization has morphed into an ethnicity marked as advantaged. Jean and Lynn's ethnicity is evident but unremarkable, their achievements extraordinary yet a matter of course. The labor that these female characters have to perform today is that of embodying professional-economic and physical optimization. As figures whose embodiment bears trans-Asia legibility, they are also tasked with linking Thailand to regional profitability. Yet the films analyzed here consistently undercut this depiction of Chinese femininity as optimized and optimal. Far from abasing the female figures in question, however, they subject the very notion of optimization to scrutiny.

The quick pacing of *Bad Genius*'s final exam scenes, the cross-cutting between spaces in the chase, and the disorienting tilt of the camera as Lynn navigates the STIC exam building and flees through the subway all enhance the notion of her algorithmic mode of operation. At the same time, this is where Lynn's functioning begins to show cracks, and the long scenes of attempting desperately to transmit the exam answers and escape the building foreground the toll that algorithmic functioning takes on her body. Cutting between her face and the exam hall, these scenes draw into relation the calculative operations in progress in the "privacy" of Lynn's intellect and the unevenly accessible, increasingly privatizing, public domain of the international education business. Concurrently, they highlight Lynn's suffering, as she exploits her own body in the attempt to beat the odds of capture. She sticks a pencil down her throat in order to vomit

6.6 Lynn interviews at a university. Film still from Nattawut Poonpiriya, *Bad Genius*, 2017.

and be excused from the exam hall; subsequently she runs madly through the exam building and the subway.

Here, the film departs from a notion of optimization.[46] The assumption of automation is replaced by an understanding of the algorithm as "an exercise in respecification rather than an application of a set of rules."[47] *Bad Genius* had included the possibility of such a break from the beginning. Lynn's mode of memorization is always artistic and frequently reverts to childhood memory. The film ultimately challenges the "common-sense idea of algorithms as recursively applied decision rules" and the operationalization of the body and mind in the name of education as a frontier of primitive accumulation in the city.[48]

At *Bad Genius*'s end Lynn appears again in the hygienic, expansive spaces of the knowledge economy. Yet this time she is there not to profit financially, or be surveilled, but to direct her intellectual capacities toward formulating a philosophy of learning. Under the bright lights of the local university building in which she interviews, Lynn has nothing to hide. Instead the lights shine on the calm idealism of her pedagogical commitment. *Bad Genius*'s denouement thereby recodes the neoliberal architectures of the knowledge industry with a non-neoliberal educational ideology (fig. 6.6).

The question is whether what started as Lynn's ambitious scheme to conquer the world isn't curbed to too great an extent by the film's ending. Her rueful decision to become a local teacher, instead of pursuing her education abroad, might be understood as the curtailing of ambition and

6.7 Lynn presents her pedagogical idealism. Film still from Nattawut Poonpiriya, *Bad Genius*, 2017.

domestication of supreme talent into a traditional femininity with nationalist overtones. Yet the wisdom that Lynn acquires by the film's end is also an advanced kind of knowledge. While she had been deeply committed to her friends and father—and committed fraud for their sakes—she now transcends individual commitment as she trades it in for the dedication to an educational mission. In order to fully grasp intellectual integrity, Lynn first had to touch its edges. As a female Bildungsroman *Bad Genius* shows that Lynn's transgressions will be forgiven because she was young. At the story's end Lynn is still young but has, in the social responsibility that she embodies, reached a precocious degree of maturity (fig. 6.7). This then is a further centering of Chinese femininity as located in the middle of society and essential to its educational enterprises. Lynn, however, surpasses paradigms of nationalist development as she now embodies fidelity to the true spirit of an egalitarian educational mission—an antineoliberal stance.

In *Bad Genius* and *How to Dump* women appear as mobile and motile agents of the future who dismantle monolithic notions of both nation and region. They are the ones in whom neoliberal aspiration is vested, yet they undercut these expectations by the ways in which they inhabit the city, new economic forms, and feminine embodiment. Dominant body-city continua are ultimately undermined in these stories: At the end *Bad Genius* no longer foregrounds Lynn's algorithmic mode of operation, and *How to Dump* highlights precisely Jean's failure to produce a minimalist psychological functionalism. Endings of de-acceleration, melancholy, and skepticism thus show Jean and Lynn ultimately pursuing paths other than those of fusing with the dictates of new urban economies.

Resisting the operationalization of gendered bodies in the BRI era, Lynn and Jean confound notions of how bodies are supposed to relate to urban space. As they transect urban space in unexpected ways, their exceptional-yet-unremarkable bodies and personas and their own psychic attachments refuse to transform "Southeast Asia" into a site of optimization. They ultimately resist the mapping of Southeast Asia as part of a thriving neoliberal region. Upscaling doesn't solve anything in *How to Dump*; in *Bad Genius*, the algorithmic potential of the young female character is deactivated, and the notion of the secessionary, primate city as the gateway to international optimization is challenged.

Contemporary Thai cinema throws into relief especially the current significations of Chinese feminine embodiment. Through two films, Chutimon plays out the contradictions of the demands made of urban femininities. Chinese femininity here appears as a question and challenge to region in the sense of undermining the economic expansionist ethos of which gendered optimization is a crucial part. Aihwa Ong and Tani Barlow have shown the ways in which "women in transition" represent the drivers of new economic forms in Asia.[49] The figures of both Lynn and Jean, as embodied by the iconic Chutimon, update this trope for the era of contemporary finance capitalism. They tantalize with their optimal potentiality, then subvert in profound ways viewer expectations for fitting into Asian economies in transition.

Conclusion

While Chinese femininities in the contemporary Southeast Asian city become instrumental in expanding the reach of capital in both material and virtual domains, they also provide inroads into alternative urban imaginaries that highlight sensory and affective plenitude and recognize cities' indelible ties to the past. By drawing attention to as-yet-obscured histories and alternative modes of sensing the present, new writing and cinema have their finger on novel ways of navigating urban and regional transformation.

Chinese female protagonists in these stories are not merely tasked with assuaging a history of denigration and exploitation. Neither do they represent triumphalist assertions of social and political ascendancy. Instead, these cultural texts make evident the demands that the neoliberal order makes of gendered, ethnicized persons, and some ultimately undermine these. To make such critical interventions, the revival sites and texts rely on counterintuitive moves, temporalities, and logics: They invoke forgetting to foreground alternative modes of remembering; center identities only to decenter them; center ethnic bodies while refusing logics of visibility; redeploy genre; and refute the linearity of heritage.

This occurs in Southeast Asia, because history remains material, and shadow memories of social plurality are abundant in this location. Their revival proceeds in multitemporal, historically differentiated modes. As the Southeast Asian texts and sites draw region and identity into new conversations, they do not merely flip relations of dominance and subordination, majority and minority, or centrality and marginality but rather tip these concepts into entirely new directions.

Women in Asia and the World

In the preceding pages a woman appeared across East and Southeast Asia, in Bangkok, Hong Kong, and Shanghai. In distressed, updated, and futuristic forms, she stands at the center of contemporary revivals in media and urban design that bring to life Chinese pasts and the aesthetics of colonial modernity. But this figure also appears in locations such as Berlin and New York. What significance might she have in those places?

In Brooklyn, New York, Vanessa Li is featured in an interview-cum-fashion-shoot at the Bushwick bar Mood Ring. Foregrounding her appearance, biography, and activist outlook, the article features co-owner Li in the space of the bar with its "lush, colorful interior, and lighting taken straight from a Wong Kar-wai film." The motile platform of Wong's 1960s Hong Kong colonial modern aesthetics here fulfills the task of actualizing a cosmopolitan Asian aesthetic in the diaspora. But, as Li explains, she created the bar also in response to "a lack of places for young, queer people of color to gather in Bushwick."[1]

In Asia figures of femininity help to deconstruct confining models of neoliberal regional governance and make available forms of belonging that extend beyond national boundaries—as well as forms of personhood that exceed templates of optimization. In this role the figure of the recuperated Asian Modern Girl or futuristic city girl is also of global significance. What makes the detemporalization and deterritorialization that she undertakes singular? After all, approaches that reflect on the logics of colonial modernity are also being applied to Europe, situating it in a larger Mediterranean region and writing new histories of religion, ethnicity, and belonging.[2] The labor that distressed figures of femininity perform in recalling cosmopolitan pasts and anticipating futures can likewise be found across the globe. Thus the work of a distressed Chinese femininity at times becomes cognate with that of female figures in Ottoman-style revivals in Mediterranean countries, or that of Jewish femininity in Weimar Germany.

Why might the world look to Asia today? Historically global desires for Asia as signaling better geopolitics are perhaps best encapsulated by the 1955 Bandung conference and its attempt to build lasting South-South alliances. Such decolonial vision now seems all but lost, and Asia seems to merely offer blueprints for lifestyle, bodily modification, self-optimization, and even governance in the present. But what appears as surface in fact bears a conceptual depth that Asia anticipates but that is instructive globally.

The particular significance of distressed-futuristic figures of Asian femininity is that their embodiment of transforming notions of economic and human value is acutely of the moment. Both in and issuing from Asia, reregionalization is taking place at an accelerated pace. In this context reterritorializations of the body and of gender come into sharp focus, bringing about an unprecedented global orientation toward Asia. As Tani Barlow states, "Much of the world is being tugged toward Asian modes of postdevelopment capitalist culture. What began as a ploy to gain market penetration is flowering into a massive, uneven, yet globally commodified femininity."[3]

Barlow revealed femininity to be at the heart of notions of eugenics and capitalist social progress in China in the early twentieth century and of notions of surplus value at its end.[4] In the twenty-first century femininity in Asia sees further "recoding" as compound value.[5] This propensity of the feminine to produce a multiplication of value—like interest on interest—makes it the prime exemplar of a contemporary finance capitalism.

What would speak against attributing the notion of multiplication of value also to representations of Asian femininity in Brooklyn, New York? The attribution of superlatives to Asia is fraught with potential colonial or (techno-)Orientalist implications. Anne Cheng's analysis of a Western racial imaginary provides a cautionary account in this regard. Cheng writes of the "yellow woman" as a figure who exceeds the human, a "form of synthetic personhood." She is found in fantasies "populated by nonsubjects who endure as ornamental appendages."[6] In Cheng's study this figure's ornamentalism "names the perihumanity of Asiatic femininity, a peculiar state of being produced out of the fusion between 'thingliness' and 'personness.'"[7]

In my reading of the Shanghai Mansion Woman, I suggested that she subverts multiple notions of the "more" with which she is associated. She does so, for one, by returning to the grounds of her abjection to redefine

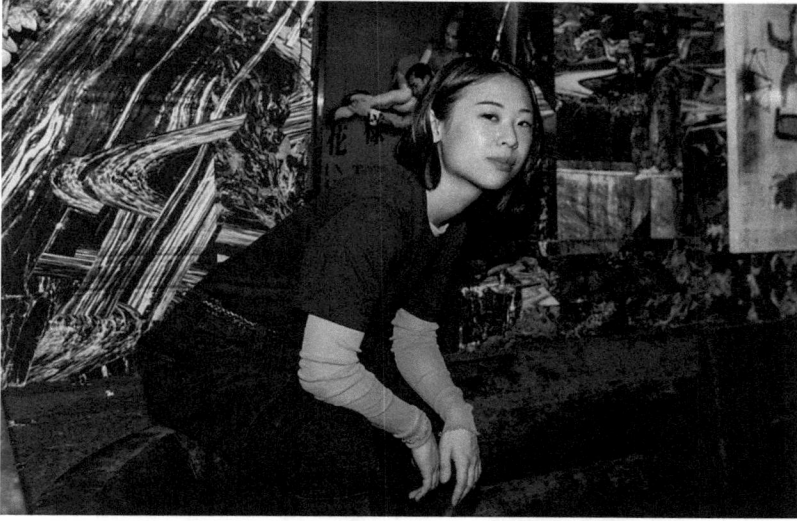

C.1 Vanessa Li, co-owner of the bar Mood Ring, Brooklyn, New York.

the historical terms that constituted her personhood. In the case of other feminine figures in Thai cultural production, I found that, though tasked with facilitating detrimental forms of urban development, they also undermine gentrification, impoverished geopolitical and social imaginaries, the ways that women have to embody pasts and futures, and ethnicized persons' subsumption into paradigms of productivity. The logic of a feminine more thus does not only facilitate unrestricted capital gain, or satisfy questionable social desires, but provides gaps in which other kinds of work can be accomplished.

In Brooklyn's Mood Ring bar, femininity fully inhabits the present, and a purported feminine more is directed toward queer and racial justice goals. The bar deploys Wong's colonial modern aesthetics—and the femininity that it foregrounds—as a platform for political, affective, and social objectives of the present. The rationale for opening the Wong-themed, Berlin-inspired queer bar—providing an *other* space "for young, queer people of color to gather"—represents a more to that which already exists and fulfills a serious social need. In this case the plenitude that the colonial modern blueprint of *In the Mood for Love* invokes underwrites an urgent politicized leisure project.

What is more, if femininity is associated with certain modes of proliferation (exemplifying the "more of the more"), the Mood Ring project leaves open the directions that such proliferation will take. A photo accompanying the interview article best encapsulates the bar's ethos. It shows Li in front of a poster of *In the Mood for Love* in which Maggie Cheung is reclining, while Li leans forward in symmetrical alignment (fig. C.1). Yet the relation between the two women is provocatively asymmetrical. Li's sartorial style replicates neither the ornate femininity of Wong's film nor the feminine optimization suggested in films such as *Bad Genius*. With her confident pose and quotidian yet elegant dress (it is a fashion shoot, after all), Li emerges neither as distressed nor futuristic. The interview's and Mood Ring's presentation thus undercuts Asian femininity's association with excess—as well as this femininity's primary association with the past and the future.

Notes

Introduction. The Revival of Bangkok as a Chinese City

1   As a symbol of Straits Chinese, or Peranakan, culture, the devotional pineapple sutures the regions of East Asia and Southeast Asia.

2   I base this formulation on the title of Kuan-Hsing Chen's *Asia as Method: Toward Deimperialization.*

3   In "Situations and Limits of Postcolonial Theory," Pheng Cheah debates China's colonial experience as well as notions of China as empire in a section titled "History of Sino-Postcoloniality: 'Chinese' 'Colonial' Experiences" (1–29).

4   In Bangkok, see, e.g., the hotels the Siam and the Sukosol (http://www .thesukosol.com); the scent company Karmakamet, which lays claim to a Chinese migrant history (http://www.karmakamet.co.th); and numerous real estate projects that reproduce colonial aesthetics as ciphers for a sophisticated, aspirationally upper-middle-class lifestyle. In Hong Kong, not only hospitality venues but also clothing brands, such as Shanghai Tang (https://www.shanghaitang.com), advertise Chinese colonial modernity as the ultimate in historically rooted, personal style.

5   A recent cinematic example is Cheang Pou-soi's *SPL II: A Time for Consequences* (Hong Kong/China, 2015). For two different perspectives on how to calibrate the deployment of temporal difference in intra-Asian media contexts, see Knee, "Thailand in the Hong Kong Cinematic Imagination," and Iwabuchi, ""Nostalgia for a (Different) Asian Modernity."

6   Stewart, *Crimes of Writing,* 67, 74.

7   Ivy, *Discourses of the Vanishing,* 68.

8   See Sedgwick, *Touching Feeling,* and Lucey and McEnaney, "Introduction."

9   Haiping Yan examines the cosmopolitanism of 1930s Shanghai literature and cinema in "Other Cosmopolitans." Bruce Robbins and Paula Lemos Horta's edited volume *Cosmopolitanisms* provides a diverse, global view of the notion of the cosmopolitan beyond any presumed European exportation of culture.

10   Lewis, "Cosmopolitanism and the Modern Girl," 1386. Christopher L. Hill's theory (described in "Conceptual Universalization in the Transnational Nineteenth Century") about how concepts attain global universality precisely by traveling corroborates such claims further. My understanding of the cosmopolitan is also informed by Sheldon Pollock's inquiry into the nature of the "Sanskrit cosmopolis," a premodern Asian cosmopolitanism. Although this is a temporally distant cosmopolitanism, Pollock's description of the Sanskrit cosmopolis's "transportability"—"the Sanskrit cosmopolis was wherever home was"—is instructive (Pollock, *Language of the Gods in the World of Men*, 16).

11   Sakai and Walker, "A Genealogy of Area Studies," 22.

12   Sakai and Walker, "A Genealogy of Area Studies," 24.

13   Walker, "The Accumulation of Difference and the Logic of Area."

14   Two book-length studies of Bangkok include Marc Askew's *Bangkok: Place, Practice, and Representation* and the 2021 publication of Lawrence Chua's *Bangkok Utopia: Modern Architecture and Buddhist Felicities, 1910–1973*. The latter includes a central focus on the ways in which Bangkok was constituted as a Chinese city.

15   Personal communication with Klaomard Yipintsoi, August 5, 2022. Only in retrospect can About Studio About Café be understood to have pioneered the revival trend.

16   Pattareeya, *Song Wat Guidebook*.

17   I take this term from Garrett, "Assaying History." Yaowarat is the name of a street in the Samphanthawong district but is frequently used to refer to (at least sections of) Bangkok's Chinatown as a whole.

18   "Tam roi kafae Ia Sae: Tamra ran amata nai chum chun Jin jud kamnoed achip hai khon phoeng tang tua" [Following the traces of 'Eia Sae Coffee': Legendary Chinese community business, vocational beginning for the just-established], *Silpa-Mag*, April 5, 2020, accessed December 11, 2024, https://www.silpa-mag.com/culture/article_27147.

19   "6 khafe satai Jin sud khlassik" [Six most classical Chinese-style cafés], *BKK Menu*, February 20, 2018, accessed December 11, 2024, https://www.bkkmenu.com/eat/stories/cafe-hopping-back-in-time.html.

20   "Lhong Tou Café," *BKK Menu*, June 17, 2018, accessed December 11, 2024, https://www.bkkmenu.com/eat/we-recommend/lhong-tou -cafe.html.

21   Chinese architectural history was recuperated in the lifestyle venue Patina Bangkok, as seen on their Facebook page, https://www.facebook .com/Patina.bkk/, accessed December 11, 2024.

22   Landsberg, *Prosthetic Memory*.

23   Sedgwick, *Touching Feeling*, 21.

24   Sedgwick, *Touching Feeling*, 14.

25   Sedgwick, *Touching Feeling*, 13.

26   "Lhong Tou Café: Hippest Chinese-Style Café @ The Market Bangkok," *Review Aroii*, undated, https://reviewaroii.com/lhong-tou-cafe/.

(This link is no longer active. The corresponding short Facebook and Twitter posts are from the end of June 2022.) While the review mainly focuses on a new branch, it accounts for the original café's location, concept, and design in Yaowarat.

27   Seremetakis, *The Senses Still*.

28   The *New Yorker*'s elaborate visual collage represents a good introduction to the film's colonial modern aesthetics and enduring global appeal. Kyle Chayka, "Wong Kar-wai's 'In the Mood for Love,'" *New Yorker*, September 1, 2023, accessed December 8, 2024, https://www.newyorker.com/culture/touchstones/wong-kar-wais-in-the-mood-for-love.

29   Teo, "Wong Kar-wai's *In the Mood for Love*."

30   Vivian Y. P. Lee formulates this as follows: "If embedded in the postnostalgic is the temptation to look back at what 'would have been,' the 'post' here implies a desire to translate what is lost into a continued questioning of what is and what will become"(*Hong Kong Cinema Since 1997*, 42).

31   Bruno, *Surface*, 38.

32   Rey Chow discusses nostalgia in "A Souvenir of Love"; Stephen Teo speaks of a heightened concern with temporality in *Wong Kar-Wai*; and Vivian Y. P. Lee investigates a postnostalgic cinema in *Hong Kong Cinema Since 1997*.

33   Lee, *Hong Kong Cinema Since 1997*, 8.

34   Lim, "Spectral Times," 290, 291.

35   Lee, *Hong Kong Cinema Since 1997*, 29–30.

36   Lee, *Hong Kong Cinema Since 1997*, 24.

37   Lee classifies Wong's films as postnostalgic on the grounds of "the films' self-reflexive intertextuality, hybrid temporal/spatial references, and stylistic flourishes" (*Hong Kong Cinema Since 1997*, 14). Critics such as Audrey Yue have also highlighted *In the Mood for Love*'s facility for movement within time ("In the Mood for Love," 129).

38   See Loos, *Subject Siam*.

39   L. Hong, "Invisible Semicolony." The Thai Marxist Udom Sisuwan (his pen name is Aran Phromchomphu) is frequently credited as having introduced the notion of semicoloniality with regard to Thailand in his book *Thai kueng mueang khuen* (Thailand: A semi-colony, 1950).

40   Wongsurawat's *The Crown and the Capitalists: The Ethnic Chinese and the Founding of the Thai Nation* contains chapters focusing on education, media, economy, World War II and nationalist narrative, and the Cold War.

41   Wongsurawat, *The Crown and the Capitalists*, 4–5. Southeast Asian Chinese history in general is increasingly researched in proximity to colonial history. See the work of scholars such as Eric Tagliacozzo, Guo-Quan Seng, and Oiyan Liu.

42   Wongsurawat, *The Crown and the Capitalists*, 5.

43   The first two books on Chinese Thai history to be published after William Skinner's *Chinese Society in Thailand* (1957) are Pimpraphai Bisalputra and Jeffery Sng's *A History of the Thai-Chinese* (2015) and Wongsurawat's *The Crown and the Capitalists* (2019). In 2023 these were joined by Sittithep Eaksittipong's *Pen Jin phro ru suek: Prawatsat suea phuen mon bai thi phoeng sang* [Being Chinese because of feeling Chinese: A very recent rags-to-riches history]. Given the centrality of Chinese migration to Thailand's nineteenth- and twentieth-century history, these publications represent very urgent contributions.

44   Pimpraphai and Sng describe the ways in which Chinese labor and business activities increased in the decades after the abolition of slavery in 1905 (*A History of the Thai-Chinese*, 255–257).

45   Pimpraphai and Sng, *A History of the Thai-Chinese*, 157.

46   Pimpraphai and Sng, *A History of the Thai-Chinese*, 211–277. The chapter is titled "Metamorphosis (1855–1925)."

47   Bernards, *Writing the South Seas*, 170.

48   According to Chua, population numbers in Bangkok in the late nineteenth and early twentieth centuries remain unclear, but he notes that "the arrival of Chinese migrants in Thailand had increased from about 2,000 persons annually in the early 1820s to 16,000 persons annually between 1882 and 1892. The figure increased exponentially to 68,000 per annum between 1906 and 1917" ("The City and the City," 936, 937).

49   Wongsurawat, *The Crown and the Capitalists*, 164n6.

50   Wongsurawat, *The Crown and the Capitalists*, 98.

51   Pimpraphai and Sng, *A History of the Thai-Chinese*, 306.

52   Pimpraphai and Sng, *A History of the Thai-Chinese*, 331–352.

53   Wongsurawat, *The Crown and the Capitalists*, 142.

54   Wongsurawat, *The Crown and the Capitalists*, 145–148.

55   By contrast, English newspapers directly named the state brutality and anti-Chineseness, and Chinese-language news combined images of violence with measured reporting. Wongsurawat, *The Crown and the Capitalists*, 148–153.

56   Wongsurawat, *The Crown and the Capitalists*, 141.

57   Wongsurawat argues against the "success story" of Chinese assimilation in Thailand in *The Crown and the Capitalists*, 158. Analyzing knowledge production about the Chinese in Thailand in "Textualising the 'Chinese of Thailand': Politics, Knowledge, and the Chinese in Thailand During the Cold War," Sittithep diagnoses a shift from viewing Chinese as the other to positioning Chinese as "the Chinese of Thailand."

58   A. Fuhrmann, *Ghostly Desires*, 92–96.

59   A. Fuhrmann, *Ghostly Desires*, 104–107.

60   A. Fuhrmann, *Ghostly Desires*, 104. The Ien Ang quotation is from "Can One Say No to Chineseness?," 236.

61   A. Fuhrmann, *Ghostly Desires*, 104.

62   See, e.g., Skinner, *Chinese Society in Thailand*; Rigg, "Exclusion and Embeddedness"; and Kasian Tejapira, "Imagined Uncommunity."

63   See, e.g., Wongsurawat, *The Crown and the Capitalists*, and Sittithep and Saichol, "An Outline for History of Emotion for the Chinese in Thailand."

64   A. Fuhrmann, *Ghostly Desires*, 104–105. The footnote in the text cites Rigg, "Exclusion and Embeddedness," 100 (on 218n41).

65   A. Fuhrmann, *Ghostly Desires*, 105.

66   Lampton, Ho, and Kuik et al., *Rivers of Iron*, 10.

67   Benjamin Zawacki, "Of Questionable Connectivity: China's BRI and Thai Civil Society," Council on Foreign Relations, June 7, 2021, https:// www.cfr.org/blog/questionable-connectivity-chinas-bri-and-thai-civil -society. Kornphanat reflects on the effects of China's contemporary official soft-power activities in Thailand, accounting for the domains of tourism, language teaching (Confucius Institutes), cultural initiatives, and media. She argues that cultural initiatives are largely welcomed and attributes their success to historical ties and the contemporary ethnic Chinese community's support. Conversely, she notes that "the increased penetration of Chinese capital is meeting resistance" ("Culture and Commerce," 167).

68   Sittithep, *Pen Jin phro ru suek*, 261.

69   Brown, "American Nightmare," 693.

70   Andrea Muehlebach writes about flexibility in labor markets in *The Moral Neoliberal*.

71   I borrow this concept from Mbembe, "Aesthetics of Superfluity."

72   Iwabuchi, "Nostalgia for a (Different) Asian Modernity," 569.

73   I take this subheading from Shih, *The Lure of the Modern*, 292.

74   See Modern Girl Around the World Research Group, *The Modern Girl Around the World*. For the Bangkok Modern Girl, see Natanaree, "The Siamese 'Modern Girl' and Women's Consumer Culture, 1925–35."

75   Berlant, *The Female Complaint*, 4.

76   Berlant, *The Female Complaint*, 4.

77   Ong, "Buoyancy," 193.

78   Harootunian, "Remembering the Historical Present."

79   See Barlow, "Femininity."

80   Mulvey, "Introduction: Fetishisms," 10.

81   Barlow, "Advertising Ephemera and the Angel of History," 113.

82   See Barlow, "'Green Blade in the Act of Being Grazed.'" I take the notion of "compounding value"—as a definition of the type of value that governs the logic of urban capitalism today—from Harvey, "The Right to the City."

83   See Barlow, "Advertising Ephemera and the Angel of History."

84   Barlow, "'Green Blade in the Act of Being Grazed.'"

85   Mbembe, "Aesthetics of Superfluity."

86   My analysis of femininity adapts notions of value and surface in the contemporary city from Mbembe's "Aesthetics of Superfluity."

87   See Ma, *Melancholy Drift*.

88   Barlow, "Debates over Colonial Modernity," 617.

89   Michel Foucault describes sexuality as a "dense transfer point" for power (*The History of Sexuality, Vol. 1*, 103).

Chapter 1. City Connectivities

1   "Kratham khwam Wong" [Doing Wong-ness], Facebook, accessed December 11, 2024, https://www.facebook.com/whysowong/.

2   See the critic Kong Rithdee's remarks on the usage of "wong" as an adjective in Thai in his discussion of the 2020 restored version of *In the Mood for Love*. Mongkol Cinema, "Wong sonthana" [Wong conversation/ Conversation round], live-stream discussion with Kong Rithdee, Prawit Taengaksorn, and Nawapol Thamrongrattanarit, Facebook, October 23, 2020, accessed December 11, 2024, https://www.facebook .com/MongkolCinemaMovie/videos/998733380633545.

3   Describing late nineteenth- to mid-twentieth-century patterns of migration, Brian C. Bernards highlights a "Swatow-Bangkok corridor" (*Writing the South Seas*, 166).

4   Mattern, *Deep Mapping the Media City*.

5   See Tagliacozzo and Chang, *Chinese Circulations*; Barlow, "Debates over Colonial Modernity"; and Barlow, "Advertising Ephemera."

6   Fu, *China Forever*; Teo, "*Wuxia* Redux"; Knee, "The Pan-Asian Outlook of *The Eye*"; Wongsurawat, "Home Base of an Exiled People."

7   See Landsberg, *Prosthetic Memory*.

8   Spivak, "Megacity"; Saskia Sassen, "Who Owns Our Cities—and Why This Urban Takeover Should Concern Us All," *Guardian*, November 24, 2015, accessed December 13, 2024, https://www.theguardian.com /cities/2015/nov/24/who-owns-our-cities-and-why-this-urban -takeover-should-concern-us-all; Mbembe, "Aesthetics of Superfluity." David Harvey, in "The Right to the City," describes the city as a product of capital, in the sense that cities represent prime transfer points for the absorption and production of surplus value.

9   Harvey, "The Right to the City."

10   Mbembe, "Aesthetics of Superfluity."

11   Mbembe, "Aesthetics of Superfluity," 374.

12   Mbembe, "Aesthetics of Superfluity," 393.

13   Mbembe, "Aesthetics of Superfluity," 394.

14   See, e.g., Mbembe's analysis of a South African casino's adoption of a Tuscan village look, in "Aesthetics of Superfluity," 396.

15   Abbas, "Cosmopolitan De-scriptions."

16   Cheung, "On Spectral Mutations," 182, 191.

17   Mbembe, "Aesthetics of Superfluity," 404.

18   Loos, *Subject Siam*; Barlow, "Debates over Colonial Modernity."

19   See Barlow, *In the Event of Women*; Barlow, "Advertising Ephemera"; and Barlow, "Debates over Colonial Modernity."

20   Barlow, *Formations of Colonial Modernity*, 6.

21   Barlow, *Formations of Colonial Modernity*, 5.

22   Kong Rithdee, "Will Gentrification Respect City's People?," *Bangkok Post*, June 28, 2023, accessed December 12, 2024, https://www.bangkok post.com/opinion/opinion/2600671/will-gentrification-respect-citys -people-.

23   L. Hong, "Invisible Semicolony."

24   For an explanation of how the Chinese entrepreneurs, the Thai monarchy, and the British empire profited from Siam's extraterritoriality in different ways, see especially Wongsurawat, *The Crown and the Capitalists*, 4–5.

25   Loos, *Subject Siam*.

26   Both quotes are from Barlow, *Formations of Colonial Modernity*, 1.

27   Stoler, *Race and the Education of Desire*; Stoler, *Carnal Knowledge and Imperial Power*. See also Hill, "Conceptual Universalization."

28   Goh and Yeoh, *Theorizing the Southeast Asian City as Text*, 4.

29   Ploy Mallikamas, "Nithasakan phap khong [Than] Phu Ying Sirikitiya Jensen" [Photography exhibition by (Than) Phu Ying Sirikitiya Jensen], *kooper*, February 7, 2020, accessed December 11, 2024, https://kooper .co/th-conversation-with-sirikitiya-jensen-hundred-years-between/.

30   See Chua, *Bangkok Utopia*.

31   See Barlow, "Debates over Colonial Modernity," and Barlow, "Advertising Ephemera."

32   Harootunian, "Remembering the Historical Present."

33   Morris, "Three Sexes and Four Sexualities," 15.

34   A review describes the venue's sister club, Sing Sing Theater, as follows: "Loosely modelled after a Chinese brothel, symmetrical elements follow principles of feng shui with walkways flowing into hidden seating areas and vantage spots." See "Sing Sing Bar and Theater," Bangkok.com, accessed December 2024, http://www.bangkok.com/magazine/sing -sing-theater.htm#.

35   Maggie Choo's, Facebook, accessed December 11, 2024, https://www .facebook.com/maggiechoos/.

36   Hershatter, *Dangerous Pleasures*.

37   Shih, *The Lure of the Modern*, 292.

38   Abbas, "Cosmopolitan De-scriptions," 775.

39   Abbas, "Cosmopolitan De-scriptions," 781.

40   Garrett, "Assaying History."

41   Ingawanij, "*Nang Nak*," 180–181.

42   Shih, *The Lure of the Modern*, 292.

43   Barlow, "Debates over Colonial Modernity," 623, 621.

44   Shih, *The Lure of the Modern*, 270.

45   Conversations with hostesses at Maggie Choo's, June 19, 2016.

46   Shanghai Mansion Bangkok, accessed December 11, 2024, http://www
.shanghaimansion.com/

47   Shanghai Mansion Bangkok, "Our Story," accessed November 24, 2020,
https://www.shanghaimansion.com/our-story/. The text has since
been revised.

48   Shanghai Mansion Bangkok, "Our Story," accessed November 24, 2020,
https://www.shanghaimansion.com/our-story/.

49   Garrett, "Assaying History," 1050.

50   Shanghai Mansion Bangkok, "Dining," accessed December 11, 2024,
https://www.shanghaimansion.com/dining/.

Chapter 2. In the Mood for Texture: Transmedia Revivals of Hong Kong's, Bangkok's, and Shanghai's Chinese Pasts and Colonial Modernities

1   See Stoler, *Imperial Debris*.

2   Garrett, "Assaying History," 1050.

3   Gina Marchetti describes this culture with precision in "Wong's Ladies
from Shanghai."

4   This dialogue is taken from the subtitles of the Criterion Collection's
DVD version of the film. For the last line of the dialogue, Denise Tang
suggests as more accurate "Am I useless?" Personal communication, November 13, 2024.

5   Garrett, "Assaying History," 1050.

6   Yue, "In the Mood for Love."

7   Pollock, *Language of the Gods in the World of Men*, 1. See George
Coedès's *Angkor: An Introduction* for a classical delineation of the significance of Angkor, and Ashley Thompson's "Performative Realities:
Nobody's Possession" for a vernacular Buddhist and feminist rereading
of Angkorian inscription.

8   In *Hong Kong: Culture and the Politics of Disappearance*, Ackbar Abbas
states that "Hong Kong has no precolonial past to speak of"; he also
notes that the city-state possesses "a postcoloniality that precedes decolonization" (2, 6).

9   In "Home Base of an Exiled People: Hong Kong and Overseas Chinese Activism from Thailand," Wasana Wongsurawat addresses "Hong
Kong's unusual non-nation status." She notes that we can "understand
Hong Kong in the Cold War years as a special space in between compet-
ing Cold War ideologies" (104).

10   Yue, "In the Mood for Love," 129.

11   Lee, *Hong Kong Cinema Since 1997*, 22.

12   Lee, *Hong Kong Cinema Since 1997*, 27.

13	See Lee's chapter on the "postnostalgic" content and aesthetic of Wong's *In the Mood for Love* and *2046* (in *Hong Kong Cinema Since 1997*, 21–42). See also Lu, "Hong Kong Diaspora Film."
14	As Audrey Yue notes, "The space between Hong Kong and China is rendered through Shanghai in the film. The story partially uses Shanghainese and is set in an immigrant Shanghainese community where everybody knows each other" ("In the Mood for Love," 132). See also Marchetti's film essay for the Criterion Collection DVD of *In the Mood for Love*.
15	See Tsai, "Singing, Dancing, and the Mass Production of Nonbelonging," 5.
16	Abbas, "Cosmopolitan De-scriptions." For a history of Shanghai that accounts for overlapping semicolonial and anti-imperial strains of ideology in the city in the mid-1920s, see Wasserstrom, "1926."
17	In "Invisible Semicolony," Lysa Hong argues that Siam declared itself postcolonial since the nineteenth century while remaining colonized by its elites until today. Siam/Thailand's coloniality is instantiated by the semicolonial condition under which it operated, which meant that its sovereignty was compromised by laws of extraterritoriality that affected its trade sovereignty. At the same time, Siam itself acted as an expansionary, colonizing power.
18	Achille Mbembe investigates the significance of the surface for the contemporary city in "Aesthetics of Superfluity."
19	Mulvey, "Introduction," 13.
20	Mulvey, "Introduction," 5.
21	Mulvey, "Introduction," 10.
22	Presentation, Kellogg Art Gallery, Cal Poly, Pomona, California, as part of "QCAMP: Queer & Critical Asian Media Projects" (2016 Eckstein Seminar, Pomona College, Claremont, California, April 15–16, 2016).
23	See Yue for a different analysis of region with regard to *In the Mood*'s deployment of the cheung sam. Thus Yue charges that Maggie Cheung's iconicity "problematises the Hong Kong cinema interface as a form of marginal imperialism in the Asian region, a genre of fusion pan-Asian kitsch in the global imagination and a structure of mood in the nostalgic present" ("In the Mood for Love," 134).
24	Wang, "The Palimpsest Body."
25	Yue, "In the Mood for Love," 133.
26	Tani E. Barlow's work on early twentieth-century Chinese modernity presents fine-honed analyses of the ways that desire, social progress, commodity, and capitalist productivity were bound up in the figure of woman. See, especially, Barlow, "Advertising Ephemera," and Barlow, *In the Event of Women*.

Lauren Berlant's analysis of the convergence and divergence of feminist and feminine complaints and desires in modern US culture also furnishes valuable frameworks for the study of this field across geographic locations. See Berlant, *The Female Complaint.*

27   Anderson, *Imagined Communities,* 24.

28   At the same time, the cheung sam points beyond these mundane temporalities to the promise for romance that capitalist modernity holds and the fusions of consumption and romance that are integral to it. See Illouz, *Consuming the Romantic Utopia.*

29   Prasenjit Duara outlines a redoubled temporality at the heart of the nation, as well as of capitalism, that includes both linear time and timelessness: "But history is not only about linear evolution; it is also about timelessness. To be recognizable as the *subject* of history, the core of the nation has to be unaffected by the passage of time" ("The Regime of Authenticity," 289).

30   As Duara explains, the temporality of capitalism is precisely not only marked by linear time: "The hegemony of linear time accompanying the transforming drive of capitalism necessitates the repeated constitution of an unchanging subject of history—a regime which stands outside time—precisely because this very combination of capital and linear time erodes it and simultaneously exposes the spectacle of this erosion" ("The Regime of Authenticity," 294).

31   On the paradoxical constitution of the modern lover's personhood, see Illouz, *Consuming the Romantic Utopia.*

32   Nguyen, *A View from the Bottom,* 115.

33   Anderson, *Imagined Communities,* 24.

34   Mulvey, "Introduction," 5.

35   Eileen Chang's *Love in a Fallen City* also prominently features a wall. See also Ann Hui's 1984 film adaptation by the same name.

36   See Anne Anlin Cheng's comprehensive rereading of the cinematic fetish of the Asian woman. Her chapter on Anna May Wong ("Gleaming Things," in *Ornamentalism*) complicates the politics of embodiment of the racialized woman by resituating the feminine fetish, objectness, and Oriental ornamentalism in the medium of cinema. Reading Wong as a signifying force, Cheng writes, "Wong sustains our imagination neither through her apparently racialized performances nor through her uncomplicated assumption of female agency but instead through her paradoxical staging and erasure of her body and of the skin that is supposed to give that corporeality meaning" (85). See also Yiman Wang's analysis of labor in Anna May Wong's work in *To Be an Actress: Labor and Performance in Anna May Wong's Cross-Media World.*

37   "Historic Qipao of Liberated Women," *Shanghai Daily,* July 6, 2012, accessed December 11, 2024, http://www.china.org.cn/arts/2012–07 /06/content_25834023.htm.

38   Shanghai Mansion Bangkok, "Explore," accessed June 14, 2020, https:// www.shanghaimansion.com/explore/.

39   Women frequently have to "stretch" to suture impossible historical and

temporal disparities. For contemporary Thai cinema, this is delineated in A. Fuhrmann, *Ghostly Desires*, 46–86.

40 Carroll, "A Historical Perspective," 75.

41 Bickers and Yep, *May Days in Hong Kong*, 1.

42 Barlow, "Asian Women in Reregionalization."

Chapter 3. Bangkok: Chinese City of Colonial Modernity

1 Marco Wilms, *Durch die Nacht mit Christopher Doyle und Nonzee Nimibutr* (Into the night with Christopher Doyle and Nonzee Nimibutr), 2010.

2 Personal communication, Sunait Chutintaranond, History Department, Chulalongkorn University, Bangkok, Thailand, June 16, 2016.

3 Wongsurawat, *The Crown and the Capitalists*, 164n6.

4 Wongsurawat, *The Crown and the Capitalists*, 140–142.

5 Chua, "The City and the City," 933.

6 See Pimpraphai and Sng, *A History of the Thai-Chinese*, 231–232.

7 See Benjamin Zawacki, "Of Questionable Connectivity: China's BRI and Thai Civil Society," Council of Foreign Relations, June 7, 2021, accessed December 11, 2024, https://www.cfr.org/blog/questionable -connectivity-chinas-bri-and-thai-civil-society.

8 Anderson, *Imagined Communities*, 11–12.

9 As Michael K. Connors writes, "By the late 1950s monarchical discourse had revived and by the 1990s and 2000s it had deepened—even as it articulated to democracy—to the point of sacralisation around the figure of the long-reigning King Bhumibol (1946–2016)" ("The Two Faces of Thai Democracy," 58).

10 See Wongsurawat, *The Crown and the Capitalists*, 153–154.

11 Wongsurawat, *The Crown and the Capitalists*, 153.

12 Chua, "The City and the City," 934.

13 Wongsurawat, *The Crown and the Capitalists*, 67.

14 Wongsurawat, *The Crown and the Capitalists*, 77. See also Sittithep, "Textualising the 'Chinese of Thailand,'" 100–109.

15 See Wongsurawat, *The Crown and the Capitalists*, 105–109.

16 As Lisa Lowe writes, "Neither free European nor the white European's 'other,' the Black slave, neither lord nor bonded, the Chinese were represented as a paradoxical figure, at once *both* an addition that would stabilize the colonial order *and* the supplement whose addition might likewise threaten the attainment of any such stability" (*The Intimacies of Four Continents*, 31).

17 Junko, "King's Manpower Constructed," 33.

18 See Arjun Subramanyan and Michael Sturma on the plight of Chinese laborers in the early twentieth-century building of the Thai-Burma railroad, in "Asian Labourers, the Thai Government and the Thai-Burma Railway."

19   See Heinrich, *Chinese Surplus*.

20   For a critique of the "Mat and Pillow" legend, see Veeraporn Nitipra-
      pha, "The Conversation: Rags to Riches Fairytales," *A Day Bulletin*, Jan-
      uary 27, 2020, 6–10 [in Thai]. Sittithep calls this trope *khon jin suea
      phuen mon bai tai rom phraborom-somphotiphan* ("rags to riches Chinese
      under royal auspices"), throughout *Pen Jin phro ru suek*.

21   Plaques in the museum describe the building as taking its style from
      the 1861–1917 phase of construction along Charoen Krung Road, while
      adopting innovations in building that used concrete and steel from the
      second phase of construction (1907–1937). The museum plaques cite
      Yongthanit, *Thanon Charoen Krung ton bon*.

22   Brochure, "Berlin Pharmaceutical Museum: Monument to Dr. Chai
      Chainuvati," Berlin Pharmaceutical Museum, Bangkok (n.d.).

23   Brochure, "Berlin Pharmaceutical Museum."

24   Brochure, "Berlin Pharmaceutical Museum."

25   Napong, "Unseeing Chinatown," 604.

26   Napong, "Unseeing Chinatown," 604.

27   Napong, "Unseeing Chinatown," 615–617.

28   Interview by author, January 11, 2018.

29   In January 2020 I was able to speak with Chupaporn Kangwanphum,
      whose family are longtime residents of Talad Noi and intimately in-
      volved in resident activism. She provided me with the publication
      Chinatown yan na doen [Chinatown: Inviting walks] (Bangkok: Pan
      Mueang, 2018). Talad Noi resident initiatives also resulted in the Thai-
      language website and app "Doen Chinatown" [Walk Chinatown],
      Khrong Kan Yan Jin Thin Bangkok [Project Bangkok Chinatown], ac-
      cessed December 11, 2024, https://www.walk.in.th. Both receive fund-
      ing from the Thai Health Promotion Foundation.

30   See Patina's web page at https://www.facebook.com/Patina.bkk/.
      Patina closed at the end of 2022. Tai Guan Café (https://www
      .facebook.com/TaiGuanCafe/) was replaced by Photohostel & Pho-
      tocafe (https://photohostel.com). The websites cited in this note were
      last accessed on December 11, 2024.

31   For a video explaining the reflection that went into the restoration
      of Tai Guan Café, see "Ban Thai Guan Eng Ki [Thai Guan Eng Ki
      House]," accessed December 11, 2024, https://www.facebook.com
      /bangkokchinatown/videos/1566028600121901.

32   See Teerapan Leelavansuk, "Dive Me Home," *The Cloud*, May 7, 2018,
      accessed December 2024, https://readthecloud.co/replace-9/.

33   Napong, "Unseeing Chinatown"; and interview with Napong Rugkha-
      pan by author, January 11, 2018. A further important structural fact is
      that before the reign of Rama X, the CPB was at least nominally external
      and at a slight remove from the monarch. With legal change initiated by
      Rama X, it is now formally the direct personal property of the monarch.

34   Personal communication, Wasana Wongsurawat.

35 Vatikiotis, "Sino Chic."

36 Sittithep, *Pen Jin phro ru suek*, 202–206.

37 Landsberg, *Prosthetic Memory*.

38 Personal communication, Wasana Wongsurawat.

39 The synopsis for *Kith and Kin* reads as follows: "At their annual ancestor worship, three generations of the Koh family discover their Fujian cemetery will be relocated. Their ancestor—Koh Bien Tiet—is buried there in a Chinese tomb." Personal communication, Salee Every, June 25, 2021.

40 See the social media for Baan Phad Thai (https://www.baanphadthai .com); Honest Mistake (https://www.facebook.com/HonestMistake Bar/); and Amdaeng Hotel (http://www.amdaeng.com). All websites were last accessed on December 11, 2024.

41 Lucey and McEnaney, "Introduction," 10–11.

42 Personal communication, Salee Every, January 10, 2018, and July 30, 2018; personal communication, Veeraporn Nitiprapha, on January 7, 2019; July 19, 2019; and January 2, 2020.

43 Personal communication, Salee Every, August 2, 2017, and January 10, 2018.

44 Tep Bar web page, accessed December 11, 2024, https://www.facebook .com/TEPBARBKK/.

45 Wallflowers Café web page, accessed December 11, 2024, https://www .facebook.com/wallflowerscafe.th/.

46 Munasinghe, "Culture Creators and Culture Bearers." See also Munasinghe, "Anxieties of Belonging"; and Viranjini Munasinghe, "An Absence of Tombs: Moral Economy of Nations and Caribbean Exception," conference paper presented at "Thinking Time," Society for the Humanities, Cornell University, April 8, 2016.

47 Seremetakis, *The Senses Still*, 7.

48 Seremetakis, *The Senses Still*, 3.

49 Ba Hao's self-presentation extends to the venue's website, Ba-Hao, accessed December 11, 2024, https://www.ba-hao.com/.

50 Wongsurawat, *The Crown and the Capitalists*, 140.

51 Thanathach Tangkhaprasert, "'Lhong 1919' tha ruea yon adid su prawatisat Thai Jin" ["Lhong 1919": The port that looks back in time to Thai Chinese history], *Matichon*, November 17, 2017, accessed December 11, 2024, https://www.matichon.co.th/prachachuen/news_734755.

52 Bangkok's port moved to its current location in the Khlong Toei district in the mid-twentieth century.

53 Shanghai Mansion Bangkok, "Explore," accessed December 11, 2024, https://www.shanghaimansion.com/explore/.

54 Shanghai Mansion Bangkok, "Dining," accessed December 11, 2024, https://www.shanghaimansion.com/dining/. The image is replicated under Shanghai Mansion Bangkok, "Bar," accessed December 11, 2024, https://www.redroselive.com/bar-page.

55   "Hidden Yaowaraj" vignette, now removed, on the Shanghai Mansion
      Bangkok website.
56   Heinrich, *Chinese Surplus.*
57   Heinrich, *Chinese Surplus*, 5.
58   Barlow, "'Green Blade in the Act of Being Grazed,'" 148.
59   Harvey, "The Right to the City." Achille Mbembe likewise avers that
      the surface of the contemporary city under neoliberalism must embody
      pricelessness, in "Aesthetics of Superfluity."
60   See also Dararat Mettarikanon, "Kha ying Jin kham chat nai prawatisat
      sangkhom Thai" [Transnational trafficking in Chinese women in Thai
      social history].
61   Ma, *Melancholy Drift*, 47.
62   See A. Fuhrmann, "*The Ghost Seer*."
63   Giuliana Bruno describes Hong Kong as "tightly wrapped in time and
      sheathed in space, somewhere in the 1960s," in *Surface*, 38.

Chapter 4. *How to Dump*: Radical Revitalization in Thai Cinema and Hospitality Venues

1   Kong Rithdee, "To Dump or Not to Dump," *Bangkok Post*, December
      31, 2019, accessed December 11, 2024, https://www.bangkokpost.com
      /life/arts-and-entertainment/1826464.
2   This is Kong Rithdee's apt translation in "To Dump or Not to Dump."
3   Chang and Teo, "The Shophouse Hotel."
4   As Minting Ye and others explain, "Tong Lau, the tenement buildings
      [were] built from the late 1800s to the 1960s in Hong Kong" ("The
      Landscape of Gentrification," 484).
5   Vatikiotis, "Sino Chic."
6   See Landsberg, *Prosthetic Memory*.
7   Cover, *A Day Bulletin*, January 27, 2020. As Thak Chaloemtiarana fur-
      ther describes this trope: "The official construction of the Chinese
      Other in Vajiravudh's nationalism defined the Chinese as poor and des-
      olate peasants who had come to Thailand with just 'a straw mat and a
      pillow [sua phuen mon bai]' to 'seek the protection of the king's righ-
      teous generosity [phueng phraboromaphothisomphan]'" ("Are We
      Them?," 163).
8   All quotes are from page 8 of Veeraporn Nitiprapha, "The Conversa-
      tion: Rags to Riches Fairytales," *A Day Bulletin*, January 27, 2020, 6–10
      [in Thai].
9   Phillips, "Freud and the Uses of Forgetting."
10   Phillips relies strongly on Freud in his essay. I also rely on Freud's no-
      tion of screen memories for my understanding of the logic of remem-
      bering in *How to Dump*. See Freud, "Screen Memories."
11   As Phillips writes, "The past is in the remaking. Remembering is a pro-

spective project. But it is as though we are continually remaking something that to all intents and purposes never existed; or perhaps because we are making copies without an original—a representable original— all the copies are different?" ("Freud and the Uses of Forgetting," 34).

12 Phillips, "Freud and the Uses of Forgetting," 30.
13 Phillips, "Freud and the Uses of Forgetting," 22.
14 See Kim, *Sidewalk City*.
15 All quotes are from the author's conversation with Supattra Vimon-suknopparat on July 12, 2017, and from personal communication, June 24, 2021.
16 As Is web page, accessed December 11, 2024, https://www.facebook.com/As.is.CoffeeStand/.
17 See Wongsurawat, *The Crown and the Capitalists*, 105–109.
18 Wongsurawat, *The Crown and the Capitalists*, 141 (both quotes). See also Anuson Chinvanno, *Thailand's Policies Towards China, 1949–1954*.
19 Wongsurawat, *The Crown and the Capitalists*, 145–153.
20 Sittithep's *Kabot Jin jon bon thanon Phlapphlachai* [Chinese revolt on Phlapphla Chai Road] presents the history of Bangkok's working-class Chinese from 1957 to 1974.
21 Phillips, "Freud and the Uses of Forgetting," 28.
22 Landsberg, *Prosthetic Memory*.
23 Cortez, "Licking for the Nation," 45.
24 Simon Rothöhler as paraphrased by Cortez ("Licking for the Nation," 45).
25 Rothöhler, "Where Film Drops Off," 141.
26 Cortez, "Licking for the Nation," 44.
27 Cortez stresses the digital's "material difference from earlier media through the sensate properties that set the digital image apart from the 'look' of a photochemical counterpart" ("Licking for the Nation," 46).
28 Cortez, "Licking for the Nation," 45.
29 Cortez, "Licking for the Nation," 45, 46.
30 Veeraporn, "The Conversation," 10. Veeraporn further uses this stance to speak out against nationalism. Analogously several other revival media, such as the Facebook page "Kratham khwam Wong" [Doing Wong-ness], also have become platforms for antinationalist antimilitarism in the present.
31 Sittithep, *Pen Jin phro ru suek*, 258, 259.
32 See Wilson, *Charming Cadavers*.
33 Quotation from Kong, "To Dump or Not to Dump."
34 Some of the work that official Buddhisms performed in a "free world" anti-communist imaginary and polity is detailed by Eugene Ford in *Cold War Monks: Buddhism and America's Secret Strategy in Southeast Asia*. For a notion of the counterpolitical work that Mahayana Buddhism can perform in this context, see A. Fuhrmann, *Teardrops of Time*.

| 35 | A. Fuhrmann, *Teardrops of Time*, 162–163. |
| 36 | See, for instance, Harootunian, "Remembering the Historical Present." |

Chapter 5. *Memories of the Memories of the Black Rose Cat*: Thai Literature as Contemporary Chinese Literature

1	All translations in this chapter are mine, except where indicated. Veeraporn Nitiprapha, keynote speech at Kunming, China, from Veeraporn Nitiprapha's Facebook page, July 26, 2019, accessed December 12, 2024, https://www.facebook.com/veeraporn.nitiprapha/posts /2955490007825512. The novel's title was modified; see Veeraporn, *Phutthasakarat*; Veeraporn, *Memories of the Memories of the Black Rose Cat*.
2	Chan, *Malaysian Crossings*, 6, 24.
3	For this work the novelist was awarded the SEA Write Award, the region's most prestigious literary award; Veeraporn is the only woman to date to have received the award twice.
4	Toh Wen Li, "Book Review: Thai Author Veeraporn Nitiprapha's Spell-binding Family Saga," *Straits Times*, June 25, 2022, accessed December 12, 2024, https://www.straitstimes.com/life/arts/book-review-thai -author-veeraporn-nitipraphas-spellbinding-family-saga.
5	Li, "Book Review"; Crosbie-Jones, "Veeraporn Nitiprapha's Super-naturally-Charged Thailand."
6	Kong, "Translator's Note," 6.
7	See Kasian Tejapira, "Imagined Uncommunity," in which he investigates the ways that Chineseness in Thailand was positioned as the other of Thainess and conflated with internal and external dangers to the nation. He begins his chapter with an analysis of the television drama *Lod lai mangkorn* that plays out the notion of gradual (masculine) social ascension. See also his book with the name of the series in its title: *Lae lod lai mangkon: Ruam kho khien wa duai khwam pen Jin nai Sayam* [Peering under the dragon's scale: Selected writings on Chineseness in Siam].
8	Thorn Pitidol, "Phutthasakarat atsadong lae khwam (rai) song jam khong khon Jin bon phaen din Thai" [The dawn of the Buddhist era and the (lack of) remembrance of the Chinese in Thailand], *101 World*, May 21, 2018, accessed December 12, 2024, https://www.the101.world /forgotten-memories-of-thai-chinese/.
9	Bernards, *Writing the South Seas*, 166.
10	Thak, "Are We Them?" The subsection "Writing the Chinese Back into Thai Historiography" (188–190) argues that left historian Nidhi Eo-seewong and writer Sujit Wongthes's "radical books give the Chinese a more prominent place and role in shaping Thai history" (188). The subsection "The Subaltern Writes Back" (190–197) analyzes two novels that "reject the existing stereotype of the meek and marginalised Chinese" (190).

11	Veeraporn, keynote speech at Kunming.
12	Veeraporn, *Memories of the Memories of the Black Rose Cat*, loc. 105.
13	Veeraporn, *Memories of the Memories of the Black Rose Cat*, loc. 116.
14	Veeraporn, *Memories of the Memories of the Black Rose Cat*, loc. 115.
15	Veeraporn, *Phutthasakarat*, 134.
16	Sakai and Walker, "A Genealogy of Area Studies," 12.
17	Conversation with Veeraporn Nitiprapha, December 15, 2023.
18	Philip A. Kuhn labels the networks that emerged with Chinese migrations to Southeast Asia as networks of "sojourners," stressing that the stay in the destination country was supposed to be temporary. Kuhn's analysis also highlights the eventual formation of diasporas, however. As such it provides a perspective on China's nonexpansionary aspirations, through the focus on relatively recent histories of migration. Individual migrations differ, of course, from large-scale governmental projects; diasporas are not congruent with national projects. Assessments of current PRC expansion should thus not be based on these nonimperial historical moves, rationales, and intentions of sojourners. See Kuhn, *Chinese Among Others*.
19	Veeraporn, keynote speech at Kunming.
20	Veeraporn, *Phutthasakarat*, 131–132.
21	Thorn, "Phutthasakarat."
22	Thus Pimpaka Towira's *Mahasamut lae susan* (*The Island Funeral*, 2015), which also contains a Chinese subtext, uses the lush geophysical setting of Thailand's south to imagine Buddhist-Muslim relations anew.
23	See, for example, Kaisan Tejapira, *Lae lod lai mangkon*.
24	Kong, "Translator's Note," 6–7.
25	Thorn, "Phutthasakarat."
26	Veeraporn, *Memories of the Memories of the Black Rose Cat*, loc. 329.
27	Veeraporn, *Memories of the Memories of the Black Rose Cat*, loc. 330.
28	Ang, "Can One Say No to Chineseness?," 233.

Chapter 6. Southeast Asia as Question: Thinking Region from Bangkok

1	Barlow, "Asian Women in Reregionalization."
2	See, for instance, Chen, *Asia as Method*; Wang Hui, *The Politics of Imagining Asia*; and Ching, *Anti-Japan*.
3	O. W. Wolters describes the region as unified by a set of assumptions around notions of power and temporality in "Southeast Asia as a Southeast Asian Field of Study." Anthony Reid asserts of early Southeast Asian rulers that they were "conscious of inhabiting a pluralistic world" (*Southeast Asia in the Age of Commerce*, 3–5). He further sees Southeast Asia as distinct because of the boundedness of its geographical territory— the fact that it is separated from China (and other places) by the sea

and from India by mountains. In the field of linguistics, see Enfield and Comrie, "Mainland Southeast Asian Languages."

4   Karatani, *The Structure of World History*.

5   Aihwa Ong reviews zonal technologies that have been developed in Asia to "secur[e] the critical spaces and connectivities that prop up sovereign power" ("Buoyancy," 193).

6   Ching, "Neo-regionalism and Neoliberal Asia," 41.

7   Duara, "The Chinese World Order in Historical Perspective," 3.

8   Duara, "The Chinese World Order in Historical Perspective," 28.

9   Yang, "Unpacking Taiwan's Presence in Southeast Asia," 6, 3.

10   See Huang, "Taiwan's New Southbound Policy."

11   Sakai, "The Microphysics of Comparison."

12   Sakai and Walker, "A Genealogy of Area Studies," 13.

13   Sakai and Walker, "A Genealogy of Area Studies," 22.

14   Sakai, "The Microphysics of Comparison."

15   Ching, "Neo-regionalism and Neoliberal Asia."

16   Bachner, "Allographies."

17   Bachner, "Allographies," 145, 146.

18   Bachner writes, "Chinese writing becomes other to itself, as the sinograph becomes its own allograph" ("Allographies," 146).

19   Bachner, "Allographies," 143.

20   Spivak, "~~Megacity~~."

21   See Mbembe, "Aesthetics of Superfluity"; Harvey, "The Right to the City"; and Saskia Sassen, "Who Owns Our Cities—and Why This Urban Takeover Should Concern Us All," *Guardian*, November 24, 2015, accessed December 13, 2024, https://www.theguardian.com/cities /2015/nov/24/who-owns-our-cities-and-why-this-urban-takeover -should-concern-us-all.

22   Ching, "Globalizing the Regional, Regionalizing the Global: Mass Culture and Asianism in the Age of Late Capital," 238.

23   Ong uses the term *territorialization*, which she defines, with Gilles Deleuze and Félix Guattari, as "the processual operation of de- and reterritorializations, in which prior flows of politics, culture, and capital are displaced and their forces reassembled as different (and often tentative) formations" ("Buoyancy," 196).

24   Barlow, "Asian Women in Reregionalization," 300.

25   Barlow, "Asian Women in Reregionalization." For Barlow, women and Chinese history are moreover so intimately connected that a history of modern China only becomes possible if it centers women (Barlow, *The Question of Women in Chinese Feminism*).

26   Wijaya, "Luminous Flesh, Haunted Future," 31.

27   Wijaya asks, "How may a work move beyond an 'area studies' model that only seems to be concerned about the area of study, without betraying the particularities of the area?" and cautions, conversely, "But if we only debated the minutiae of Chineseness within the context

and history of Chineseness, we risk forming a closed circle without relationality to other areas of research" ("Luminous Flesh, Haunted Future," 38).

28   Ang, "Can One Say No to Chineseness?," 233.

29   David Ehrlich, "'One for the Road' Review: Wong Kar-wai Produces Overwrought Thai Melodrama," *Indiewire*, January 29, 2021, accessed December 12, 2024, https://www.indiewire.com/2021/01/one-for-the-road-review-1234612076/.

30   This is different from previous generations. See Thak Chaloemtiarana's account of the gradual transformation from the status of "other" to a position integral to Thai society. He concludes that "today, the idea that 'we' the Thai are gazing (down) at the Sino-Thai 'them' has been subverted to the point where the critical distinctions between the two categories are no longer clear" ("Are We Them?," 209).

31   See the analysis of a trans-Asia Chinese femininity recuperated as desirable in the Thai Chinese lifestyle magazine *Dajiahao* in A. Fuhrmann, *Ghostly Desires*, 93–96.

32   See also Wongsurawat, "Educating Citizens."

33   See Chow, *The Protestant Ethnic and the Spirit of Capitalism.*

34   Munasinghe, "Culture Creators and Culture Bearers"; and personal communication, December 14, 2020.

35   In a different historical and cultural context, Anne Cheng argues that the conditions of embodiment for the Asian racialized female body *onscreen* are always subject to a different logic. She stresses that this cinematic body exceeds the conventional logic of the fetish and reduction to enhanced corporeality: "It is precisely the overcorporealized body that may find the most freedom in the rehearsal of corporeal dematerialization or, alternatively, of synthetic self-extension" (*Ornamentalism*, 85). As Cheng argues, "Through the refraction of light, the 'Oriental woman' as objet d'art has been derealized. Shine offers less a description or quality of light than an active mode of relationality: a dynamic medium through which the organic and the inorganic fuse, and through which the visual spills into the sensorial" (78).

36   Shu-mei Shih is most closely associated with Sinophone studies. A recent reader coedited by Shih assembles a variety of scholars working in this domain. See Shih, Tsai, and Bernards, *Sinophone Studies*. As Brian Bernards writes, "The term 'Sinophone' denotes Chinese-speaking individuals and communities, yet it implies that their locations and histories are heterogenous . . . and the languages they speak . . . varied and multiple" ("Sinophone Literature," 72).

37   Astolfo, "Unpacking Bangkok Urbanism," 37. In "Regional Educational Disparities in Thailand," Gerald W. Fry and Rosarin Apahung list Bangkok and Bangkok Metropolitan Region provinces as ranking highest in the "education quality index" (383).

38   Ranwarat Kobsirithiwara (Kasetsart University, Department of Liter-

ature) notes that last names and business names that include the components *sue trong*, *phak di*, and *sutjarid* may well have been devised to counter Thai bias against Chinese migrants. Personal communication, July 18, 2022.

39 For "Amélie," see Huang, *Urban Horror*, 70.

40 Huang, *Urban Horror*, 71.

41 Huang, *Urban Horror*, 73.

42 Barlow, "Femininity," 391.

43 On the ways that "culture" is appropriated by state-business formations, see Yue, "Creative Queer Singapore."

44 Ziewitz, "A Not Quite Random Walk," 4.

45 Ziewitz, "A Not Quite Random Walk," 10, 2.

46 This also allows *Bad Genius* ultimately to avoid, or undercut, the trope of the "yellow woman's" proximity to the technological and the synthetic that Anne Anlin Cheng outlines in her chapter "Dolls" (*Ornamentalism*, 127–151).

47 Ziewitz, "A Not Quite Random Walk," 11.

48 Ziewitz, "A Not Quite Random Walk," 10.

49 See Ong, *Spirits of Resistance*, and Barlow, "'Green Blade in the Act of Being Grazed.'"

Coda. Women in Asia and the World

1 "This Bar Owner Has a Drink for Your Every Mood," O.N.S., accessed October 30, 2024, https://ons-manual.onsclothing.com/fashion/bar-owner-drink-every-mood/.

2 See M. Fuhrmann, *Port Cities of the Eastern Mediterranean*.

3 Barlow, "Femininity," 391.

4 See Barlow, "Advertising Ephemera and the Angel of History"; and Barlow, "'Green Blade in the Act of Being Grazed.'"

5 Barlow writes of femininity's "recoding as money" in "Femininity," 391.

6 Cheng, *Ornamentalism*, 14, 17.

7 Cheng, *Ornamentalism*, 18.

Bibliography

Abbas, Ackbar. "Cosmopolitan De-scriptions: Shanghai and Hong Kong." *Public Culture* 12, no. 3 (2000): 769–786.

Abbas, Ackbar. *Hong Kong: Culture and the Politics of Disappearance*. Minneapolis: University of Minnesota Press, 1997.

Anderson, Benedict. *Imagined Communities: Reflections on the Origin and Spread of Nationalism*. London: Verso, 1983.

Ang, Ien. "Can One Say No to Chineseness? Pushing the Limits of the Diasporic Paradigm." *boundary 2* 25, no. 3 (1998): 223–242.

Anuson Chinvanno. *Thailand's Policies Towards China, 1949–1954*. Basingstoke: McMillan, 1992.

Askew, Marc. *Bangkok: Place, Practice, and Representation*. London: Routledge, 2002.

Astolfo, Giovanna. "Unpacking Bangkok Urbanism." In *Bangkok: On Transformation and Urbanism*, edited by Giovanna Astolfo and Camillo Boano, 37–53. London: Bartlett Development Planning Unit, 2016.

Bachner, Andrea. "Allographies." In *Beyond Sinology: Chinese Writing and the Scripts of Culture*, 129–164. New York: Columbia University Press, 2014.

Barlow, Tani E. "Advertising Ephemera and the Angel of History." *positions: asia critique* 20, no. 1 (2012): 111–158.

Barlow, Tani E. "Asian Women in Reregionalization." *positions: asia critique* 15, no. 2 (2007): 285–318.

Barlow, Tani E. "Debates over Colonial Modernity in East Asia and Another Alternative." *Cultural Studies* 26, no. 5 (2012): 617–644.

Barlow, Tani E. "Femininity." In *The Palgrave Dictionary of Transnational History*, edited by Akira Iriye and Pierre-Yves Saunier, 388–392. London: Palgrave Macmillan, 2009.

Barlow, Tani E. *Formations of Colonial Modernity in East Asia*. Durham, NC: Duke University Press, 1997.

Barlow, Tani E. "'Green Blade in the Act of Being Grazed': Late Capital, Flexible Bodies, Critical Intelligibility." *differences: a journal of feminist cultural studies* 10, no. 3 (1998): 119–158.

Barlow, Tani E. *In the Event of Women*. Durham, NC: Duke University Press, 2022.

Barlow, Tani E. *The Question of Women in Chinese Feminism*. Durham, NC: Duke University Press, 2004.

Berlant, Lauren. *The Female Complaint: The Unfinished Business of Sentimentality in American Culture*. Durham, NC: Duke University Press, 2008.

Bernards, Brian C. "Sinophone Literature." In *Sinophone Studies: A Critical Reader*, edited by Shu-mei Shih, Chien-hsin Tsai, and Brian Bernards, 72–79. New York: Columbia University Press, 2013.

Bernards, Brian C. *Writing the South Seas: Imagining the Nanyang in Chinese and Southeast Asian Postcolonial Literature*. Seattle: University of Washington Press, 2016.

Bickers, Robert, and Ray Yep. *May Days in Hong Kong: Riot and Emergency in 1967*. Hong Kong: Hong Kong University Press, 2009.

Brown, Wendy. "American Nightmare: Neoliberalism, Neoconservatism, and De-Democratization." *Political Theory* 34, no. 6 (2006): 690–714.

Bruno, Giuliana. *Surface: Matters of Aesthetics, Materiality, and Media*. Chicago: University of Chicago Press, 2014.

Carroll, John M. "A Historical Perspective: The 1967 Riots and the Strike-Boycott of 1925–26." In *May Days in Hong Kong: Riot and Emergency in 1967*, edited by Robert Bickers and Ray Yep, 69–85. Hong Kong: Hong Kong University Press, 2009.

Chan, Cheow Thia. *Malaysian Crossings: Place and Language in the Worlding of Modern Chinese Literature*. New York: Columbia University Press, 2022.

Chan, Judy (Yuwadi Tonsakulrungruang). *A Walk Through Spring* [*Roi Wasan*]. Bangkok: Praphansarn Publishing, 2010.

Chang, Eileen. *Love in a Fallen City*. Translated by Karen S. Kingsbury and Eileen Chang. New York: New York Review Books, 2006.

Chang, Eileen (Zhang Ailing). "Love in the Fallen City, 1943." In *Dragonflies: Fiction by Chinese Women in the Twentieth Century*, edited by Shu-ning Sciban and Fred Edwards, 31–70. Ithaca, NY: East Asia Program, Cornell University, 2003.

Chang, T. C., and Peggy Teo. "The Shophouse Hotel: Vernacular Heritage in a Creative City." *Urban Studies* 46, no. 2 (2009): 341–367.

Cheah, Pheng. "Situations and Limits of Postcolonial Theory." In *Siting Postcoloniality: Critical Perspectives from the East Asian Sinosphere*, edited by Pheng Cheah and Caroline S. Hau, 1–29. Durham, NC: Duke University Press, 2022.

Chen, Kuan-Hsing. *Asia as Method: Toward Deimperialization*. Durham, NC: Duke University Press, 2010.

Cheng, Anne Anlin. *Ornamentalism*. New York: Oxford University Press, 2019.

Cheung, Esther M. K. "On Spectral Mutations: The Ghostly City in *The Secret*, *Rouge* and *Little Cheung*." In *Hong Kong Culture: Word and Image*, edited by Louie Kam, 169–191. Hong Kong: Hong Kong University Press, 2010.

Ching, Leo T. S. *Anti-Japan: The Politics of Sentiment in Postcolonial Asia*. Durham, NC: Duke University Press, 2019.

Ching, Leo T. S. "Globalizing the Regional, Regionalizing the Global: Mass Culture and Asianism in the Age of Late Capital." *Public Culture* 12, no. 1 (2000): 233–257.

Ching, Leo T. S. "Neo-regionalism and Neoliberal Asia." In *Routledge Handbook of New Media in Asia*, edited by Larissa Hjorth and Olivia Khoo, 39–52. London: Routledge, 2016.

Chow, Rey. *The Protestant Ethnic and the Spirit of Capitalism*. New York: Columbia University Press, 2002.

Chow, Rey. "A Souvenir of Love." In *At Full Speed: Hong Kong Cinema in a Borderless World*, edited by Esther Yau, 209–230. Minneapolis: University of Minnesota Press, 2001.

Chua, Lawrence. *Bangkok Utopia: Modern Architecture and Buddhist Felicities, 1910–1973*. Honolulu: University of Hawai'i Press, 2021.

Chua, Lawrence. "The City and the City: Race, Nationalism, and Architecture in Early Twentieth-Century Bangkok." *Journal of Urban History* 40, no. 5 (2014): 933–958.

Coedès, George. *Angkor: An Introduction*. Translated and edited by Emily Floyd Gardiner. New York: Oxford University Press, 1963.

Connors, Michael K. "The Two Faces of Thai Democracy." In *Routledge Handbook of Contemporary Thailand*, edited by Pavin Chachavalpongpun, 55–70. London: Routledge, 2020.

Cortez, Iggy. "Licking for the Nation: Auntie Genealogies in Apichatpong Weerasethakul's *Rak ti Khon Kaen*." *Journal of Cinema and Media Studies* 60, no. 3 (2021): 37–61.

Crosbie-Jones, Max. "Veeraporn Nitiprapha's Supernaturally-Charged Thailand." *Art Review*, August 10, 2022. https://artreview.com/memories-of-the-memories-of-the-black-rose-cat-by-veeraporn-nitiprapha-translated-by-kong-rithdee-river-books-9-99-softcover/.

Dararat Mettarikanon. "Kha ying Jin kham chat nai prawatisat sangkhom Thai" [Transnational trafficking in Chinese women in Thai social history]. *Sinlapawathanatham* 21, no. 4 (2000): 26–39.

Duara, Prasenjit. "The Chinese World Order in Historical Perspective: The Imperialism of Nation-States or Soft Power." *China and the World: Ancient and Modern Silk Road* 4, no. 2 (2019): 1–33.

Duara, Prasenjit. "The Regime of Authenticity: Timelessness, Gender, and National History in Modern China." *History and Theory* 37, no. 3 (1998): 287–308.

Enfield, N. J., and Bernard Comrie. "Mainland Southeast Asian Languages: State of the Art and New Directions." In *Languages of Mainland Southeast Asia: The State of the Art*. Berlin: De Gruyter, 2015.

Ford, Eugene. *Cold War Monks: Buddhism and America's Secret Strategy in Southeast Asia*. New Haven, CT: Yale University Press, 2017.

Foucault, Michel. *The History of Sexuality, Vol. 1: An Introduction*. 1976. New York: Vintage, 1990.

Freud, Sigmund. "Screen Memories." In *The Standard Edition of the Complete Psychological Works of Sigmund Freud, Volume III (1893–1899)*, translated by James Strachey, 303–322. London: Hogarth Press, 1962.

Fry, Gerald W., and Rosarin Apahung. "Regional Educational Disparities in Thailand." In *Education in Thailand: An Old Elephant in Search of a New Mahout*, edited by Gerald W. Fry, Hui Bi, and Rosarin Apahung, 373–391. Singapore: Springer Singapore, 2018.

Fu, Poshek, ed. *China Forever: The Shaw Brothers and Diasporic Cinema*. Urbana: University of Illinois Press, 2008.

Fuhrmann, Arnika. *Ghostly Desires: Queer Sexuality and Vernacular Buddhism in Contemporary Thai Cinema*. Durham, NC: Duke University Press, 2016.

Fuhrmann, Arnika. "*The Ghost Seer*: Chinese Thai Minority Subjectivity, Female Agency, and the Transnational Uncanny in the Films of Danny and Oxide Pang." In *Ghostly Desires: Queer Sexuality and Vernacular Buddhism in Contemporary Thai Cinema*, 87–121. Durham, NC: Duke University Press, 2016.

Fuhrmann, Arnika. *Teardrops of Time: Buddhist Aesthetics in the Poetry of Angkarn Kallayanapong*. Albany: State University of New York Press, 2020.

Fuhrmann, Malte. *Port Cities of the Eastern Mediterranean: Urban Culture in the Late Ottoman Empire*. Cambridge: Cambridge University Press, 2020.

Garrett, Bradley L. "Assaying History: Creating Temporal Junctions Through Urban Exploration." *Environment and Planning D: Society and Space* 29 (2011): 1048–1067.

Goh, Robbie B. H., and Brenda S. A. Yeoh. *Theorizing the Southeast Asian City as Text: Urban Landscapes, Cultural Documents, and Interpretative Experiences*. Singapore: World Scientific Publishing, 2003.

Harootunian, Harry. "Remembering the Historical Present." *Critical Inquiry* 33, no. 3 (2007): 471–494.

Harvey, David. "The Right to the City." *New Left Review*, no. 53 (2008): 23–40.

Heinrich, Ari Larissa. *Chinese Surplus: Biopolitical Aesthetics and the Medically Commodified Body*. Durham, NC: Duke University Press, 2018.

Hershatter, Gail. *Dangerous Pleasures: Prostitution and Modernity in Twentieth-Century Shanghai*. Berkeley: University of California Press, 1997.

Hill, Christopher L. "Conceptual Universalization in the Transnational Nineteenth Century." In *Global Intellectual History*, edited by Samuel Moyn and Andrew Sartori, 134–158. New York: Columbia University Press, 2013.

Hong, Lysa. "Invisible Semicolony: The Postcolonial Condition and Royal National History in Thailand." *Postcolonial Studies* 11, no. 3 (2008): 315–327.

Huang, Erin Y. *Urban Horror: Neoliberal Post-Socialism and the Limits of Visibility*. Durham, NC: Duke University Press, 2020.

Huang, Kwei-Bo. "Taiwan's New Southbound Policy: Background, Objectives, Framework and Limits." *Revista UNISCI*, no. 46 (2018): 47–68.

Illouz, Eva. *Consuming the Romantic Utopia: Love and the Cultural Contradictions of Capitalism*. Berkeley: University of California Press, 1997.

Ingawanij, May Adadol. "*Nang Nak*: Thai Bourgeois Heritage Cinema." *Inter-Asia Cultural Studies* 8, no. 2 (2007): 180–193.

Ivy, Marilyn. *Discourses of the Vanishing: Modernity, Phantasm, Japan*. Chicago: University of Chicago Press, 1995.

Iwabuchi, Koichi. "Nostalgia for a (Different) Asian Modernity: Media Consumption of 'Asia' in Japan." *positions: asia critique* 10, no. 3 (2002): 547–573.

Junko, Koizumi. "King's Manpower Constructed: Writing the History of the Conscription of Labour in Siam." *South East Asia Research* 10, no. 1 (2002): 31–61.

Karatani, Kojin. *The Structure of World History: From Modes of Production to Modes of Exchange.* Translated by M. K. Bourdaghs. Durham, NC: Duke University Press, 2014.

Kasian Tejapira. "Imagined Uncommunity: The *Lookjin* Middle Class and Thai Official Nationalism." In *Essential Outsiders: Chinese and Jews in the Modern Transformation of Southeast Asia and Central Europe,* edited by Anthony Reid and Daniel Chirot, 75–98. Seattle: University of Washington Press, 1997.

Kasian Tejapira. *Lae lod lai mangkon: Ruam kho khien wa duai khwam pen Jin nai Sayam* [Peering under the dragon's scale: Selected writings on Chineseness in Siam]. Bangkok: Khob Fai, 1994.

Kim, Annette Miae. *Sidewalk City: Remapping Public Space in Ho Chi Minh City.* Chicago: University of Chicago Press, 2015.

Knee, Adam. "The Pan-Asian Outlook of *The Eye.*" In *Horror to the Extreme: Changing Boundaries in Asian Cinema,* edited by Jinhee Choi and Mitsuyo Wada-Marciano, 69–84. Hong Kong: Hong Kong University Press, 2009.

Knee, Adam. "Thailand in the Hong Kong Cinematic Imagination." In *Hong Kong Film, Hollywood and the New Global Cinema: No Film Is an Island,* edited by Gina Marchetti and Tan See Kam, 77–90. London: Routledge, 2007.

Kong Rithdee. "Translator's Note." In Veeraporn Nitiprapha, *Memories of the Memories of the Black Rose Cat.* Translated by Kong Rithdee. Bangkok: River Books, 2022. Kindle edition.

Kornphanat Tungkeunkunt. "Culture and Commerce: China's Soft Power in Thailand." *International Journal of China Studies* 7, no. 2 (2016): 151–173.

Kuhn, Philip. *Chinese Among Others: Emigration in Modern Times.* Singapore: NUS Press, 2008.

Kwan, Stanley, dir. *Rouge.* DVD. Hong Kong: Golden Harvest Company and Golden Way Films Ltd., 1987.

Lampton, David M., Selina Ho, Cheng-Chwee Kuik, et al. *Rivers of Iron: Railroads and Chinese Power in Southeast Asia.* Berkeley: University of California Press, 2020.

Landsberg, Alison. *Prosthetic Memory: The Transformation of American Remembrance in the Age of Mass Culture.* New York: Columbia University Press, 2004.

Lee, Vivian P. Y. *Hong Kong Cinema Since 1997: The Post-Nostalgic Imagination.* New York: Palgrave Macmillan, 2009.

Lewis, Su Lin. "Cosmopolitanism and the Modern Girl: A Cross-Cultural Discourse in 1930s Penang." *Modern Asian Studies* 43, no. 6 (2009): 1385–1419.

Li, Shaohong, dir. *Baober in Love*. DVD. Beijing: Rosat Film and TV Production Co. Ltd., 2004.

Lim, Bliss Cua. "Spectral Times: The Ghost Film as Historical Allegory." *positions: asia critique* 9, no. 2 (2001): 287–329.

Loos, Tamara. *Subject Siam: Family, Law, and Colonial Modernity in Thailand*. Ithaca, NY: Cornell University Press, 2006.

Lowe, Lisa. *The Intimacies of Four Continents*. Durham, NC: Duke University Press, 2015.

Lu, Sheldon H. "Hong Kong Diaspora Film and Transnational Television Drama: From Homecoming to Exile to Flexible Citizenship." In *Chinese-Language Film: Historiography, Poetics, Politics*, edited by Sheldon H. Lu and Emilie Yueh-Yu Yeh, 104–121. Honolulu: University of Hawai'i Press, 2005.

Lucey, Michael, and Tom McEnaney. "Introduction: Language-in-Use and Literary Fieldwork." *Representations*, no. 137 (2017): 1–22.

Ma, Jean Yun-chen. *Melancholy Drift: Marking Time in Chinese Cinema*. Hong Kong: Hong Kong University Press, 2010.

Marchetti, Gina. Film essay. In *In the Mood for Love*, DVD. Criterion Collection, 2000.

Marchetti, Gina. "Wong's Ladies from Shanghai." In *A Companion to Wong Kar-wai*, edited by Martha P. Nochimson, 205–231. Chichester: John Wiley and Sons, 2016.

Mattern, Shannon. *Deep Mapping the Media City*. Minneapolis: University of Minnesota Press, 2015.

Mbembe, Achille. "Aesthetics of Superfluity." *Public Culture* 16, no. 3 (2004): 373–405.

Modern Girl Around the World Research Group. *The Modern Girl Around the World: Consumption, Modernity, and Globalization*. Durham, NC: Duke University Press, 2008.

Morris, Rosalind C. "Three Sexes and Four Sexualities: Redressing the Discourses in Gender and Sexuality in Contemporary Thailand." *positions: asia critique* 2, no. 1 (1994): 15–43.

Muehlebach, Andrea. *The Moral Neoliberal: Welfare and Citizenship in Italy*. Chicago: University of Chicago Press, 2012.

Mulvey, Laura. "Introduction: Fetishisms." In *Fetishism and Curiosity*, 1–15, Bloomington: Indiana University Press, 1996.

Munasinghe, Viranjini. "Anxieties of Belonging: East Indians and the Cultural Politics of the Nation in Trinidad." In *India Beyond India: Dilemmas of Belonging*, edited by Elfriede Hermann and Antonie Fuhse, 67–82. Göttingen: Göttingen University Press, 2018.

Munasinghe, Viranjini. "Culture Creators and Culture Bearers: The Interface Between Race and Ethnicity in Trinidad." *Transforming Anthropology* 6, nos. 1 and 2 (1997): 72–86.

Napong Tao Rugkhapan. "Unseeing Chinatown: Universal Zoning, Planning Abstraction and Space of Difference." *International Journal of Urban and Regional Research* 40, no. 3 (2016): 601–620.

Natanaree Posrithong. "The Siamese 'Modern Girl' and Women's Consumer Culture, 1925–35." *Sojourn: Journal of Social Issues in Southeast Asia* 34, no. 1 (2019): 110–148.

Nattawut Poonpiriya, dir. *Chalad Kem Kong [Bad Genius]*. DVD. Bangkok: GDH 559, 2017.

Nawapol Thamrongrattanarit, dir. *How to Ting... Ting yang rai mai hai luea thoe [Happy Old Year]*. DVD. Bangkok: GDH 559, 2019.

Nguyen, Hoang Tan. *A View from the Bottom: Asian American Masculinity and Sexual Representation*. Durham, NC: Duke University Press, 2014.

Ong, Aihwa. "Buoyancy: Blue Territorialization of Asian Power." In *Voluminous States: Sovereignty, Materiality, and the Territorial Imagination*, edited by Franck Billé and Debbora Battaglia, 191–203. Durham, NC: Duke University Press, 2020.

Ong, Aihwa. *Spirits of Resistance and Capitalist Discipline: Factory Women in Malaysia*. Albany: State University of New York Press, 2010.

Pattareeya Puapongsakorn. *Song Wat Guidebook: A Love Letter to the Neighborhood*. Bangkok: Patcharin Srichanwanpen, 2023.

Phillips, Adam. "Freud and the Uses of Forgetting." In *On Flirtation*, 22–38. Cambridge: Cambridge University Press, 1994.

Pimpraphai Bisalputra and Jeffery Sng. *A History of the Thai-Chinese*. Singapore: Editions Didier Millet, 2015.

Pollock, Sheldon I. *The Language of the Gods in the World of Men: Sanskrit, Culture, and Power in Premodern India*. Berkeley: University of California Press, 2006.

Reid, Anthony. *Southeast Asia in the Age of Commerce, 1450–1680*. New Haven, CT: Yale University Press, 1993.

Rigg, Jonathan. "Exclusion and Embeddedness: The Chinese in Thailand and Vietnam." In *The Chinese Diaspora: Space, Place, Mobility, and Identity*, edited by Lawrence J. C. Ma and Carolyn Cartier, 97–116. Oxford: Rowman and Littlefield, 2003.

Robbins, Bruce, and Paula Lemos Horta. *Cosmopolitanisms*. New York: New York University Press, 2017.

Rothöhler, Simon. "Where Film Drops Off: Michael Mann's High-Definition Images." In *Screen Dynamics: Mapping the Borders of Cinema*, edited by Gertrud Koch, Volker Pantenburg, and Simon Rothöhler, 137–149. Vienna: Österreichisches Filmmuseum and Synema, Gesellschaft für Film und Medien, 2012.

Sakai, Naoki. "The Microphysics of Comparison: Towards the Dislocation of the West." *Transversal Texts*, June 2013. https://transversal.at/transversal/0613/sakai/en.

Sakai, Naoki, and Gavin Walker. "A Genealogy of Area Studies." *positions: asia critique* 27, no. 1 (2019): 1–31.

Sassen, Saskia. "Does the City Have Speech?" *Public Culture* 25, no. 2 (2013): 209–221.

Sedgwick, Eve Kosofsky. *Touching Feeling: Affect, Pedagogy, Performativity.* Durham, NC: Duke University Press, 2003.

Seremetakis, C. Nadia. *The Senses Still: Perception and Memory as Material Culture in Modernity.* Chicago: University of Chicago Press, 1994.

Shih, Shu-mei. *The Lure of the Modern: Writing Modernism in Semicolonial China, 1917–1937.* Berkeley: University of California Press, 2001.

Shih, Shu-mei, Chien-hsin Tsai, and Brian Bernards. *Sinophone Studies: A Critical Reader.* New York: Columbia University Press, 2013.

Sittithep Eaksittipong. *Kabot Jin bon thanon Phlapphlachai* [Chinese revolt on Phlapphla Chai Road]. Bangkok: Matichon, 2012.

Sittithep Eaksittipong. *Pen Jin phro ru suek: Prawatsat suea phuen mon bai thi phoeng sang* [Being Chinese because of feeling Chinese: A very recent rags-to-riches history]. Bangkok: Matichon, 2023.

Sittithep Eaksittipong. "Textualising the 'Chinese of Thailand': Politics, Knowledge, and the Chinese in Thailand During the Cold War." PhD diss., National University of Singapore, 2017.

Sittithep Eaksittipong and Saichol Sattayanurak. "An Outline for a History of Emotion of the Chinese in Thailand." *Asian Ethnicity*, August 26, 2020, 1–19.

Skinner, G. William. *Chinese Society in Thailand: An Analytical History.* Ithaca, NY: Cornell University Press, 1957.

Solomon, Jon. "Rethinking the Meaning of Regions: Translation and Catastrophe." *Transversal Texts*, March 2008. https://transversal.at/transversal/0608/solomon/en.

Spivak, Gayatri Chakravorty. "~~Megacity~~." *Grey Room*, no. 1 (2000): 8–25.

Stewart, Susan. *Crimes of Writing: Problems in the Containment of Representation.* New York: Oxford University Press, 1991.

Stoler, Ann Laura. *Carnal Knowledge and Imperial Power: Race and the Intimate in Colonial Rule.* Berkeley: University of California Press, 2002.

Stoler, Ann Laura, ed. *Imperial Debris: On Ruins and Ruination.* Durham, NC: Duke University Press, 2013.

Stoler, Ann Laura. *Race and the Education of Desire: Foucault's History of Sexuality and the Colonial Order of Things.* Durham, NC: Duke University Press, 1995.

Subramanyan, Arjun, and Michael Sturma. "Asian Labourers, the Thai Government and the Thai-Burma Railway." *Journal of Contemporary History* 56, no. 2 (2021): 364–385.

Tagliacozzo, Eric, and Wen-Chin Chang, eds. *Chinese Circulations: Capital Commodities and Networks in Southeast Asia.* Durham, NC: Duke University Press, 2011.

Teo, Stephen. *Wong Kar-Wai.* London: British Film Institute, 2005.

Teo, Stephen. "Wong Kar-wai's *In the Mood for Love*: Like a Ritual in Transfigured Time." *Senses of Cinema*, April 2001. http://sensesofcinema.com/2001/wong-kar-wai/mood/.

Teo, Stephen. "*Wuxia* Redux: *Crouching Tiger, Hidden Dragon* as a Model of Late Transnational Production." In *Hong Kong Connections: Transnational Imagination in Action Cinema*, edited by Meaghan Morris, Siu Leung Li, and Stephne Chang Ching-kiu, 191–204. Durham, NC: Duke University Press, 2005.

Thak Chaloemtiarana. "Are We Them? The Chinese in 20th Century Thai Literature and History." In *Read Till It Shatters: Nationalism and Identity in Modern Thai Literature*, 155–210. Acton: Australian National University Press, 2018.

Thompson, Ashley. "Performative Realities: Nobody's Possession." In *At the Edge of the Forest: Essays on Cambodia, History, and Narrative in Honor of David Chandler*, edited by Anne Ruth Hansen and Judy Ledgerwood, 93–119. Ithaca, NY: Southeast Asia Program Publications, 2008.

Tsai, Po-Chen. "Singing, Dancing, and the Mass Production of Nonbelonging: Musicals, Melodramas, Migration, and the Transnationalization of Hong Kong Cinema, 1940s–1960s." PhD diss., University of Chicago, 2013.

Vatikiotis, Michael. "Sino Chic: Suddenly, It's Cool to Be Chinese." *Far Eastern Economic Review*, January 11, 1996, 22–25.

Veeraporn Nitiprapha. *Memories of the Memories of the Black Rose Cat*. Translated by Kong Rithdee. Bangkok: River Books, 2022. Kindle edition.

Veeraporn Nitiprapha. *Phutthasakarat atsadong kab song jam khong song jam khong maeo kulab dum* [Dusk of the Buddhist era and remembrance of the memory of the black rose cat]. 2nd ed. Bangkok: Matichon, 2018.

Walker, Gavin. "The Accumulation of Difference and the Logic of Area." *positions: asia critique* 27, no. 1 (2019): 67–98.

Wang Hui. *The Politics of Imagining Asia*. Cambridge, MA: Harvard University Press, 2011.

Wang, Yiman. "The Palimpsest Body and the S(h)ifting Border: On Maggie Cheung's Two Crossover Films." *positions: asia critique* 20, no. 4 (2012): 953–981.

Wang, Yiman. *To Be an Actress: Labor and Performance in Anna May Wong's Cross-Media World*. Berkeley: University of California Press, 2024.

Wasserstrom, Jeffrey. "1926: A City in the Streets." In *Global Shanghai, 1850–2010: A History in Fragments*, 62–76. London: Routledge, 2009.

Wijaya, Elizabeth. "Luminous Flesh, Haunted Future: The Visible and Invisible Worlds of Chinese Cinema." PhD diss., Cornell University, 2018.

Wilms, Marco, dir. *Durch die Nacht mit Christopher Doyle und Nonzee Nimibutr* [Into the night with Christopher Doyle and Nonzee Nimibutr]. Berlin: Arte and Avanti Media Film- und Fernsehproduktion, 2010.

Wilson, Liz. *Charming Cadavers: Horrific Figurations of the Feminine in Indian Buddhist Hagiographic Literature*. Chicago: University of Chicago Press, 1996.

Wolters, O. W. "Southeast Asia as a Southeast Asian Field of Study." In *Early Southeast Asia: Selected Essays*, edited by Craig J. Reynolds. Ithaca, NY: Southeast Asia Program Publications, 2008.

Wong Kar-wai, dir. *In the Mood for Love.* DVD. San Francisco: Criterion Collection / Janus Films, 2000.

Wongsurawat, Wasana. *The Crown and the Capitalists: The Ethnic Chinese and the Founding of the Thai Nation.* Seattle: University of Washington Press, 2019.

Wongsurawat, Wasana. "Educating Citizens: Building a Nation." In *The Crown and the Capitalists: The Ethnic Chinese and the Founding of the Thai Nation,* 12–46. Seattle: University of Washington Press, 2019.

Wongsurawat, Wasana. "Home Base of an Exiled People: Hong Kong and Overseas Chinese Activism from Thailand." In *Sites of Modernity: Asian Cities in the Transitory Moments of Trade, Colonialism, and Nationalism,* edited by Wasana Wongsurawat, 103–117. Berlin: Springer-Verlag, 2016.

Yan, Haiping. "Other Cosmopolitans." In *Cosmopolitanisms,* edited by Bruce Robbins and Paula Lemos Horta, 254–270. New York: New York University Press, 2017.

Yang, Alan H. "Unpacking Taiwan's Presence in Southeast Asia: The International Socialization of the New Southbound Policy." *Issues and Studies: A Social Science Quarterly on China, Taiwan, and East Asian Affairs* 54, no. 1 (2018): 1–30.

Ye, Minting, Igor Vojnovic, and Guo Chen. "The Landscape of Gentrification: Exploring the Diversity of 'Upgrading' Processes in Hong Kong, 1986–2006." *Urban Geography* 36, vol. 4 (2015): 471–503.

Yongthanit Phimonsathian. *Thanon Charoen Krung ton bon: Akhan thi mi khunkha khuan kae kan anurak boriwen* [Upper Charoen Krung Road: Buildings of heritage preservation value]. Bangkok: ICOMOS Thailand, 2009.

Yue, Audrey. "Creative Queer Singapore: The Illiberal Pragmatics of Cultural Production." *Gay and Lesbian Issues and Psychology Review* 3, no. 3 (2007): 149–160.

Yue, Audrey. "In the Mood for Love: Intersections of Hong Kong Modernity." In *Chinese Film in Focus: 25 New Takes,* edited by Chris Berry, 128–136. London: British Film Institute, 2003.

Yuwadi Tonsakulrungruang (Judy Chan). *Roi Wasan [A Walk Through Spring].* Bangkok: Praphansarn Publishing, 2010.

Ziewitz, Malte. "A Not Quite Random Walk: Experimenting with the Ethnomethods of the Algorithm." *Big Data and Society* 4, no. 2 (2017): 1–13.

Index

Page numbers followed by *f* indicate figures.

belonging, 7, 23, 35, 63, 84, 147, 169

Berlant, Lauren, 20–21

body/bodies: Asian racialized female body, 191n35; body-city continua, 161, 166; in China/Peoples Republic of China, 22, 94, 160; ethnic body, 157, 168; immigrant body, 85, 157

Bowring Treaty, 15, 37, 80

Britain, 13, 15, 36; British empire, 37, 55

Buddhism: detachment in, 124–25, 126; Mahayana Buddhism, 125, 126–27, 128; in Thailand/Siam, 38, 75, 189n22; Theravada Buddhism, 126

Burmese people, in Thailand, 18

Cambodia, 54; Modern Girl in, 20; Phnom Penh, 2, 65

capitalism, 58, 59, 157; critique of, 161; electronic capitalism, 34, 36, 152; femininity and, 59, 95, 170; finance capitalism, 21, 22, 32, 152, 170; late capitalism, 41; neoliberalism, 19, 22, 23, 151, 158, 159–60, 165, 186n59; temporality of, 60–61; urban capitalism, 35

Chai Chainuvati (Tsai Yen-Kiang), 78–79

cheung sam/qipao, 40, 64, 91, 182n28; class and, 93–94; *In the Mood for Love* and, 57–60f, 61–62; in Shanghai, 63, 65f

Chiang Kai-shek, 56, 63

China, 134–35, 141–43, 144, 149, 153; Qing Empire, 15; Tribute Order, 150. *See also* People's Republic of China

Chinatown, in Bangkok, 8, 25, 43, 71, 112; Bang Rak district, 36, 39, 73, 82, 100; Berlin Dispensary Co. Ltd. and Pharmaceutical Museum, 78–79f; Charoen Chai district, 80; Charoen Krung Road, 74, 78, 79, 184n21; Chinatown Gate, 74, 75f, 79, 97; Crown land ownership and, 78, 80, 81, 184n33; description, 73; industrial character of, 111; neighborhoods, generally, 74; Pom Prap Satru Phai district, 8, 73, 82, 100; redevelopment and, 79–80, 81, 84, 112; Samphanthawong district, 8, 45, 73, 74,

80, 82, 100; sex trade in, 95; Soi Nana alley, 85, 87, 107, 110; Sou Heng Tai Mansion, 80–81f; Talad Noi district, 80, 81, 105, 107, 113, 184n29; Yaowarat Heritage Center (Samphanthawong Museum), 76, 78, 79, 97, 101; Yaowarat (Yaowaraj) neighborhood, 9–10, 11, 16, 45, 64, 78, 83–84, 94

Chinese cosmopolitan/colonial modernity, 5–6, 31, 61, 67, 173n4; aesthetics of, 38, 39, 101, 171; of Bangkok, 8, 49, 63; as basis for critique, 3, 32, 84, 97, 102, 109, 110, 187n30; definition, 2; as desirable, 20; the Modern Girl and, 22, 169

Chinese femininity, 5, 17; as basis for critique, 166–67, 171; Chinese revival in Bangkok/Thailand and, 21, 23, 148, 157; and cities, 40, 94; consumption and, 91–93; cosmopolitan/colonial modernity and, 63, 65, 90, 124, 169; as denigrated/desired, 96, 154, 164; as distressed, 22, 44, 49, 169; Shanghai femininity, 46; in Thai cinema, 167

Chinese language, 110, 151–52, 154; Cantonese dialect, 56; Hokkien dialect, 90; Mandarin dialect, 56, 67, 71, 82, 100; Shanghainese dialect, 56; Sinophone cultural production, 137, 141, 153, 157–58, 191n36; Teochew dialect, 71, 82, 90

Chinese migration to Thailand/Siam, 142; as culture bearing, 85; as diaspora, 18; narratives of, 16–17, 76, 77, 127; peak of, 15; and Thai historical narratives, 117

Chinese people, in Southeast Asia, 26, 143; identity and, 151–52; migrations, 189n18; shophouses and, 100, 102; Straits Chinese, 1, 173n1

Chinese people, in Thailand/Siam, 14; as agents of modernity/development, 17, 72, 78–79, 111, 116, 164; assimilation/nonassimilation of, 17–18, 115, 117; "Chinese dream"/*suea phuen mon bai* ("Mat and Pillow" legend) concerning, 77, 102, 110, 143, 144; as Chinese Thais, 82–83, 124, 128; cultural production of, 153–54, 158; dialect cultures of, 71, 82, 100, 101; economic importance of, generally, 102, 159; history of, 85, 99, 120, 135, 145, 155; identity and, 7, 12, 96, 136, 146, 153, 157; *Jews of the Orient* and, 16, 17, 77; as knowledge workers, 156; labor of/as laborers, 15–16, 73, 77, 94, 102, 104; memory and, 121, 146; as merchants, 37; minoritarian status of, 25–26, 76–77; political dissent and, 16, 17, 112; population numbers, 15–16, 73, 176n48; as racialized others, 77, 111, 116, 188n7, 191n30; as transnational, 33, 37, 67, 73, 111, 157; women as sexualized, 91, 95

Chinese revival, in Bangkok/Thailand, 18, 19–20, 26, 80, 123, 136; *In the Mood for Love* and, 11, 14, 72; phases/ types of, 82–83, 84, 101; remembering/forgetting and, 104, 116, 117, 120; temporality of, 115, 120–21; urban redevelopment and, 100, 113; women/ femininity and, 21, 23, 148

Chupaporn Kangwanphum, 184n29

Chutimon "Aokbab" Chuengcharoensukying, 129, 153–54, 167

citizenship, 25

city, 66; body-city continua and, 161, 166; digital realm and, 90; gentrification in, 171; lifestyle as driving development of, 34–35; materiality of, 5–6, 22, 115; as mediatized locale, 32–33; neoliberalism and, 160, 186n59; patina and, 10, 22, 80; personhood and, 3, 19; secessionary urban culture, 152; urban decay, 52; value absorption/production and, 95, 101, 178n8; women/femininity and, 21, 40, 90, 158, 160. *See also* Bangkok; Chinatown, in Bangkok; Hong Kong; Shanghai

class, in Thailand, 93–94, 156; critique of, 155; working class, 102, 110, 111, 112, 158

clothing, 5, 12, 45, 96, 155, 161, 172, 173n4. *See also* cheung sam/qipao

Cold War, 4, 15, 27, 67, 86–87, 126, 148

colonialism, 3, 37

coloniality: "anticoloniality" of Thailand/ Siam, 63; of Bangkok, 8, 64, 67; of East Asia, 20; of Hong Kong, 55; post-coloniality of Thailand/Siam, 181n17; semicoloniality, generally, 36; semicoloniality of Shanghai, 2; semicoloniality of Thailand/Siam, 13, 14, 31, 36, 175n39; of Thailand/Siam, 14

communism, 15, 56, 63, 86; postsocialism, 160

Cortez, Iggy, 122, 123

cosmopolitanism, 48, 174n10; Chinese cosmopolitanism, 38, 55, 59; defined, 6; of premodern Asia 54, 67; in Southeast and East Asia, 3, 45, 50, 58

Crown Property Bureau (CPB), 80, 81, 100, 184n33

cultural production: in Bangkok/ Thailand, 1, 12, 21, 149; in Southeast and East Asia, 3, 7, 35

culture: cultural practices, 8, 10; cultural recovery, 82, 124; cultural survival, 100; culture bearer, 85

de Gaulle, Charles, 54, 64

Deleuze, Gilles, 190n23

desire, 2, 4, 34, 43, 53; in Buddhism, 125, 127; for decolonization, 64; distressed Chinese femininity and, 23; and memory/nostalgia, 62, 104, 145; for transregional colonial modernity, 5, 18, 20, 25, 31, 33, 49, 66

diaspora/diasporic, 72, 85, 140, 147; center/diaspora relation, in Southeast and East Asia, 18, 19, 121, 146, 153, 158; Chinese diaspora, 26, 134, 143, 189n18

difference, 137; Chinese persons in Thailand and, 17, 25–26, 76, 128; of Southeast Asia, 141, 148, 151, 152

distressing/distressed, 5, 22; of city spaces, 35; distressed Chinese femininity, 44, 49, 169

Doyle, Christopher, 49, 50, 72

Durch die Nacht mit Christopher Doyle und Nonzee Nimibutr (Into the night with Christopher Doyle and Nonzee Nimibutr) (Wilms), 49, 50, 68

East Asia, 148, 173n1; global orientation toward, 170; racialization of women of, 182n36, 192n46; within-region orientation of, 151

fantasy: Bangkok as site of, 3, 12, 14, 23, 50, 63, 96, 121; Southeast Asia as site of, 147
feminism, 84, 145, 153
femininity, 63; agency and, 60–61; Asian femininity, generally, 170, 171; and capitalism, 59, 95; and the city, 40; colonial modern femininity, 39, 43; and economic productivity, 20, 22, 23; as fetish, 56–57, 64, 65; the Modern Girl, 6, 20–24. *See also* Chinese femininity; women
fetish/fetishization, 20, 46, 56–57, 64, 65, 182n36
film, 38; Chinese cinema, generally, 6, 39, 153; digital cinema, 123; memory and, 10, 83; Thai cinema, 167; women in, 57, 153–54, 182n36, 191n35. *See also* Hong Kong cinema
France, 36
Freud, Sigmund, 57, 104, 120
future/futurity, 5, 8, 12, 21, 23, 42, 64, 169; decolonial futurity, 67; future-present, 11, 38, 55, 56, 66, 109

gender, 148, 152, 155–56
genre, 10, 140, 168; distressed genre, 5; and gender, 20; Modern Girl as, 21
Ghostly Desires: Queer Sexuality and Vernacular Buddhism in Contemporary Thai Cinema (Fuhrmann), 17
good life, in Southeast and East Asia, 3, 12; as experienced by women, 21
Grassi, Joachim, 37
Guattari, Félix, 190n23

Happy Old Year (*How to Ting . . . Ting yang rai mai hai luea thoe* [How to dump? . . . How to dump so that there will be nothing left of you]) (Nawapol Thamrongrattanarit), 99–101, 108f, 118f, 119f, 125f, 129f; analog vs. digital in, 122, 123; Buddhism and, 124–27; class representation in, 102; as critique of neoliberalism, 161, 165; ethnic representation in, 107, 154; female agency in, 154, 158, 160, 165; history/memory and, 104–5, 116–20, 121, 128, 156–57; Jean (character), 116–20, 122, 125–27, 154, 160–61, 164, 167; mobility as theme in, 159, 165; transregionalism and, 129, 152–53
Hark, Tsui, 14
heritage: gender and, in Southeast Asia, 136; renovation of, 87–88; revival of, 42, 101–2. *See also under* Chinese people, in Thailand/Siam
history, 35, 157; of Chinese presence in Bangkok/Thailand, 8–9, 11, 14–18, 104; diasporas as preserving, 72, 85; distressed genres and, 5, 12; the fetish and, 57, 65–66; of labor in Thailand, 77, 111; materiality and, 86, 87; Modern Girl and, 21; traumatic events in, 23, 95, 146; women and Chinese history, 190n25
Hong Kong, 1–2, 10, 23, 67, 72; aesthetics of, 3, 12, 31, 43, 49, 102, 169; colonial/postcolonial temporality of, 6, 51, 55; doubling of with Bangkok and Shanghai, 2, 4, 5, 57, 97; Kowloon Walled City, 83; manufacturing in, 59; Modern Girl in, 20; 1997 transition, 13, 14, 62, 63; and real estate market, 35; riots (1967), 64, 65; shophouses in, 100; Star Ferry protest (1966), 64, 65; Thailand and, 3, 33
Hong Kong cinema: New Wave 13–14, 55; Shanghai cinema and, 55–56; Shaw Brothers, 33; Thailand and, 66–67; as urban critique, 35. *See also* film; *In the Mood for Love*; Wong Kar-wai
hong thaeo. See shophouse

hospitality industry: in Bangkok/
Thailand, 1–2, 5, 7, 35; in Southeast
and East Asia, 3
How to Dump. See Happy Old Year
How to Ting. . . . See Happy Old Year
Ho, Yim, 14
Hui, Ann, 14
Hundred Years Between (exhibition), 38, 41

identity, 7, 151, 157. *See also under* Chinese
people, in Southeast Asia; Chinese people, in Thailand/Siam
India, under British rule, 37
Indonesia, 153
intersubjectivity, 10–11
In the Mood for Love (Wong), 2, 5, 33, 56,
102; aesthetics of, 169, 171; capitalism,
as depicted in, 60–61; Chan So Lei
(character), 56, 57, 60; cheung sam in,
39, 57–60, 61–62, 64; Chinese femininity in, 22, 40, 66; Chinese revival in
Bangkok and, 11, 14, 72; futurity in, 55,
56; as invoking colonial modernity, 41,
67; Hong Kong, as depicted in, 12, 55,
57, 67; making of, 49; political critique
in, 64, 65; as postnostalgic, 14; regional
vision in, 68; the ruin and, 50, 51–54,
66; Shanghai and, 56, 57, 67; Southeast
Asia, as depicted in, 67; temporalities
in, 13, 55, 60–61; transnational Chinese
history and, 58, 62–63

Japan/Japanese, 15, 62, 63, 67
Johannesburg, 34–35

Kasian Tejapira, 188n7
knowledge/technological industry, in
Thailand, 79, 156, 157, 158, 162, 165
Kong Rithdee, 99, 126, 135, 145
Korea, 151
"Kratham khwam Wong" Facebook page,
31–33, 34, 66
Kuhn, Philip A., 189n18
Kuomintang, 16, 63, 73
Kwan, Stanley, 14; *Rouge*, 13

labor/laborers: Chinese people as, in
Thailand/Siam, 15–16; racialization of
labor in Asia, 95; surplus of in Southeast and East Asia, 20; women's labor in
Southeast and East Asia, 21, 94, 169
Lee, Vivian, 55
leisure, 3, 21, 35, 171
leisure/hospitality venues, in Bangkok,
33, 36, 149; About Studio About Café,
8, 174n15; As Is Café, 110–12, 113f, 115;
Ba Hao, 85–87, 97, 107; Chinese femininity and, 22; Eia Sae, 9f, 10, 93; Foo-
John Building, 8, 83, 84, 105–7f, 109f,
110, 115; history, use of by, 35, 64, 68,
83, 97, 101, 117, 120, 123; Lhong 1919, 87,
88f, 89f, 97; Lhong Tou Café, 8, 10, 11;
Maggie Choo's, 8, 39–41f, 42–43, 56,
136, 179n34; Mother Roaster, 112–16f;
Shanghai and, 38; texture, use of by,
84–85. *See also* Shanghai Mansion
Bangkok
lifestyle industry, 3, 9, 112, 113; cities in
Southeast and East Asia and, 34, 85,
173n4
Li, Vanessa, 169, 171f, 172
loss, 99, 120, 122, 144, 160; of home, 63,
56, 141–43
Love in a Fallen City (Chang [Zhang]), 62

Ma, Jean, 23, 96
Malaysia: Malaysian Chinese (Mahua) literature, 134, 151; Penang, 100
manufacturing, in Asia, 21, 59
Mao Zedong: Long March of, 143
Marx, Karl, 6, 57
materiality: affect and, 126; of cities, 5, 6,
22, 113; of history/memory, 86, 115, 119;
of the ruin, 66
Mattern, Shannon, 32–33
Ma Zhou, 87, 89f, 90
Mbembe, Achille, 34–35
media, 3; analog, 101, 122; digital, 31–35,
90, 101, 122; memory and, 10, 83; photography, 38; social, 39. *See also* film;
"Kratham khwam Wong" web page

Thailand/Siam, relations with China/
 Peoples Republic of China, 74–75, 76,
 84, 87, 101, 147, 152; economic relations,
 82–83; projects in Thailand, 19
trade networks, 2, 5, 59
transnationalism, 13, 18, 20, 38, 101, 150;
 culture of, 102, 126; economic activity
 and, 34, 37, 82, 111; language and, 151;
 migration and, 33; modernity and, 57,
 61; as response to hegemony, 67
trauma, 23, 57, 58, 96, 141, 146
treaty ports, in East and Southeast Asia, 5,
 68; culture of, 3, 31, 63, 87, 88, 90
Tsai Yen-Kiang. *See* Chai Chainuvati

Udom Sisuwan (Aran Phromchomphu),
 175n39
United States, 15, 86

value: compounding of, 94, 95, 170,
 177n82; the Modern Girl and, 22; pricelessness, 34, 186n59; production/
 absorption of, by cities, 95; surplus
 value, 22, 101, 170, 178n8
Veeraporn Nitiprapha, 84; Chineseness
 as concern of, 134, 136, 141, 146–47;
 A Day Bulletin interview, 102, 103*f*, 117,
 124; migration as concern of, 134–35.
 *See also Memories of the Memories of the
 Black Rose Cat*

Wang Lee family, 87, 90
Waraluck Hiransrettawat. *See* Salee Every
Wijaya, Elizabeth, 153
women, 46, 56–57, 182n39; agency of, 43,
 155, 158; as agents of critique, 164–65,
 171, 187n30; bodies of, 22, 58, 157, 160,
 161, 165, 191n35; economic function
 of, 40, 42, 167; film and, 57, 153–54,
 182n36; and ideas of surplus, 22, 94–95;
 labor of in Southeast and East Asia,
 21, 60, 94, 169; mobility/motility of,
 159–60, 162; sexualization of in Thailand, 91, 95; as tellers/agents of history
 in Southeast and East Asia, 23, 96, 136,
 152, 190n25; "yellow woman," 170. *See
 also* Chinese femininity; femininity;
 gender
Wong, Anna May, 182n36
Wong Kar-wai, 5, 56, 109; Bangkok as setting for films of, 7–8, 11, 38, 72; films of,
 generally, 31, 169, 175n37; language, in
 films of, 56, 67; *2046*, 39, 56. *See also In
 the Mood for Love*
Wongsurawat, Wasana, 14–15, 48, 71, 73,
 112
World War II, 27, 148
Wuhe, 151

Yuwadi Tonsakulrungruang: *Roi Wasan*,
 112